DATE DUE

JUN 1 1 1998			
2/19/11			
NOV 0 6 2014			

The Library Store   #47-0103

WOMEN IN EUROPE SINCE 1750

WOMEN IN EUROPE SINCE 1750

PATRICIA BRANCA

ST. MARTIN'S PRESS   NEW YORK

© 1978 Patricia Branca

All rights reserved. For information write:
St. Martin's Press Inc., 175 Fifth Avenue, New York, N.Y. 10010
Library of Congress Catalog Card Number: 77-20202
ISBN 0-312-88739-6
First published in the United States of America 1978

Library of Congress Cataloging in Publication Data

Branca, Patricia.
  Women in Europe since 1750.

  Bibliography: p.221
  Includes index.
  1. Women – History. I. Title
HQ1121.B65   301.41′2′09   77-20202

ISBN 0-312-88739-6

Printed and bound in Great Britain by
Billing & Sons Limited, Guildford, London and Worcester

CONTENTS

To Howard because I love you

PREFACE

Encountering the table of contents of this book, a reader could conjecture that, given the youth of women's history, the undertaking was a mite presumptuous as a field of scholarly endeavour. A moment, then, for my sense of purpose. In eight years of researching and teaching in the field I have continually tried to come to grips with what has seemed to me at times to be the riddle of the sphinx. What is women's history? Each year new works of scholarship are published on diverse aspects of this subject: biographies of eminent women, monographs on suffrage movements, studies of women's economic roles and family position along with polemics on the culture of womanhood. What I wanted to know was how did all these pieces fit? Was there any relationship between the history of the mill girl and the experience of a woman like Parnell's mistress, Catherine O'Shea? Was there any conceptual framework that would help one to understand better the diverse experiences of women's growing-up in modern society. Thus I set out to write this book.

The task inevitably involved dealing with controversies. This presentation clashes at times with the theses of a number of historians of women. However, the point of this book was not to find fault. It is concerned primarily with the development of a framework for beginning to integrate the dynamics which have marked the modern experience of women. The emphasis is on interpretation. Thus, in order to avoid undue interruption of the conceptualisation, controversy has been limited to footnote discussion wherever possible. In addition the bibliography includes a listing of secondary works in fields where contention is most acute. Hence a point of view, an interpretive study follows and it will not accord with everyone's previous work. But that is the only way a real history of women can be constructed. To many the empirical base will seem wanting. This book is designed to facilitate new thinking in new directions.

Having briefly given due to the book's *raison d'être,* I would like to express my sincere thanks to all my students whose questions and enthusiasm throughout the years made this project worthwhile. I would like to thank David Crawford and Vicki Erd for their efforts at transcribing my cryptic thoughts into type. A word of appreciation goes to David Croom whose advice on how to make myself understood better was taken to heart. Thanks also to my dear friends, Theresa McBride, Jeffrey Kay, Gerald Chait and Fred Samuels. A personal note of deep feeling for constant support and belief in me I give to Howard Smalley. And finally I thank my loving daughter Nancy whose growing up has given me new visions.

1 THE WHY OF WOMEN'S HISTORY

Whatever one's image of modern women there is the underlying consensus that the history of modern women is really very new. For some it is an accounting of current events. At most it is the story of twentieth-century Anglo-American women, with a few bows to nineteenth-century precursors. Within these boundaries the relevant question seems to be whether there is a *history* of modern women given their recent emergence into the public realm. What is there to know about a past that is so short? Short it is but not as short as some historians would have us believe. The purpose of this book is to show that the history of modern women, while still unfolding, has a rich and varied past, with its roots in the late eighteenth century and indeed even earlier for some women of the upper classes.

Modernisation is a concept rarely applied to women. Recently it has been the subject of a semantic debate and has suffered harsh criticism essentially from anti-modernists. This book is not meant to debate the usefulness and validity of the concept of modernisation. Modernisation is only a word that is used to describe the dynamics of social change brought about by the transformation of the Western economy over the last two hundred years. It is not used as a philosophical statement of how things *should* be but as a way of measuring the rate of this change.

The process by which this tranformation occurred is most complex. Basic to it all was the transformation of society into an industrial framework. Common people began to find that agriculture was not the only means of making a living. Newer types of work — mechanised work in factories, jobs in offices, government bureaucracies, even schools — were developed. Modern society became urban. In the nineteenth century millions of people in Western Europe uprooted themselves from their centuries-old rural setting in favour of moving to urban centres. But these were only the outer trappings of change. Modern living involves more than simply how people work or where they eat and sleep; it involves their perception of the world and their place in that world. A new state of mind prompted people to seek new residence and new work roles. Obviously it is difficult to articulate the states of mind that this produced. The artist is better suited for this task than the historian. But history, if it does anything at all, must try to capture the intangible for us. Only by getting inside evolving mentalities can we begin to feel for the past.

In very general terms modern people think rationally and believe in progress and self-determination. While this undoubtedly sounds quite simplistic, we know it represents a vital transformation. Progress inevitably implies change and for centuries change was not only discouraged but was prevented by traditional strictures both materially and spiritually. Equally as distinctive, modern people think as individuals. Their motivations, their expectations are by and large determined by a desire to enhance personal well-being. As a result modern people are secular, even materialistic, reducing the hold of traditional structured religion in their lives. An expression of this new sense of individuality is the surge of political consciousness. People came to believe that they had rights of participation in the state which is formed to guarantee their individual welfare.

Defining a modern life style is complicated further by the fact that it is an ongoing process; its chronological limits are never set. Within this open framework it involves different stages for different groups in society.

Having said all this we need to address ourselves directly to the question of where women fit into this scheme. An effective argument could be mounted that women have not modernised, in that the industrialisation of work roles has been dominated by males. At the same time women have only been able to participate formally in politics during this century; since 1917 in England, 1919 for American women and in 1945 for French women. However, a key factor in understanding women's self-development is that it differed substantially from the pattern set by men during the same period. Emergence into the modern world for women involved political consciousness, directed not primarily at political rights but first at sheer legal recognition. More important than these incidents of change was the alteration of the female perspective, the struggle for individuality. The forthcoming pages will evolve around this very important question of self-image, and the difficulties females had and continue to have because of their sex in coming to terms with defining an image for themselves.

For the most part women's history does not fit into the conventional historical timetable; that is, it cannot neatly be divided into 1789-1815; 1815-48; 1848-70; 1870-1914, etc. Periodisation in women's history presents several complexities. Conventional studies of modernisation focus on the period 1800-1850 as the most productive. Certainly at this time women were involved in new things; most obviously they were found in increasing numbers in the burgeoning textile industry. However, this new sector of the female population was minute, never comprising more than ten per cent. For the early years of the nineteenth century most women found themselves bound by the traditions of pre-modern society. As we will see, changes in the life style of the average woman were most clearly implemented only after the mid-nineteenth century. The focus in this study is therefore on the later nineteenth and twentieth centuries.

Several recent historians of women have found the modern period to be important but have come away with the impression that pre-modern society was more significant for women. Contrary to the opinion that modern times brought progress, some believe that modernisation for women clearly entailed regression. The contention is that women's position in society deteriorated markedly with the advent of modernisation cum industrialisation cum capitalism. There seems to be only one basis for such a pessimistic overview of the female experience: work. Pre-modern woman's work role was highly productive: as she supplied society with its basic neccessities she received appropriate power positions. With the advent of industrial society and its male-oriented machines and factories women's work role was diminished. As a result her position in society became inferior to the male, now the only producer and thus the only holder of power. But in exploring the pre-modern woman's position in society we must try to perceive her work role as she did. All evidence suggests that the nature of work in pre-modern society was bleak, especially for women — constant physical strain yielding little material sustenance. This was particularly so in her role as mother. To be sure, the pre-modern woman was productive but the rewards must be viewed through her eyes, which were more often than not weary and strained.

In evaluating the process of modernisation of women some aspects are more difficult to assess than others. One of the more important developments affecting the lot of the common woman was improved health. No one seriously argues against the fact that women today are healthier. At the same time we realise that women still agonise over diseases peculiar to their sex, such as breast cancer. But when we move to still more intimate aspects of a woman's experience, for example, her sex life, we run into much controversy.

Is the modern woman *sexier* than her traditional counterpart? Women's modernisation depended as much on sexual liberation as on political and economic breakthroughs. Yet how does the historian begin to measure sexual fulfilment for women? Vital statistics can provide us with some crude measure. The increase in the number of illegitimate births in the late eighteenth and nineteenth centuries, for example, has been hailed as the sexual revolution for women. There are many problems with this thesis. Vital statistics tell us little about the *quality* of sex a woman experienced which is essential for an overall evaluation of the impact of change. Until quite recently there have been no records of the number of orgasms a woman enjoyed or how she attained them. The lack of quantifiable accounts however does not mean that a woman's sex life has remained tradition bound or is untraceable historically. As we will see, an integration of a variety of sources shows that sex was becoming an important consideration for the modern woman's self-image. We can never be sure if she reached orgasm but we can be sure that she came to recognise her right to orgasm. Sexual awareness for women began to· rise in the nineteenth century and the process has been much accelerated in the twentieth century but the revolution is not complete. The right to female orgasm is now widely acknowledged but not fully acted upon. The recent establishment of sex clinics and the proliferation of sex surveys show that we are still grappling with the problem. Yet, a change has occurred and for the majority of women it has meant new opportunities, either experienced or eagerly anticipated.

There are a number of ways to view the overall repercussions of women's modernisation. Three are most relevant for our purposes: the contemporary, the ideal and the historical. Through contemporary eyes women's history is viewed as one of repression: women in the past were forbidden to own property; forbidden to sue in court; forbidden to work outside the home; forbidden to vote; forbidden to enjoy sexual pleasures. The second set of standards is somewhat different but comes to the same conclusion. The idealist can see only the persistent inequities which confront women preventing self-fulfilment. Both perspectives serve useful functions, most specifically consciousness-raising. But they both distort.

The historical approach offers a more encompassing context as reference can well illustrate. Later chapters will discuss the degree of sexual fulfilment possible for a woman living below subsistence level. How important were erotic pursuits for a woman who was hungry, cold and weary most of the time? How freely did women indulge in sexual delights when the fruit was a nine-month pregnancy draining her already limited energy, and inevitably involving a painful and dangerous delivery for herself and the baby? Committed generalisation about the male conspiracy depriving women of their pleasures does not do justice to the full drama of the female experience.

An evaluation of the female experience must also take another point into consideration. Just as modernisation affected women differently than men, it also evoked different responses in varying segments of the female population. Women's history is sometimes conceived as the sisterhood of all women. Women are generally treated as one social group. It is true that women did and continue to share common social experiences; for example, most define their lives through marriage and motherhood. But as we will see, the female experience, even in something as basic as motherhood, was conditioned by social class. Yet class distinctions are difficult to define in women's history. How does a women fit historically into a class structure that is articulated according to male criteria? In spite of the difficulty an attempt must be made, for it is a grave injustice to women's history to ignore these differences. The problems of the working-class woman do not define the middle-class woman's experience or vice versa.

However, it is difficult in women's history to come to terms with a precise definition of working or middle-class. Class differences go beyond income and occupational structures. Class consciousness is as much a mental state, determining behaviour and self-perception. Differences in attitudes and practices regarding sex, education, child-rearing, family size are all important dimensions in coming to terms with class differences among women. Understanding the subtle but real differences in personal relationships, particularly husband-wife, mother-daughter, will contribute also to a richer definition.

The need for the comparative perspective goes beyond class differences: what area of the modern world should one focus on? To date most historical accounts have concentrated almost exclusively on the Anglo-American woman as the prototype of the modern woman. The reasons for this concentration are understandable. England and America produced the more articulate women in the nineteenth and twentieth centuries (i.e., the radical feminists), with the exception of areas of Scandinavia. These women were more than isolated figures on the conventional historical stage. Naturally their life histories, diaries and ideas on reform have been seized upon as a means of interpreting the female experience in modern society.

The Anglo-American model is made even more attractive by the fact that it offered us drama and action. The violence of the women's protest movement in these countries strikes pride in the hearts of modern women intellectuals. But these stories confront the women's historian with two important ideological implications. First the stories of articulate women, the protesters, can too easily be regarded as the whole of women's history. This was not true even for American and

English women. In fact the history of women is for the most part the story of the non-violent, the inarticulate. The second limitation of the Anglo-American approach is that all women's history is made to relate to this model. When it does not it is dismissed as either unimportant or backward. Consequently we know much less about the Continental European experience except that European women did not launch a vigorous political campaign. This book attempts to look at the European woman's experiences through a serious consideration of the French woman. The English and the French woman's experiences were compared in order to determine whether there is a modernisation model or at least the need to construct variants within its framework. France was chosen as the basis for comparison since it underwent changes similar to those in England but not as abruptly. Whether these two case studies are appropriate for Eastern or Third World cultures, awaits further study, although some suggestions are offered.

This brings us to our final and most complex problem. How can one explore the world of women who never left us with direct accounts? Women's history is in essence the history of the inarticulate. However a balance of quantitative and qualitative sources offers a variety of information. Vital statistics tell as much about the anonymous female. Through marriage, birth and death records we can hypothesise about her life, when she married, how many children she bore, how long she lived and how she died. Another important source which must be handled with care is cultural artifacts: the material women read or was intended for their reading; household manuals, women's magazines, health and child care manuals, newspapers and advertisements. These tell us much about the outer and inner dimensions of the female experience in modern society. The things she surrounded herself with, her home, her furniture, her clothes, also tell us something about her world and her self-perception. While the sources present problems of representativeness and do not lend themselves to sophisticated quantification they are invaluable nonetheless. They capture the abstract that numbers alone fail to relate — the human element of the modern experience.

The design of the book is to reflect upon the experiences of the whole woman. We cannot pretend to offer a balanced, and comprehensive discussion of all aspects of the female experience since 1750. Space and research limitations would prohibit such a sweeping claim to expertise. Thus certain topics such as women's fashion and leisure actvities could only be touched upon. Likewise the impact of religion on women's lives has not been explored. Also too little is said about the experiences of older women. How women have coped with the demographic realities that they will outlive men is not explored fully. More important, how death affects women whose very being is closely tied to giving and sustaining life are further areas that make this study far from complete. The particular history of upper-class women's experiences is also not specifically addressed in this study. Impressionistically, upper-class women, like their middle-class counterparts, have been more often characterised than seriously studied. Many of the problems that beset middle- and working-class women were realities for the upper ten per cent as well. Broken health, the tragedies of infant and maternal mortality, absent husbands tore at the hearts of the women who enjoyed the good life as well as those who did not.

Since the underlying theme of our period is change, those aspects of women's life style that were affected most dramatically have been highlighted. Three areas stand out above all others: women's work role; women's family role; and women's public role. Taken together these topics cover the most telling aspects of the female experience in modern society.

The first topic for investigation is women's work roles. The importance of the subject is unquestionable. The central question here surrounds the problems women encountered in the new world of work as it developed beyond the domestic sphere. What did industrialisation do to the woman's economic position *vis-à-vis* society? The purpose of the discussion is not only to illustrate its significance for the modern woman but to integrate the work experience into her life cycle. While work roles are a significant factor in the development of the modern woman (particularly with the working-class woman) they have fluctuated in importance with changes in the female life cycle. For most of the nineteenth century and early twentieth century, only young single women ventured to do battle in the economic jungle. Gradually but most importantly after World War II work came to dominate a major part of a woman's life. Rather than being viewed as a separate stage, more often a stepping stone to marriage, it has become an integral aspect of many women's lives. Today work impinges upon the bulk of the female population. It has demanded an increasing and innovative response from all women, middle class as well as working class, married as well as single.

From work we move to the most central issue of the modern woman's life, her family role. This aspect has not only been underestimated but often denigrated. This study will try to evaluate the experience as felt by the woman herself. The importance of the complexities of the family role are two-fold. First it is a role that the majority of women will have to confront; as marriage rates continue to be over 90 per cent and the age at marriage is younger than ever before. Thus marriage will shape the expectations and motivations of the majority of women and for most of their lives. Second, and more important, changes in the family role have been the key to the woman's adaptation to the modern social structure. Through a study of family and women we receive a vital insight into areas that affect us all, from sexuality to the impact of vacuum cleaners.

The final major section deals with the more familiar: women in the public arena and the political, legal and educational struggles that have beset her. All three topics are linked in a final section on the contemporary woman. The trends and breaks in women's history since 1750 are all brought to bear on the experience of the woman today.

2 WOMEN AT WORK: BEASTS OF BURDEN

The Women Workers in the Pre-Modern Economy

With rare exceptions (the disabled, the very rich), all women worked in pre-modern society and all women work now. However the work experience has changed dramatically. This section focuses on those women in pre-industrial society who did productive or service labour for which they received some remuneration. The central themes are the development of working conditions, wages and training, along with the number and quality of new jobs opened to women. At the same time the evolution in the nineteenth century of a new and distinctive work ethic is explored; a work ethic which was so pervasive that it defines even the contemporary work patterns of many women.

Until recently, the labour history of women has largely been ignored. Conventional treatments of workers note the importance of women in early industry but do not focus on women as labourers.[1] There are several reasons why women's labour history has fared so badly. Firstly, it has normally been studied strictly in comparison to men's work, which produces interesting results but inevitably leads to 'the conclusion that women workers are inferior to men.[2] These studies ignore the different conditions which formed part of a more complex female work ethic which may actually have been more successful than that of the male. Secondly, women have been neglected in labour history because female labourers rarely participated in labour movements. However, we cannot explain why women behaved differently until we explore female labour against the background of their entire experience rather than simply dimissing them when they do not conform to the male labour model.

The most fundamental feature of women's work in pre-modern times was its familial base. As the key economic unit of production every member of the family was employed. There was scant hope of survival outside the family for either male or female; those who did not marry usually worked as family dependents. For both husband and wife, the family defined economic effort; each worked for the goals of the unit, not as an individual. The family dictated the type of work performed and the conditions and rewards accorded to each member. However the female was at a great disadvantage because the predominantly manual labour of the land placed severe restraints on her work roles.

Women's work was, however, vital giving her importance if not primacy in the family. The fact that women's work was crucial does not mean it was equal and it certainly does not mean that it was pleasant or rewarding. Work roles were segregated with women typically given less important jobs; in this sense continuing segregations and low pay constitute throwbacks to pre-industrial conditions which industrialisation has in fact modified.[3] The lot of the pre-modern woman greatly depended on her health, energy and family position in adolescence. Work was physically demanding. Those who could supply the brawn survived. From the age of ten, when hard labour dominated the child's ordinary day, to marriage at the age of 25 to 28. Much had to be achieved by a girl working as part of a family unit. Reference to the working *girl* rankles with many of us today because of its overt sexist connotations. Yet it reflects a cultural reality for the pre-modern woman. *Womanhood* was not attained through work as was manhood. A girl became a woman only when she married. Thus the goal of work, not always realised but attractive beyond any conceivable alternative was marriage. Work fitted into the lives even of young women as a means to an end. Hard work, demonstration of the ability to endure physical stress and strain increased marriage chances; above all, an economically successful family would alone be able to assure a dowry, the key to marriage for any daughter.

While the goal was clear, the means of reaching it were far from direct. A girl did not work as an individual. If wages were earned, they were a supplement to the family economy, not for the young girl's personal use. Given the nature of subsistence agricultural labour, the work experience of most girls was confined to service, generally service in someone else's home, from the age of 10 to 25-28. Only younger daughters were kept at home, to look after ageing parents; unlikely to marry, they thus began a life of uninterrupted dependence which would carry on when they were left to the mercies of a brother's wife.

Whether at home or 'in service', the land provided the major source of employment for women. Well into the nineteenth century, agriculture was the largest single employer of women, single, married, young or old. Yet, agriculture had special connotations for the woman. The type of labour required for working on the land put the woman in an inferior position. Some of the inequalities are familiar. Rarely could a woman own or expect to own the land on which her livelihood depended. Widowhood or inheritance in a family with no sons provided

the only exceptions, which were not always enviable as it was difficult
for a single woman to maintain a farm where physical labour was so
varied and demanding. Women's work while crucial to the more
typical family unit, was formally dependent. Further, agricultural
employment for the woman was largely confined to domestic duties
associated with servanthood rather than directly *productive* labour;
only men concentrated on the latter.

Young girls whose labour was not needed at home generally worked
close by, often for an uncle or an older brother. Their tasks included
cooking, cleaning, washing clothes, feeding the domestic animals and
milking cows; in pressure periods of the agricultural year they went
into the main fields for planting, particularly to glean and gather hay.
Working conditions were by any standard poor. Work continued from
sunrise to sunset and there was no end to it. The pattern continued for
most married women, in their own homes. Here too women rarely
worked alongside their men, as they spent most of their own long days
in fields at some distance from the house.

Subsistence agricultural labour was physically demanding for all but
especially so for the female. As farm servants or as working wives,
women's health suffered severely for hard work was combined with
irregular, often inadequate nutrition. We may cherish the image of the
rosy-cheeked peasant girl singing in the sunny field, while taking an
occasional swipe at golden grain. We may cherish it, but we can not
really believe it. Rosy cheeks there were, but more often than not the
result of fever and broken health caused by poor diet and exhausting
labour. A more accurate picture of peasant girls would show worn
faces, rough and blistered hands. An old English woman who was put
out to service at the age of nine recalls her work experience in the
early nineteenth century:

> I used to be employed when I was apprenticed in driving bullocks to
> the field and fetching them in again; cleaning out their houses and
> bedding them up; washing potatoes and boiling them for pigs;
> milking in the field, leading horses or bullocks to plough. . I was
> employed in mixing lime to spread, digging potatoes, digging and
> pulling turnips, and anything that came to hand. . .I reaped a little,
> not much; loaded pack horses, went out with horses for furze. I got
> up at five or six, except on market mornings twice a week, and
> then at three. I went to bed at half-past nine.[4]

Regional variations provided some women with specialised work, as in the case of wine-growing areas or areas specialising in dairy farming. Both industries relied upon the skills of the woman. The whole dairy business was in the hands of women. Their knowledge was purely empirical, the art of butter making and cheese making handed down from one generation to another. Here, as in most aspects of women's work, there was little formal training and no concept of skills. And even in the dairy, the bucolic image of the young dairy maid in her pretty white apron 'dabbling in the dew' is far from reality. The French dairy maid found her work was never done. Her day began at three or four in the morning, depending on the season. Cows had to be milked directly in the pasture, which required the girl to walk some distance from the farm. With the milk brought back, over the same long distance, the actual making of butter and cheese began. The girl churned until three and then returned to the cows, only to repeat the earlier procedure; the whole process lasted well into the evening. The situation was similar throughout Europe. Of cheesemaking in Cheshire, England, an observer reported that 'the labour of turning and cleaning cheese is performed almost universally by women; and that in large dairies, where the cheeses are upwards of 140 pounds each upon an average; this they do without much appearance of exertion. . .which is a matter of surprise even in this country.'[5] Even if apparent ill effects of heavy work were not seen it is known that when the plight of agricultural women was first brought to public attention, in the early nineteenth century, dairy women were noted to suffer the most from over-exertion and the consequences of lifting heavy objects. Making butter was less arduous than making cheese as it only required churning two or three days a week. There was also some compensation for the labours of the commercial dairy in the fact that female dairy workers were better paid than women in any other branch of agriculture.

In poor regions, a certain number of young girls served as migratory workers, going off for two to four weeks at a time primarily for harvest work. In France a common migration pattern involved the movement from the northern regions of the Massif Central into the southern wine-growing areas for grape picking. The work was long and pay extremely low, but it was a vital resource for girls from the barren mountains – and one could have all the grapes one could eat. A smaller-scale migration was directed to the olive harvest, while other migrants worked in the mulberry and silk worm industries. Grain harvests, in contrast, were more often worked by families than by single girls. Husbands contracted to reap, while wives gleaned. This again was back-breaking work for long hours, but the wages were better than in grape picking. A woman with gleaning rights could collect a significant amount of grain, often of better quality than that available at home.[6]

Another migratory pattern, often involving longer periods of employment, took girls to the city. Some in fact remained, but the initial intent was for the girl to work only for a period, earn money for family use, and then return to the village. In the city proper, a few women were apprenticed to craftsmen, serving as bakers' assistants or even goldsmiths. Urban guild restrictions tended to be highly discriminatory against women; few crafts mixed significant numbers of single men and women. Far more girls were employed in trades connected with textiles, working as milliners, mantua makers, embroiderers and seamstresses. Yet most young girls in the city entered domestic service, rather like their country cousins though in this case most commonly for artisan families. In service a girl might pick up useful skills, as well as some earnings, which would enhance her marriage prospects.

The artisan's wife could be an instructive tutor as she enjoyed a particular economic role. She was fully acquainted with her husband's business, serving as 'mistress of the managing part of it' and she could often maintain the business even if her husband died.[7] In some instances, she helped with preparatory stages of production but usually concentrated on marketing the goods. For most urban girls, then, whether of urban or rural origin, the happiest employment ladder involved service leading to marriage to a craftsmen and with this in turn distinct economic duties.

This same ladder by necessity had lower rungs. At the bottom were beggars, thieves, paupers and prostitutes, and many a young girl struggled to stay alive. For the girl who entered the trade of prostitution there was often no way out; as one historian puts it, 'prostitution...was a one-way ticket'.[8] The experience involved pain and indignity and commonly led to premature death. Many a prostitute was a victim of rape, a servant seduced by her master; and, deprived of a chance for 'decent' work she took to the street to keep alive and prevent the baby from starving.

For a small handful prostitution offered some variety.[9] Our impression that prostitution and destitution are synonomous was the ugly truth for the majority. It emerged largely from the women who ended dying in the public hospitals or beggars' homes; and the image has been heightened by the indignant blasts of moralists. Some prostitutes served as mistresses to wealthy men and lived comfortably;

among pre-industrial cities, Bordeaux, for example, was noted as being particularly rewarding in this area.[10] Ranging down from this were girls who worked out of their own apartments, girls who worked in public houses, and outright streetwalkers in port districts or army garrison towns. Conditions and earnings varied widely. A girl working in a high class house could earn more money from her 'respectable' clients than a servant. Prostitution could even continue the motif of the family economy; Jeanne and Marguerite Vidal entertained their customers in their parents' home while the rest of the family waited outside, appreciating the extra source of income. But overall this was a hazardous profession, whatever its initial attractions. The danger of disease was fearsome at any level of the trade, for there was no cure and the victims were left to die a pauper's death.

Urban employment before industrialisation had a number of distinctive characteristics. A girl had to earn money, in contrast to the agricultural setting where cash earnings were rare. Opportunities were more formally limited than in the countryside. Females were largely confined to service rather than production roles though, as in the case of craftsmen's wives, these roles might be both important and prestigious. Textile production was the only exception, the one manufacturing outlet widely open to women. Under these circumstances it was difficult to develop a special job commitment or sense of skill, as male artisans could. With little to begin with and little to gain many girls slipped from one occupation to another. Part-time prostitution enters the story here, and would continue to do so well into the nineteenth century. Servant girls or textile workers not infrequently took to streetwalking to tide them through a period of unemployment or to win a bit of extra money for a new dress or some other necessity. With ingenuity one could get by. Prostitution, our extreme example, might be degarding, even fatal, but it might also provide earnings which could make up a dowry and hence be the escape into marriage. The fact remains that for the majority of working women, it was at least as true in city as in countryside that marriage was essential to secure one's economic position. The older single woman in the city could rarely earn enough for more than bare survival. Happy was she who managed to exploit the social contacts and small savings possible from servanthood to gain a marriage where her economic functions would actually increase. Failing this, happy was she who brought back a bit of money into the more embracing family economy of the countryside.

In the city or in the village, the work experience of the pre-modern woman was extremely tenuous. More than men, females were subject to underemployment. Most women worked intensively for peak periods, at harvest time or during the fashion season for urban seamstresses, and then found their functions and, if single or widowed, their earnings substantially reduced. Many of the burdens we have described — hard physical toil, uncertain and intermittent reward — applied to men as well. Pre-industrial labour was a golden age for few of either sex. But it is clear that patterns of job segregation were already clearly established. The framework of the family economy cushioned married women against the worst potential disadvantages of distinctive and inferior work roles, though its effects were less benign for daughters or spinsters who were marked, at best, for definite dependence. But married women were supplementary, not primary workers, as they were non-producers in an economy where the bulk of attention had to be given to production.

Women's work situation began to change toward the mid-eighteenth century, with the expansion of the domestic manufacturing system. This was not a new system, but it had not recruited widely before. Now, it became a necessity for, with massive population growth, women, already underemployed, were threatened with an inability even to subsist. In France hard-pressed peasants could not gain sufficient land to make do and had to look for ancillary sources of income. In England different circumstances produced the same need, in the context of an even more rapidly expanding population. Domestic manufacturing was to provide a source of temporary relief. Although both sexes participated, it is unquestionable that never before did such a large percentage of women participate in productive labour. Women monopolised the spinning of wool, cotton, linen and silk and other branches such as lace making and the knitting of stockings. Ironically, discrimination continued. Women were barred, into the nineteenth century, from most weaving operations, the most lucrative in textiles, though they did do preparatory work. Here again physical disabilities put the woman in an inferior position. Greater strength requirements and higher earnings made weaving largely a male preserve. But a beginning was at hand for the female labourer. The transformation of female work opportunities was genuine, which is why the period has been seen as a brief but glorious age.

Novel elements were many. Domestic manufacturers required some specific training — about a year for lace makers, for examples. The concept of skill was becoming more relevant for female work. Domestic manufacturing brought money earnings, also, a new experience for many rural workers; a new sense of independence, what has been called a 'market mentality',[11] could result, particularly if the earnings were comparatively high as was often the case. The acquisition was much slower for the woman for adaptation was complicated as we will see. Cottage industries broadened personal contacts as well. A city merchant, usually in textiles, sent a middle man, the 'putter-outer', to contract work in the countryside, supplying a peasant woman with materials and the design required. He then returned to pick up the finished product and pay a piece rate wage. For many a country woman this was the first contact with urban people and their values, all associated with a market setting. Some domestic manufacturers actually went to cities themselves to sell their goods; here, contacts with a wider variety of people were to be still more diverse.

Yet the domestic manufacturing system operated in a traditional setting in vital respects, which returns us to a final judgement of the pre-industrial economy. It was home centred. Money earnings were turned over for family use. Male dominance of the family economy continued, whether the husband or father remained in productive agricultural work or took on weaving or one of the better paid jobs in the spreading domestic system. Work for both sexes remained extremely laborious. Women spinners often worked in damp, dark rooms – conditions believed essential in order to keep textile fibres supple. The power provided to their tools came from their physical exertions alone. Single women remained dependent, for though domestic manufacturing gave new opportunities, earnings were rarely sufficient for a girl to remove herself from the family economy or family direction. For wives, a minority of the female working population when one counts them against single girls and the large number of permanent spinsters, the situation was more complex. Without question a married woman's work was crucial to the family's existence, whether it took the form of supplementary agricultural or artisan roles or the new, money-earning productive functions available in domestic industry. But the physical hardship of work bore heavily on married women who had also to bear and nurture children. If some found a sense of purpose, few could find any individual self-fulfilment; indeed the concept is anachronistic for the pre-industrial economy. The family unit defined existence for married women and working daughters, and work was secondary, not an end in itself but a means to fulfil familial goals. It was from this early work pattern that women would move slowly to meet economic change.

The First Transition: The Domestic Manufacturing System

The basic nature of European society began to be transformed from the mid-eighteenth century onward. Literal revolution, beginning with the American and French risings in the eighteenth century, is now seen as part of more basic upheavals: the immense surge in population growth, the spread of commercial economic relationships and ultimately the industrial revolution itself. Outlines of these dynamic developments have been sketched mainly as they affected men, although women perforce, as bearers of children, are granted a role in the population revolution. Where to begin to measure the impact of the political, social and economic revolution on women is not at all clear. Many historians have correctly seen this important period as one of violent upheaval. While the early years were most difficult we need to look at the whole phenomenon. In fact, women not only played a vital role in society's transformation, as workers as well as mothers, but also carefully and constructively adapted to the new economic setting.

The initial increase of population from 1750 placed immense burdens on women as mothers who gave birth more frequently and had more surviving children to care for. The swelling ranks of people created economic pressures, thereby forcing the family to innovate in order to fulfil traditional support functions. The brunt of the increased economic burdens was taken by the males. Women's economic roles did not change fundamentally, although their work methods altered substantially. Far longer than men, who continued to work for the family but now increasingly outside its physical confines, women continued the literal definition of the family economy, working to supplement husbands' earnings and usually, if married, within the home itself.

Traditional holds were most binding for the female as agriculture remained the largest single employer of women until at least 1850 and in many areas beyond that date. Some historians have argued for a decline in agricultural labour during this period, claiming for example that the encroachment of enclosure on smallholdings in England left women without their usual means of employment.[12] However it has been suggested that agriculture, even on new large estates, became more labour intensive than ever before.[13] While new techniques were developed they spread very slowly; manual labour was not quickly displaced. With the spread of new crops such as the potato, women's agricultural functions increased, for cultivation of root crops had always been their prime responsibility. As cities began to grow, some women earned money wages in market gardening or dairy farming designed to supply new markets. Thus agriculture remained a prime employer for women with all its traditional trappings even in changed economic conditions. As late as the 1890s one can find French girls launching on the same career — as servants for a neighbour, hopefully to be capped with marriage and the specialised economic functions of the peasant wife — as their counterparts of a century and a half before.

Domestic manufacturing, during the century of transition was second to agriculture as an employer of women. Its numerical importance derives in part from the fact that it, like agriculture, demanded the least possible change, in terms of values, for the woman worker. It was by definition home-centred, easily a part of the family economy. However, within traditional confines it offered a chance for innovation in economic values as well as methods of production which was why domestic manufacturing was more beneficial to women than agricultural jobs. Here was a training ground in contacts with strangers, with handling money, with developing some sense of personal skill. It would serve women well if later they had to move beyond the home or into factories; it gradually changed women's outlook even if they remained in the system. The extraordinary persistence of domestic manufacturing well into the nineteenth century shows its appeal to women, who adapted to steady innovations in economic method — including ultimately the use of sewing machines and other powered equipment — in order to preserve the setting.

From the beginning the domestic manufacturing system involved a number of industries. In addition to textiles, the system served the gold, silver, iron, tin and jewellery industries. Women made tools, nails, bolts, screws, stirrups and spurs. Women metalworkers included some highly skilled operatives, though more commonly training was limited and much labour consisted of unskilled work as stampers or metal polishers. The typical female metalworker was young, apprenticed between 7 and 10 years of age and then continuing work until marriage in her early twenties. Girls who made pins went out still earlier, for it was assumed that pin-heading 'can be done by a child as soon as it acquires the use of its arms and legs' — typically around the age of five.[14] In compensation, metals paid relatively well for women. But access was difficult, and metalwork represented only 2.2 per cent of the female industrial labour source as late as the 1890s in Britain.[15] Male resistance was high, for metalwork had been a male preserve. The substantial training required discouraged many a woman because of other commitments; why spend years preparing, when the goal of work was marriage after which manufacturing could at most be only a sideline? The trade was costly to enter, for tools as well as raw materials surpassed the income of most peasant households, particularly the income that could be afforded to set up a woman at work. Economically it did not make sense in a peasant family to invest in an apprenticeship for a daughter. Finally, key metal industries early moved out of the domestic system, into factories, because of new equipment and the need for closer supervision of labour. Women, reluctant to work outside the home, rarely followed, and perhaps as a result it was in factories that male resistance to female entry would be most vigorously expressed.

Thus textiles with its reliance on traditional skills and no cost training remained the typical manufacturing outlet for women. Wool and silk are illustrative of the workings of domestic manufacture of textile goods. In both industries production equipment was relatively inexpensive. In neither industry was technical advance rapid (save in wool spinning) so not only did female domestic labour remain competitive but it was indeed essential for the maintenance of the industries. Women provided not only needed numbers of workers but but also adaptability. Their work remained in the home, but particularly in silk they moved into jobs that had previously been male domains, such as weaving. The evolution of the domestic system must be viewed as a combination of the familiar and the novel. Women's transition was made possible with the adaptation to new economic pressures within a setting that was their own.

The woollen industry was the staple manufacture for women in England, France and Belgium. In England it was said that 'there was probably not a town, village or hamlet throughout the length and breadth of the country which was not connected at some time or other with the manufacture of cloth'.[16] Women were supplied with the raw wool by the 'putter-outer' for washing and picking and then combing or carding. Spinning remained the female speciality, and well into the nineteenth century the spinning wheel was a basic piece of furniture in the cottager's home. This was a simple affair. In England it could be purchased for as little as half a crown. By the same token spinning was laborious and dull; it was estimated that a woman walked an equivalent of thirty-three miles in one week's worth of spinning, though gradual improvements on the hand-operated wheel increased the operative's productivity. How many women spun commercially cannot precisely be determined but at the height of domestic spinning the number ran into the hundreds of thousands. There were 36,000 in the English country of Suffolk, alone.[17] In France around 1800 there were 145,000 female hand spinners in the Nord.[18] Women unquestionably outnumbered men in this immense industry, and by a considerable margin.

Material conditions were poor, however. The willingness of women to work at home when at all possible made them easy targets for exploitation, for their key advantage to the employer lay in numbers and related low cost. In England in the second half of the eighteenth century a full-time spinner earned about 7 to 8 shillings a week, a married woman with other household or farming chores much less, about 2 to 3 shillings.[19] It is commonly accepted that these wages were 'inferior'. A spinner's wage would not allow a woman to survive by her labour alone. But she did not intend to; and in fact few men in domestic manufacturing could survive alone either, though their wages were higher. Without denying misery and exploitation, the key point about the domestic system for women is that it made sense. Rural women had never expected to survive on their own; this was what the family economy was all about. The mentality simply continued. And there were advantages apart from the sheer fact of being able to work at home, even while caring for a family. Hours of work would vary according to the family's need. This meant that in times of crop failure, when need was great, women might work up to sixteen hours a day to keep the family alive. But in other times they might ease off, deciding their own pace. Women could also measure their situation by comparing it to that of their grandmothers; with better equipment, women by 1800 were normally earning more than their mothers or grandmothers had. They were also earning more than a common agricultural labourer and, despite periods of unemployment, usually on a more regular basis. Domestic manufacture thus suited the work values of many women even though the conditions seem miserable to us.

Few men were involved with the spinning process so the question of sexual discrimination on the job is not as important here, though one can find individual cases of men earning more than female spinners, in part because, with greater strength plus freedom from household chores, they simply produced more. Male/female labour relations become more dramatic, however, in the case of weaving. Although weaving had traditionally been a male preserve, women became increasingly involved in it from the late eighteenth century onward. Initially this was simply because job opportunities expanded so fast. Women could easily work the narrow loom, which required less strength; hence whole production branches, such as the serge trade in Devon, were dominated by women.[20] Broadloom weaving was more common, however, and here men outnumbered women for several reasons. The broadloom required two workers, one an assistant. Given traditional peasant thinking, where the woman played a supplementary role, it was natural for her to serve as second to her husband, father or brother. Furthermore, broadlooms were expensive, large and difficult for cottagers to buy or accommodate their use spread rapidly to shops, where married women were reluctant to go. The considerable strength involved was the final factor. The weaver had to sustain the brunt of the loom with his chest, and women were simply not built for the job. Thus the relative lack of female weavers was due to a host of factors, ranging from physique to the values that made both women and men find it natural for married women to avoid work outside the home if possible and to serve as assistants rather than principals in complex operations. The result was that men working in the wool trade definitely earned more than most women, for as weavers their product was more valuable, the skill and strength required greater. Frankly, while options were at all open women preferred to be spinners, because the task was physically easier and could be more readily interrupted to allow attention to other duties.

In sum, while one could harp not just on exploitation but discriminatory exploitation in the wool industry, this would ignore what women sought from their work. Perhaps they should have moved to become principal breadwinners, but they never expected to take the leading productive role. With opportunities expanding amid a continuing desire to use work as a vital supplement to assure family survival (and not maximisation of earnings, either for self or family), what might be judged discrimination seemed natural, if it occasioned any thought at all.

The silk industry presents a slightly different case within the same basic framework, for here innovation and work on an equal footing with men became increasingly important. Women took part in all stages of silk production and so the industry became increasingly important to women. In England as late as the 1890s, for example, 30,000 women worked in silk production in the countryside, compared to 20,000 in wool. But in the heyday of domestic manufacturing, silk, as a luxury product, could not offer the number of jobs available in wool or cotton. It was further restricted by climatic conditions to certain regions, such as southern France. In the area around Lyons, however, silk manufacture employed up to a quarter of the population.[21] And its employment expanded, in contrast to some other fibres where factory production stabilised or even reduced available jobs. In Lyons and its surroundings expansion occurred, particularly in the countryside. There were about 16,000 looms in the city in 1790, and only 30 in the countryside; by 1870 there were 30,000 in the city and 90,000 in rural cottages.[22]

Silk manufacture was exceedingly delicate and women proved adept at all stages of the process. From the woman's standpoint silk proved particularly advantageous. The whole process could be carried on at home. It was common for women to grow their own worms, pull and reel the silk and finally weave the cloth. The work was light and clean, weaving involving a small loom that took up little space in the cottage. Men still tended to dominate weaving while women concentrated on preparing and spinning, but the sex differential never matches that found in the other fibre industries. In Lyons in the 1830s there were over 7,000 women weavers, and here and in England women averaged between a third to a half of the total (concentrating however mainly on the plainer kinds of cloth).

Domestic manufacturing offered an array of conditions depending on the industry. Sex differentials persisted to some degree in most industries, but the example of silk shows that women could close the gap. Pay levels were seldom high, for particularly after 1800, when machine competition became extensive, the domestic system depended on cheap labour, but for many women this was the first wide exposure to money wages. More important, the industry made sense in terms of traditional economic expectations. It is probable that for many women the system confirmed an attitude toward work that would persist even when circumstances no longer warranted acceptance of inferior pay and subordinate work roles.

Yet the domestic manufacturing system made a positive contribution to women's experience of work. Through domestic manufacturing women could preserve a substantially traditional environment, enabling them to adapt (however slowly) to a new social and economic setting. It allowed a steady shift into productive work away from the pre-modern service work. Pay was better and in many cases work more regular than pre-modern levels. These, rather than comparison with male conditions, were the important issues for women especially as both sexes still participated in the same family economy. Domestic manufacturing allowed traditional goals to be fulfilled more completely and in different ways; marriage could occur at a younger age, and more women could marry when they were earners in their own right. Domestic manufacturing certainly does not represent the modern woman at work but it provided a transitional stage, helping women to move from a purely agricultural role to industrial society.

The long term impact of domestic manufacturing on the female work experience should not be underestimated. Its significance was two-fold. First, the values women maintained or developed in domestic manufacturing were carried over into other kinds of work; the mixture of tradition and innovation is a key aspect of women's economic development. The second point is the amazing vitality of this particular type of work. As women moved to the cities they brought their 'cottage industry' with them. But now it was called 'home work' and generally involved sewing rather than spinning. Domestic manufacturing remained a viable work alternative for women, particularly married women, well into the nineteenth century, and in some areas into the twentieth century.

There was in fact no set pattern, but variation from one region and one country to the next. Without undue simplification we can posit two models that outline the role of domestic manufacturing in women's economic history. In the first, domestic manufacturing began to succumb to the factory system by the second half of the nineteenth century, first in the cotton industry, and then in the wool and linen trades. This is the model applicable to England and Germany. In England, cotton manufacturing quickly gained over the more entrenched rural production of wool and linen. Cotton itself was at first rural, and a heavy employer of women, but it rapidly moved into the factories. Germany simply found her traditional textile industry over-whelmed by British competition, resulting, again, in a reduction in employment opportunities for women after a brief effervescence of the domestic system.

In the second model, strong tradition, adaptive rural workers, and in certain cases (such as French silk) a vigorous export market in cloth difficult to mechanise long supported the domestic system. France, Belgium and Northern Italy fit into this pattern, for in all cases domestic manufacturing maintained itself as an employer of women into the twentieth century. France benefited from slower population growth than England and Germany, which allowed more people to stay in the countryside; manufacturers had to seek their work there or do without. But in France, Belgium and Italy the traditional formal employment of women in agriculture remained extremely high, so that female labour remained a vital part of these economies until well into the twentieth century.

The Second Transition: Work in the City

Advancing industrialisation in the nineteenth century sharpened the distinction between single and married women in the work force. The distinction was not new. Had a census taker travelled over England in the early 1700s he might have concluded that many married women were not formally employed. It had always been single women who dominated employment categories such as agricultural labour and servanthood. Married women worked hard, but in and around the home. Married women suffered the greatest economic loss with the transference of the home-production unit to the factory system in the city. Despite overwhelming pressures married women proved amazingly adaptive to the new situation. The major means of adaptation was the remaking of the 'cottage' industry in the city tenement. Married women in the city sought those work opportunities that allowed them to maintain the primacy of their domestic roles. Thus the typical experience throughout the nineteenth century and well into the twentieth century was 'home work': producing ribbons, artificial flowers and textile goods, often on a part-time basis. Another important avenue of revenue for the married woman was in caring for lodgers. Up to a third of the women in the urban working class took in lodgers in order to supplement the family income.

More lucrative was retailing. While the husband was out in the factory or shop, women with a bit of capital set up small shops, even bars; demand for small retail outlets increased greatly. The common arrangement, which is still very much a part of the European experience particularly in the smaller cities, was for the family to live in an apartment off the store. Thus for the woman and her children the economic unit was still primarily home-centred. Even those women who lacked the resources to set up a small store or provide room for a lodger found work. They commonly sought jobs such as washing and ironing, some occasionally did charring, others might take in children to care for.

Thus while the typical married woman in the urban working class was not formally employed and therefore not represented by economic statistics, i.e. the census, work they did. In countries like England and Germany only about ten per cent of all married women were reported as formally employed throughout most of the nineteenth century. The figure was higher, up to a third, in France where the agricultural and domestic manufacturing sector loomed larger, but within the urban working class the figure would have been comparable to England's. The only area to employ significant numbers of married women was textile manufacturing where up to a third of all working women were married. It has been said that the married woman who was employed was a woman with a husband dead, drunk or disabled. In the cities, formal employment, which involved earning a wage and labour outside the home was not acceptable or feasible to working-class culture. Men, and presumably women, found it inappropriate and degrading for married women to take outside jobs. Thus the working-class family, well into the twentieth century maintained itself on the wage of the husband and older children alone.[23] This shift in economic functions was to significantly affect the working-class woman's dealings with the workings of modern society.

How one begins to measure the impact of the new situation is a difficult question to answer. This is in essence the key point of debate in the equation of industrialisation with deterioration in women's role. There is no clear cut answer. If one considers the fact that the physical dimensions of the woman's lot were somewhat alleviated by the decrease in the necessity for her to find regular employment plus the fact that she could devote more attention now to her primary responsibility, her family, her position would appear to be better off. Without the burden of wage earning the woman could work at being a better wife and mother thus improving her position in the eyes of her family and, given her own sense of purpose, in her own eyes as well. At the same time, it is true that the absence of employment removed a potentially important outlet for self-expression. The male's dominance over economic matters indeed made the woman more dependent. Ultimately this would prove a problem for the working-class woman, particularly as a new culture developed stressing the desire for self-fulfilment. But this was a problem for the twentieth century, not the nineteenth. The problem of self-image for the working-class woman has only very recently been recognised. It is quite possible that the nineteenth century experience of heightened dependence retarded the working-class woman's struggle for a self-image. While noting this problem, it is important to keep in mind that this was a period of profound upheaval. Working-class women were confronted with many new problems – the lack of viable economic opportunities was only one. Until we examine her other problems, most important those arising with the increased numbers of children she bore and nurtured, we cannot perceive the full realities of the working-class woman's experience.

All this in turn means that the history of working women in nineteenth-century cities is the history of young single girls, spinsters and widows. For this group, particularly the young, economic opportunities increased steadily. The young female labourer's response to the modernisation of work was the same all over Europe and set the values that women would long apply to the job, and which apply to a great extent even now.

Two alternatives were particularly important in the nineteenth century — domestic service and factory labour. The first was vastly more important in terms of numbers. There can be no understanding of women's labour history without a grasp of the life of the domestic servant, despite the fact that historians have only recently recognised the importance of this work role.[24]

Servanthood: a Path to Modernisation

Domestic service came to rank second only to agriculture as an employer of women, and it was the first essentially new work opportunity to open up. Urban service was not entirely new, but women had only a modest foothold in pre-industrial times. During the nineteenth century women came to dominate domestic service and the locale switched from artisan household to middle-class household. Up to a third of all women worked as servants at some point in their lives by the mid-nineteenth century in France and Britain.

The vast expansion of domestic service is obviously related to the problem of economic alternatives. Women were pushed into innovation by the failure of other traditional fields to keep up with the growing population, and domestic service was an appropriate activity because it represented the least abrupt switch from tradition. For many girls it only seemed to involve a change in locale: domestic service instead of agricultural service. Daughters of an overcrowded rural cottage decided whether they would venture to the city or try to make do in the countryside. More important were the positive attractions of urban service which helps explain why, for example, it was chosen over factory work.

The popularity and persistence of servanthood stemmed largely from the transitory service it provided the young woman labourer. Domestic service allowed one to confront the new while maintaining familiar trappings; it maintained a family environment. Many tasks in the household were familiar. Girls who sent their earnings back to their family in the countryside clearly maintained their sense of the customary familial economy. Yet at the same time, the nineteenth-century servant girl was vastly different from her pre-industrial counterpart, and some girls entered service in part because they wanted their lives to be different. Migration to the city was of course the first change, and servant girls often moved great distances to find positions farther than factory workers whether male or female. Their social horizons inevitably expanded with the trip itself and then life in the city. The urban servant furthermore now worked for a family from a very different social stratum, not like the farm girl who simply had gone off to another peasant household. The middle-class setting added greatly to the changing experience of domestic service. Above all the domestic servant of the nineteenth century proved far more mobile than her pre-industrial counterpart. She not only travelled much further, but also changed positions constantly, on the move from job to job as often as once a year. In contrast the pre-industrial servant usually was committed to the same position for seven years or more. The servant experience thus became a distinctive one.

Actual conditions of servanthood varied immensely from one situation to another. In a formal sense a clear hierarchy existed: housekeeper on top, followed by lady's maid or chambermaid, head nurse, cook, upper housemaid, still room maid, nursemaid, under laundry maid, kitchen maid and scullery maid. Wages, living quarters and prestige differed greatly with position in the hierarchy. The duties of a chambermaid centred on the mistress's personal needs, keeping her clothing in order and good repair, arranging her hair, helping her dress. The cook not only prepared meals but was responsible for shopping and cleaning both kitchen and dishes, though she might have assistance from a young girl, called in France the 'aide de cuisine'. The most specialised group of servants were the nurses, whose chief ward was the children. Nurses included women who were wet nurses, breast-feeding the newborn infant; the *bonne d'enfants,* or nanny, who cared for the child during its first years; and finally, most privileged of all, the governess who ordered the child's primary education.[25] Within the servant hierarchies, as in all hierarchies, careful snobbery was practised. Although both servants, the housekeeper and scullery maid recognised the wide gulf between them; many a housekeeper found it beneath her station to speak to one so lowly, conveying orders through an intermediary servant. Wages confirmed the social network. A housekeeper earned more than four times as much per year (at £18 to £40) as the scullery maid (at £6).[26] At the same time, for a lucky few, hierarchy also meant mobility hopes and opportunities, for a diligent young maid could rise in station.

Most domestic servants, however, remained outside this complex hierarchy, and this is the most important point, against common impressions of lavish households and servant multitudes. Only the upper class could afford a servant hierarchy, and the expanding opportunity for women came mainly in the middle-class households. Here most servants, working alone or with at most one colleague, found their duties extremely varied, doing all of the work the many servants in the retinue of a nabob accomplished. The range of duties was suggested in the title, the English maid-of-all-work or the French *bonne à tout faire*. Upper servants must not be neglected. Their numbers increased rapidly as the ranks of the entrepreneurial class surged upwards. Yet the upper servants combined, male and female, were vastly outnumbered by the lowly general servants, who comprised two-thirds of all servants in France, three-quarters in England.

The ability of the middle-class family to afford but a single, unskilled servant meshed at least in part with the background of most girls entering service. The girls were novices, with no relevant training. In a typical pattern the young country girl left home at 14 or 15 to make her way to the city. Few servants had been born in the city. In Versailles in 1820, over half of all servants came from outside the department and only 15 per cent had been born in Versailles itself; by 1872, with the explosion in servant numbers, 81 per cent came from outside the department and only 8 per cent had been born in Versailles. In Lyons in 1872, 20 per cent of the servants had been born in the city, the rest outside. In Paris, the largest centre of domestics, at least 60 per cent of the girls were from rural districts, here particularly often travelling great distances from the mountainous extremities of France or from impoverished Britanny.[27]

With predominantly rural backgrounds, the first problems of the new servant were shaped in advance, for the contact of country ways with the expectations of the urban middle-class was typically abrupt, causing tension on both sides. Mistresses frequently tried to train their rough employees giving curt orders and criticising sloppiness.

These country girls were not, however, typical country girls in that their willingness to travel many miles suggests girls with unusual spirit and an unusual range of motivations. Cities attracted the venturesome young, now that the tight network of the rural family economy was under seige. The cities paid the highest wages and offered a new social world, with the gay life of cafés and theatre; as witnessed by Juliette Sauget, a positive drive to get to Paris, 'where life seemed more enjoyable'.[28] Thus many girls who could have worked closer to home in factories passed instead to the big city using servanthood as their means of urbanisation.

Servanthood provided the wandering stranger with a sense of identity or at least a sense of the familiar. The identity was provided by the family context, the continuity with rural tradition in which young girls expected to work in a situation of personal dependence.

Here was protection against the scale of city life for a girl separated from her own family. And few, even with no prior training, had to wait for work, as job opportunities increased steadily.

More important, there was a concrete economic advantage in servant-hood. At first glance domestic wages appear appallingly low, even in contrast to factory labour. In France a female cotton spinner earned about 780 francs per annum in the latter nineteenth century, a servant 390 francs. In England the same pattern prevailed, where a factory worker could earn as much as £35 annually compared to the £14 of the maid-of-all-work. But the servant's wage came on top of additional remuneration that provided a higher net gain. The servant received room and board, which a factory hand had to provide for herself. English records suggest that the cost of feeding a servant alone amounted to £30 per year; another estimate at the turn of the century mentioned £20,[29] but even with this lower figure the servant was already matching the factory hand, before housing and other advantages were added. Thus in France servant wages, room and board amounted to 1,300 to 1,400 francs a year, close to double the earnings of the female factory worker; in England servants received the average equivalent of £45 annually.[30] There were further advantages beneath the formal figures. Bonuses were expected, such as the Christmas box in England or the New Year's gift in France. Many girls received travel expenses when they first took a job plus a small bonus for signing the work contract.[31] While in service a girl might receive used clothing from her mistress — and a smart girl found other ways to supplement income. Quite commonly servants arranged kickbacks, called poundage in England and *sou pour livre* in France, with local tradesmen: a percentage of the total bill was remitted in return for regular patronage. Servants also could sell ashes and fats for additional money. An increasing stream of complaints suggests that many young girls were more proficient at learning these practices than in mastering domestic chores *per se* — another sign that a new acquisitive motive was entering the female work experience. Certainly many servants, combining regular wages with side earnings, could amass modest savings.

And with savings new motivations continued, though leavened with tradition. Usually, some money was sent home to the girl's family. More, however, was retained for her own dowry. Here was a customary practice now in a new context, for the dowry was more clearly one's own, as was the choice of one's own mate. Domestic skills learned in the middle-class household could further enhance the marriage prospects of a servant girl. With savings, knowledge of household management and new standards of cleanliness, and frequently the ability to read and write, the servant girl could find upward mobility through marriage. In France at least a third of all servant girls married well above their original station to small businessmen or prosperous artisans. How many servants were drawn to their job with the hope of making a good marriage we do not know. But this was the clearest, long-range potential advantage of servanthood.

There were inherent problems and indeed one reason that marriage proved such a desirable outcome was that an entire life of service, although necessary for a small number of spinsters, would have been difficult to contemplate. Living conditions were often crowded and unhealthy, particularly in France where middle-class families lived in small apartments. In England, where town houses were more common, servants might find a bit more comfort and privacy. The French servant often had only the crawling space under the roof of the sixth floor of an apartment building or was bedded in a corner of the hallway or kitchen. The attic rooms lacked heat and ventilation — cold in the winter, blisteringly hot in summer. Often three or four girls, serving different families in apartments below, might be crowded in a single bed. Diets were probably a bit better than the lower-class average, but many mistresses skimped here and servants could see that they did not eat as well as their employers. The work load constituted the most onerous aspect of service. At an extreme a girl was expected to labour 15 to 18 hours a day, six and a half days a week with an additional whole day off per month. The work was routine and long hours were only mitigated by a slow pace. The mornings were the worst, for the day began at five or six in the morning with setting the fires and preparing breakfast; then came dusting, making beds, cleaning floors. In the afternoon there was shopping, and a bit more freedom; a girl might meet friends and escape the eye of her mistress. Still the work load and lack of privacy were severe disadvantages, even if not entirely unexpected to a girl raised in the rural tradition.

The plight of domestics gained public attention in both England and France. English women's magazines ran articles week after week depicting starved teenaged girls abused by callous mistresses who treated them as unfeeling machines. By the 1860s service was being compared to slavery. French concern was not as high, but the need for reform in housing conditions was widely discussed. In neither country was there much practical result from the reformer's concern. A few homes were founded to help servant girls who became pregnant and lost their jobs. Vocational training schools were set up to improve skill levels, but attendance was low. A few governmental regulations over housing were passed by the end of the century. Yet for the most part conditions continued to depend on the resources and character of the middle-class mistress. The fact that hundreds of thousands of girls continued to pour into servanthood well into the twentieth century suggests the ongoing attractions of the job, at least among available alternatives. Wages improved, as a means of attracting service, at least until the later nineteenth century, and probably working conditions eased a bit. But immense drawbacks were inherent in the work.

This is where servants themselves entered the fray, for they were not without some power to improve their lot. Formal organisations of servants were established in the later nineteenth century but they drew few members and accomplished little. The servant, isolated within private households, did not feel herself part of a class, and her remedies were typically individual. Some elements of the middle-class mentality of self-help might stimulate renewed venturesomeness on the part of a girl who grew accustomed to the city after a year or two. Finding conditions unacceptable the servant voted with her feet. The rate of turnover was extremely high, as girls rarely spent more than a year or two in any one home. This was one way to cope with the severe burdens of servanthood. Even if objective conditions did not improve with a job change, at least there was a brief period of hope and a slightly different setting. Here, first expressed in servanthood, was a key nineteenth-century female adaptation to urban work: short-term periods of employment with frequent changes of scene. Capping this in turn, was the view of work itself as a stage of life, a temporary occupation, to be followed not by other formal employment but by marriage. Servanthood helped a higher percentage of girls to marry than ever before, blending traditional goals with new methods of fulfilment.

The Girl at the Mill

Factory work involved a dramatically more novel setting than servanthood. This feature, along with certain economic disadvantages, made it less attractive but women who did enter factories developed work responses surprisingly similar to those of servants. Women, too easily seen as malleable pawns under a severe household mistress or a factory owner looking for cheap, docile labour, produced defences of their own. Within an admittedly limited context, they were not out of control of their situation.

The numerical importance of factory work varied with time and place. Countries like England ultimately had a large number of women in factory work. Where domestic industry retained greater vitality, as in France or Belgium, and more women had formal jobs overall, the percentage not only of employed women but of all women over the age of twelve working in factories was lower. Thus in England by 1871, some 580,000 women worked in textiles, at least two-thirds of them now in factories, whereas in France no more than 200,000 women worked in textile plants though textiles in general, counting the segment still using the domestic system, employed more women than in Britain.[32] In Britain, where factories came to have real importance, the incursion of large numbers of women came only after 1850. A few key mechanised industries, such as cotton spinning, employed a high *percentage* of women earlier; by the 1840s upwards of 40 per cent of all cotton spinners in French factories were women, and the figure may have been higher in Britain. But precisely because mechanisation was so productive in spinning only a small *absolute* number of workers was required. While recognising the importance of women's labour to certain early factory industries one must keep in mind that factories and women's work developed very slowly only and incompletely as far as the bulk of the female work force was concerned.

Tradition inhibited the expansion of women's work in the factory. Most women entered those areas in which they had previously worked in the countryside, notably textiles and, later, food processing. In textiles, tradition was maintained as women stuck mainly to the spinning plants. At first, simple weaving machines drew young female workers, but soon they were largely replaced by males. Important aspects of the family economy were maintained in the factory setting. Many girls in the early factories lived at home or returned there for weekends or at harvest time; their work in the city was considered temporary and supplemental, any extra earnings were supposed to go to the family kitty. Even when a more distinctly urban working class emerged, female work remained dependent on the family. Hence spinning was regarded as supplementary to weaving, the task assigned now to the main breadwinners: the husbands, fathers, and brothers. One result was that the weavers proved more tenacious than spinners in resisting technical changes that might eliminate jobs; the female task being only ancillary to the family economy.[33] With few exceptions, mainly involving young girls in the early phases of industrialisation, women were barred from male production lines even as these were mechanised: hence they were rarely seen in the mines and almost never in metallury or the working of metals.

As with domestic service, however, innovation was unavoidably a part of the factory setting. Most important from the female view point was the introduction of machines. Women historians like labour historians continue to argue about the impact of machines. Some hold that machines severely limited women's economic role.[34] Where a large number of jobs in domestic industry were eliminated, as early occurred in spinning, the argument has some force, particularly in Britain and Germany where the percentage of women formally employed undoubtedly declined. In this case we must await a fuller assessment of the non-work role of the married women. However, most single women found work, and underemployment among women seeking jobs actually declined. Further, once the initial impact of industrialisation was absorbed, the percentage of women employed held up well and even increased. As child labour declined, by mid-century in Britain and France, due to legislation but also the growing complexity of machines, women were able to take over a greater share of textile manufacturing processes in the factories. Wage trends indicate women's gains clearly, for the average pay of female operatives, though inferior, rose more rapidly than that of men.[35] Demand tended to exceed the supply of interested women. Certainly women, unlike some men committed to traditional methods, did not attack machines directly; there is scant evidence of female Luddites.[36] Those women who entered the factories at all adapted to machines readily, a trend we will see also in later white-collar work and in the household. If women were displaced by early machines they were not of the right age nor usually in the right place to comment on the source of their difficulties. Those women who did go into factories could see machines as a source of improving wages and lighter physical work loads.

Most female factory workers were young and single; in 1841 in England 50 per cent were under 20 years of age.[37] The number of married women who continued factory work was confined almost entirely to the textile centres, where the type of work had greatest contact with tradition. Over 20 per cent of all married women might continue on the job in textiles in contrast to domestic service and in contrast to centres of mining or metalwork, where outside employment almost invariably ended with marriage. The lighter work made possible by machines helped maintain a minority of married women in textiles in the factories, and could prove better than harvest work or seed drilling. The pay was definitely superior. Some women also enjoyed the social contacts, the chance of meeting a variety of people found in the factories.

Factory work inevitably involved greater difficulties than domestic service. Surrounded by billowing smoke and stench, deafened with the noise of machinery, the factory could easily scare off a young farm girl even if she had to endure the work only until she could find a husband. The rigorous time schedule and tight supervision of the factory made many a mistress of servants look almost benevolent. The lack of personal contact with employers, at least in the larger plants, was particularly troubling to women who were used to dependence but on an individual basis, not in anonymity.

The horrors of the nineteenth-century factories are familiar. Many factories were literally death traps, lacking light and ventilation and offering no protection from dangerous equipment. Women in textile firms worked in hot boxes, most windows were kept closed to keep the fibre supple. Hours of work were long, at worst up to sixteen a day with few breaks, more commonly thirteen to fourteen in the early textile factories. Injuries were common, and if the work was physically lighter it was more intense. A moment spent in idle dreaming could mean torn clothing or a lost hand. Sexual assaults by foremen and other workers were grim realities.

The married woman faced added difficulties in the factory.[38] Exhausting work and long hours outside the home left little time or energy for housework, yet domestic chores had to be done. Child care was particularly difficult, though some factories allowed children to stay near their mothers — a double benefit in keeping experienced women on the job and preparing children themselves for factory work at an early age. Broken health and broken families were the price paid by many married working mothers in the early throes of industrialisation. The impact of the factory extended well beyond its interior hell. Where work had to continue problems were passed from generation to generation. Children in textile centres suffered worse health compared to those in other working class communities. Mothers at the mills could not attend to their children's minimum needs. Poor health in childhood insured a disabled adulthood, the inability to do heavy work, which confined much of the next generation to the low-paid textile centre where they had been raised. A vicious circle entrapped the most vulnerable — the women and the children.

The problems posed by women's factory work drew early attention from contemporary reformers, far more abundant and effective than in the case of domestic service which, properly or not, was regarded as 'natural' for women. In the early 1830s the British Sadler Commission recounted horror after horror, to a wide audience, and these efforts, which prompted the first legislation generally limiting child labour, were followed by recurrent public campaigns to protect the abused woman. An 1847 law limited hours of work for women as well as children to ten per day, and while imperfectly enforced it did begin to reduce the sheer physical burdens of factory work. France limited hours of female labour during the revolution of 1848, though durable and effective legislation awaited the 1870s. Germany and Denmark first offered specific protection for female factory workers in the 1870s, Belgium and Holland and the Scandinavian countries within the next two decades. Meanwhile regulation of sanitary and safety conditions, beginning in Britain in the 1850s, reduced some of the most obvious on-the-job dangers.

Legislation applying specifically to women was ambiguous in several respects. In singling out the factories it missed the majority of women labourers who endured long hours of arduous toil in the domestic system and in domestic service. Also restrictions on women's participation in the economic sector were not new (one need only look again to the guild restrictions put upon women). The nineteenth century reforms were part of a large scale reform movement in general which was concerned with the age-old abuses of a subsistence level of agriculture which were not to be perpetuated in the industrial nexus. Thus children's labour was controlled even more vigorously than women's. The rate of reforms most clearly reflected the widespread cultural belief that women's work outside the home and in the city was basically unnatural, a belief dear to middle-class reformers but shared by many workers as well.

By the late half of the nineteenth century, with the rise of a new consciousness among some women, a new concern developed over the discriminatory impact of laws that applied only to women.[39] Women, for example, who were not allowed to work as long as men, or at night, were kept from key jobs – doomed to a perpetual state of economic subordination. The sentiment was put well by a twenty year old worker in England who objected that 'she would sooner work longer hours for more wages than shorter hours for less; and she was accustomed to only work and did not mind it.'[40] By the early years of the twentieth century efforts at regulation were beginning to be applied to workers in general. Another bias in legislation which is still with us today is that women are often unprotected, in pension and insurance plans, which are based on relatively high levels of earnings and a long period of work for the same company.

In evaluating the effect of protective legislation for women workers one should keep in mind several points. First, as noted earlier, the demand for women operatives rose faster than the supply during the very period when special legislation was at its height. Second, the early factory laws were the first to take account of the special problems of women at work, of the realities of the dual roles, at home and on the job. Neither legislators nor employers had ever considered women's many burdens before. Finally, the full impact of the regulatory legislation for women workers was not felt immediately since it did not affect those areas of work that women found most suitable. Rather its long term implications were to be most damaging to the development of women as individuals.

Nineteenth-century factory legislation did not alter the fundamental values applied to work by the female labourers. For as with servant-hood, factory work for most girls was only a brief experience, confined to young girls who would tolerate many unsatisfactory conditions because they did not plan to build their lives around the job. The female factory operative's main objective in working was to get married and be able to stop working. Within reason, long hours, unsanitary conditions, even crude foremen could be endured. During the six to eight years spent in the factory there were compensations. Wages were high, and if one lived with one's family there was extra to spend or save. Some factory girls who turned over money to the family might find that their status in the family was enhanced. They might be consulted more often when the family had to make decisions; and they were viewed as knowing more about the modern world than their mothers, born to rural ways, could claim. Gradually, as in England by the second half of the nineteenth century, factory girls could keep back some of their earnings for their own use, giving them a chance to save up a dowry and/or buy something for themselves. Girls might value the factory also as a place to meet people, including prospective mates. Never, save in harvest work which was by definition episodic, had girls developed job experience so rich in social contacts. So we need not view the time spent on factory jobs as one unmitigated horror. Without question the whole experience was tempered by the hope that it was temporary — even if, for a minority of women, the knowledge proved false and work had to continue.

Like servants, factory girls changed jobs frequently, a sign of their distinctively low sense of specific job commitment and desire for variety. In any given occupation, they changed jobs more often than men. Similarly, factory girls normally ended work with marriage. With their own earnings and with much easier social contacts, they in fact married far earlier than was the pattern among servants (although the gap was greater in France than in England, where servants were more quickly urbanised and more anxious to leave employment).

Urban work of all sorts was thus directed toward marriage. The widely-sung horrors of factory life and the dependent position of the domestic service without doubt contributed to the new urgency in getting married. Had jobs been more rewarding, chances for equality in pay and promotion greater, a different pattern might have developed. The question is, however, academic for the historian. Marriage remained a desired goal. What the new work patterns did allow for was more women to attain this goal than ever before; aided by their independent earnings which served often as the initial family savings and the increased social contacts.

The most subtle changes occurred with marriage. With girls now free to make choices as individuals, the romantic element began to compete with the age-old paradox determinant economics. A new self-consciousness, fed by the work experience, slight as it was, modified a traditional institution, even though marriage itself might dampen the sense of individualism over the years.

Acceptance of marriage in some combination of traditionalism and individual self-expression obviously rebounded on the female work experience itself. Women did not acquire the job experience or skills necessary to advance, with rare exceptions such as the women who climbed in the servant hierarchy, accepting this by desire or necessity as a permanent career. Significant advancement was irrelevant since the urban job experience was by definition temporary. Without doubt greater efforts at advancement would have encountered discriminatory resistance. Perhaps women sensed this. But few probed deeply enough to experience the problem directly. There is evidence that employers would have welcomed a more stable female labour force and would have increased wage levels to attain it — if the device would have worked. Few women were ready to oblige. Whatever the mixture of pleasure and shock that new urban jobs offered, there was no desire to enjoy or suffer it permanently.

Relative lack of concern over poor conditions and unequal pay scales stemmed from traditional conditions plus the marriage escape hatch. From pre-industrial times women were accustomed to segregated job roles and, where pay had been involved at all, lower wages. Industrialisation actually increased the variety if not the number of jobs available and exposed more women to individual and usually rising wages. Measured by the past, it was hard to find this entirely bad. Above all, work was a means to an end; it was temporary. So why worry about annoyances, why even consider equality, so long as one could hope to get out after five to ten years? Participation in unions activity, particularly strikes, could easily seem counterproductive, for someone whose working years were going to be short; why disrupt earnings now for relatively remote goals? Equality had particularly little meaning for a women who planned to form her own family economy, relying primarily on a man's earning power, as quickly as possible. Women, who had traditionally had distinctive work roles, now, in the industrial cities, translated this into a lack of deep job commitment.

The result was a circle that was difficult to break into. Unions, male-dominated, became hostile to women because of their indifference to job gains. Many discouraged female membership, so those women who came to find grievances on the job lacked the most obvious outlets for expression; many would decide that the standard pattern was best, dropping their grievances in favour of looking for a husband.

Yet, precisely because the job experience of nineteenth-century women, combined with pre-industrial tradition, failed to nurture the same work orientation that men developed, we must be careful to attempt an assessment appropriate in women's own terms. It may have been undesirable to break into the circle. We may err in judging the female work experience by male standards, where it is inevitably found wanting. Women simply did not define their lives through work. Even as they were pressed into newer work roles that initial industrialisation imposed, even when they began to participate haltingly in some protest efforts, they never, as a group, lost the primary identification with the family. Their work contributions, in jobs old and new, their work within the urban family which we have yet to assess, were vital to the industrialisation process. The possibility of dual identifications, for married women who could continue work, might enhance life; so might the simple experience of successive life stages in which work gave way to family in primacy. The distinctive female work ethic developed in the nineteenth century was a fairly successful adaptation to the initial impact of the upheavals in modern economy.

Labouring Women: The Turn of the Century, a Time of Trial and Triumphs

By the later nineteenth century most male and female workers, even in the countryside, were involved in the so-called 'market economy'. Many were accustomed to new machines and new units of work. Urban growth continued but more slowly, so fewer people had to adapt afresh to city ways. In these and other respects the new economic structure had matured and the first shock of rawness and alienation had worn off.

For women workers, however, the late nineteenth century brought certain elements of crisis. The ingredients of crisis are these:

1. From the mid-1870s onward agricultural prosperity declined in Western Europe, bringing with it an absolute decline in the number of people employed. This affected women severely, particularly countries such as France and Italy where it had remained the major employer; even in England, where the agricultural population had long been a minority, this was an important blow to women's jobs.

2. At the same time domestic industries reeled from what was virtually the final blow. In Germany, for example, domestic manufacturing employed 15 per cent of all workers as late as the 1890s; but by 1907 the figure had plummeted to 6 per cent. Major branches of textiles, leather (including shoe manufacture) and woodworking were converted to factory production. Even the mechanisation of button manufacture could displace tens of thousands of workers.[41] Women were disproportionately affected by this change; more than men they had depended on maintenance of home based, rural employment, and this was now sorely challenged.

3. Though less important numerically, married women who earlier might have hoped to set up a small retail shop found their opportunities reduced. Female retailers still expanded but at a slower rate than before, as large department stores edged into what had been an important activity for many women.

4. The employment levels in those few factory industries where women provided significant labour stagnated or declined. This was true particularly in textiles, now afflicted with growing international competition and a new round of technological improvement. Men fled the industry faster than women, who could try to hang on to what was usually a temporary or supplementary job. The absolute number of women employed in textiles did not drop. But the industry could not absorb what was still a rising population, as more and more women came of the age to enter the work force.

5. The growth of the servant class slowed in Germany, came close to stagnation in England, while in France the absolute number of servants began to decline by the 1890s. This means that all of the major sources of employment for women typical of pre-industrial and early industrial times had lost their resiliency if they were not on a definite downgrade. The case of servanthood, however, differs from the others, in that the decline resulted in part from new choices by women workers

themselves. And if new motives were in play here, they might be involved in other economic sectors or at least aid in adapting to a new onslaught of change.

This was the context for the relative decline of servanthood. More middle-class families decided that servants posed an undue burden on their budget, that an occasional charwoman to help out with cleaning chores would suffice. As a result, servant wages tended to stagnate, which reduced and then eliminated the economic advantage of the occupation over most forms of factory work. We have suggested that servants were early aware of economic advantage, and growing experience with the urban market economy could only sharpen their calculation. Increasing numbers of working-class girls or even peasants newly in from the countryside decided that they did not want to serve as live-in maids; their decision might precede that of the middle-class housewife. In England, Germany and elsewhere, former servants began to pop up in factories, proclaiming their new found freedom. The Germans noted that 'the foremen are not nearly so coarse as the gracious ladies', while English servants noted that they found 'more life' in the factories.[42] The number of servants actually transferring was small, but the number of girls not entering the occupation at all, in contrast to their mother's choice or their elder sister's choice, was significant in a growing female labour force. Particularly as any economic advantage was removed, girls could express a new sense of personal independence, which preferred the comparatively remote supervision of the factory to a household routine. The trend noted earlier, that few girls born in cities entered servanthood, became most prominent; servant job-changing was now switched to avoiding the occupation altogether, for a number of girls. At the same time factory conditions improved in the latter part of the nineteenth century, even in textiles. Hours were firmly limited, to twelve at the most; sanitary and safety measures, enforced by regular inspection, helped make these jobs more suitable for women. With rising wages in addition, the decline of servanthood, at least in its percentage of women employed, made considerable sense.

With this, we face a series of questions: did the end of the nineteenth century usher in a crisis for women's employment, a relatively gentle modification in patterns, or a revolution in opportunities?

It has been suggested that what was happening toward 1900 was that women were forced for the first time to confront industrialisation head on, as their menfolk had done fifty years or more before.[43] In fact, however, there is little evidence of a major crisis. Instead we see a surprising but largely successful readjustment in women's work patterns, but nevertheless echoing the female work ethic established earlier in the nineteenth century. Without question percentages of women employed in the previous leading employment categories diminished but newer fields were quickly adopted and more then compensated for any loss.

A significant number of women were able to hold on to traditional types of jobs and very few were forced out of jobs on which they were well launched, except in the case of servants who moved to factories by personal choice. Nowhere save in Belgium did women's hold in the formally employed labour force diminish; in most countries it rose. This suggests that the crisis in traditional occupations was modest *and* that many women were capable of adapting to new jobs.

Domestic industry declined in many branches of production, for example, but not in all. In France the percentage of workers in the domestic system remained stable, as women switched from textiles and leather, where opportunities were shrinking, to the manufacture of clothing. This was indeed an extreme case, which other countries, such as Belgium, could not match. Equally important for our understanding of the evolution of women's work is that the decline of domestic industry and agriculture was sufficiently gradual to allow women to meet the challenge successfully; in countries such as Germany, where domestic employment had been hit hardest earlier, further decline was more than compensated for by new opportunities for women in factory production. Servanthood, similarly, must not be written off. It stopped growing, but it still was the largest single employer of urban women, hundreds of thousands of them in all the major industrial countries. We are talking of a modification of the early industrial job pattern, not an upheaval in job choice and certainly not in work values. Even the distinction between the English and French patterns remained. Despite increases in female employment in the former, the percentage of women employed in countries like France remained higher. Nor, finally, was there a significant breakdown in the tradition that married women should not work outside the home, despite the stagnation of outlets such as small shop retailing or domestic manufacturing. Only in Germany did the number of married women at work exceed their growth in the population before World War I. Between the wars the pattern was dented further, as workers had to modify their culture and allow wives to work when possible to meet the challenges posed by inflation and then depression to their standard of living. But traditional values remained strong, and the typical woman worker was young and single.

The change that kept the percentage of employed women rising in most countries combined a slight increase in the numbers working in manufacturing, including branches of industry which women had not penetrated previously with the growth of massive new job opportunities in white-collar work. The white-collar job proved particularly suitable to the female wage-earner, in part because it retained significant similarities with traditional work patterns. For this reason another impulse, long expressed, remained generally valid: the desire or need for most employed women to look outside the factory for work. The new work roles conformed neatly to what was now becoming a pervasive female work ethic: frequent job changing, a view of work as supplementary and temporary, and above all, a desire to combine work with a quest for personal contact, for socialisation. The preference for a personalised work context had long showed in the desire to cling to home-based manufacturing or even servanthood. This was still the case. In England, the growth rate of factory employed women between 1871-91 was but 20 per cent, compared to 106 per cent in domestic service; as late as 1911 textiles and dressmaking combined claimed only 800,000 women, while domestic service still drew 1,302,438.[44] More important for the future, even if still overshadowed numerically by older kinds of job choices, white-collar work gave women the impression at least of a personal touch plus the broader social vistas which they were now increasingly eager to enjoy.

Note must be made of the shift in factory employment, though the numbers involved were relatively slight. Women in manufacturing increased in percentage terms as well as in number in England and Germany, where domestic industry had already been reduced and even to a great extent in France. But with textiles stagnating, there was a modest tendency to head toward printing, metals, machine tools, chemicals and the production of furniture. By way of example the growth rate of the female labour force in English metals from 1891-1911 was over 4 per cent per year (compared to 1.1 per cent for both sexes combined); in printing, 3.6 per cent; in chemicals, 6.7 per cent. German expansion was even greater, as fewer women had entered factories previously: hence metals showed an 8.6 per cent increase, printing 12.8 per cent, machine building 20.5 per cent — all higher than male growth rates in these industries.[45]

Impressive as these figures are, they represent only a minor upsurge in women's work in general. Manufacturing labour of all sorts, by no means all of it in factories, still claimed less than half of the female work force even in England. And the new industries into which women ventured could not begin to rival traditional standbys such as textiles and dressmaking, which together employed over 85 per cent of all women in English manufacturing in 1911. The impressive German growth rates in a few new industrial branches contributed to an expansion of little over 3 per cent per year in women's jobs. For the absolute numbers of women involved in the new industries remained small. In none of these industries did women rise to over 10 per cent of the total labour force. New machine techniques in printing and metalwork did bring a growth of semi-skilled jobs, of which some women took advantage. Their entry was noted, and resented, by men; and in some immense industries, such as construction and mining, women made no impression at all. A French printer summed up the common sentiment, which kept women out of many unions in new industries even when it did not totally bar them from shops and factories:

> They're too impulsive. One day they're enthusiastic for our work, the next day they've changed their minds. The only way to resolve this problem would perhaps be by absorption. Each male typographer would marry a female typographer. That would be the solution.[46]

What was happening, then, was a minor readjustment. Women very slightly increased their total role in the manufacturing labour force and in factories particularly: 17 per cent of all manufacturing workers in Germany in 1895, they constituted 18 per cent in 1907; 21.5 per cent in 1891 in Britain, they were 23 per cent in 1911.[47] A few women gained new experience and new earnings as semi-skilled workers in industries that had always, even before industrialisation, been closed to them. But male attitudes toward women at work did not change. And women's own outlook, dampened perhaps by male resistance, did not change markedly either. Manufacturing was still not women's preferred work. Married women showed almost no sign of increased entry to the factories. Well into the early decades of the twentieth century women strove to accommodate work to their primary role of getting married and then raising families.

The White Blouse Revolution

Yet, within the context of a mini-crisis in the traditional fields of female labour, a revolution took shape in one economic sector, white-collar work. The kind of job a country girl newly arrived in the city would seek and obtain *began* to change; so, even more, did the range of jobs open to the daughter of a working-class family. Even middle-class women began to enter the labour force, launching a trend that today involves as many middle- as working-class women in formal employment. As in factory labour, the rise of white collar and even professional jobs involved a skill upgrading ranging from a high level of mechanical skills such as typing at the clerical position to formal training as teachers and nurses. Women's growing-up process was put into a higher gear in the field of work, though ties to traditional values remained a problem.

The time schedule in the maturation of women's work can still be illustrated by the differences in the English and French patterns. England experienced the first impact of new work roles, if only because there had long been fewer traditional job outlets and because industrialisation was farther advanced. Yet there was a quick response from women in the French pattern which was in many ways more remarkable, given their long-standing attachment to home based, even rural surroundings.

Women made the adjustment to new jobs with relatively little active protest. There was no outburst comparable to that of male workers before World War I. Cultural indoctrination to be passive, and exclusion from many male unions are obvious factors here, but we will see that women could be quite demanding when they found the cause important, not only in formal feminist agitation but with issues that were most central to their lives, as in fighting infant and maternal suffering. Work innovation was welcomed because it did meet the mini-crisis in jobs and because it confirmed many of the values women had long sought in employment, thereby preventing thorough alienation.

One of the key areas of work to open up for women was in domestic retailing. By 1914 in England there were half a million female shop assistants. Essentially this job was replacing domestic service (and allowing most women still to bypass the factories). Instead of serving in a middle-class home, girls now served middle-class retailers and customers. There was still no need for elaborate training. Many early shop assistants were in fact provided with room and board, which maintained a contact with tradition for a while. But despite long hours and often strict rules of behaviour and dress (none of which was new to women workers), there was a growing sense of independence and variety in retail work, which is why more and more girls came to view domestic service as beneath them.

Even at this level an important element was added to the criteria by which a young woman chose her job: respectability. For the majority of female wage earners this was more important than maximising pay. Thus women preferred work in retailing to more lucrative but physically more demanding and dirtier jobs in factories. Often respectability amounted to nothing more than a facade, involving work for up to ninety hours a week (far longer than factories ever required); in the smaller shops there were no formal meal breaks, and girls ate only when there were no customers to serve. Sanitary conditions might be foul, for her, as with hours, state regulation did not yet apply; one girl in London's East End reported that she had to share a small and barren room with eight others.[48] Legislation was slow in coming for the young female retail clerk. The contrast with factory laws was striking. An 1873 bill in England to limit the hours of women and children in shops was quashed. In 1886 a bill got through because of its mildness, limiting hours for women under 18 to 75 per week. In the early twentieth century more stringent legislation on hours and sanitary conditions (and requirements that chairs be provided for retail clerks, who had often been compelled to stand all day to appear alert and ready for the doubtful customer) was passed, but it applied to both sexes. This was an important development. White-collar work, perhaps because it was newer, involved less blatant sexual discrimination. Thus when legislation was passed women did not automatically lose their positions because of special disabilities.

Given these sombre conditions of work, why were women so seemingly eager to take retail jobs? Despite the growth of department stores, most worked in medium sized shops employing three to ten clerks. Therefore the element of familiarity and the opportunity for close personal contact was preserved. These were service jobs, and the key to respectability was in a sense the distinction between service and manufacturing work. In a service job one dealt with people from various social classes; one wore a decent dress (even if it was the only good dress one owned). Disparities between the sexes were minimal (save for the fact that supervisors were largely, though not exclusively male), for here as in many of the new jobs women quickly came to monopolise the field. Retailing kept ties with tradition; even monopolisation of a form of work by women, who worked largely with each other, harked back to pre-industrial forms. Work values developed during earlier industrialisation were also served: the desire for wider social contacts including the chance to find an attractive mate. Here, retailing had the clearest edge over servanthood and factory work. Newer values still, respectability and independence (compared at least to the confines of domestic service), were at least partially expressed. Long hours, nothing new to the woman worker were therefore endurable. Low pay, no novelty either, persisted as well. For women retail clerks still changed jobs frequently, still viewed their work as temporary, and thus tolerated the abuses.

One does not want to stress the tolerance level of the new woman worker too much. The level of tolerance was quickly qualified. Earlier and more clearly than in factories, female clerks participated in unions to improve their positions. The National Union of Shop Assistants (later the National Amalgamated) formed in the 1880s in England, admitted women on an equal basis from the start, in marked contrast to most manufacturing groups. Women were simply too numerous to be denied. They could even be elected to any union position. Discriminatory efforts existed but they were fought. As a consequence, they were not as blatant as those found in the traditional work channels. Efforts to establish minimum pay for shop assistants in the early 1900s at first dealt only with men, but it was soon realised that these efforts would be a mere sham if women were not considered as well; by 1906 the English campaign included women, on the basis of a minimum wage 75 per cent that of men. Early unions and job campaigns were weak in retailing, however. The isolation of small shops made cohesion difficult; so did the great variety of conditions from one shop to the next. Thus weak unionisation followed patterns characteristic of earlier factory industry. Perhaps even more important was the fact that most women did not want to unionise, even though male opposition was minimal. Less than 10 per cent of female retail clerks were organised by 1914 in Britain. This was a conscious decision made for very familiar reasons. The female shop assistants were young and single; well over a half were under twenty-one years of age. Their expectations and goals were not found within the union's platform. They expected to marry and stop full-time work, and as such their motivations were short-term. If their wages let them support themselves (as always, many lived with their parents, at most paying room and board), and, save for eventual marriage, as long as the job provided social contacts and some sense of personal autonomy, grievance levels were low. Especially in its formative years, unionisation had to be based on long-term commitment to a life of work, in which temporary sacrifice was obviously worth the effort. For women, work remained a means to an end, not an end.

As retail work expanded a 'white blouse' revolution was occurring in clerical employment that was to prove even more fundamental in changing women's job patterns. In England the rate of expansion of female clerks was 446 per cent from 1861 to 1911. Women flocked by the thousands to the new jobs created by the expansion of bureaucracies in government and private enterprise, virtually displacing men in key branches of clerical work. Here was women's clearest economic haven after the transitional phase of servanthood, for with the progress of industrialisation the number of clerical workers increased more rapidly than that of actual production workers.[49] The growth of banks and insurance companies as well as industrial bureaucracies provided new jobs, and in filling them women workers became more pervasive and indispensable to the economy of modern society than ever before in their work history.

The key to women's success in clerical jobs which, in the early industrial period, had been monopolised by men, was dominance in developing essential new skills. Never before had women presented so many varying levels of skill. Most relevant in the clerical world were shorthand and typing — prosaic abilities, perhaps, but these were well in advance of traditional female skill levels and were also skills men proved reluctant to master. Many a male clerk was fired or retired protesting the intrusion of typewriters and adding machines into the world of handwritten ledgers. New skills, as in factories involving adaptability to new machines, were essential to offices of all types by the turn of the century. And women did not let their skills become obsolete as they conquered the advancing technology that was steadily introduced into office work. After a slight lag, the telegraph provided thousands of jobs for women and the telephone was almost immediately a female device; in the 1870s one might hear a male voice at the switchboard, but this was not to be true again until the 1970s.

Women were right in step with clerical mechanisation, and the reward was not simply jobs but, again, respectable jobs. The work was light and clean compared to factory labour or domestic service. And as typical of the newer white-collar jobs there was less blatant discrimination by sex. The positive aspects of clerical work included better human surroundings. Office buildings provided increasingly impressive and comfortable physical working conditions. In contrast to retail work as well as factories, hours of work were relatively modest; clerks did not have to start work until eight or nine in the morning, again a first in the history of employed women. Wages varied — highest in insurance and banking, lowest in transport (where women provided the smallest number of clerks in any event). In England female clerical workers averaged between £50 and £100 per year depending on skill, experience and age. Finally, in terms of most women's expectations, clerical work provided considerable interest. There was more independence from supervision, less need for deference, than in any work open to masses of women. Secretaries, even switchboard operators could meet more people than factory girls could, and people of a wider range of social backgrounds. Even new office machinery could prove a challenge, for, except in some factories, women's work had typically been confined to the simplest of tools.

Nonetheless office work was still work. Increasingly large units, with rows of typists and rules purporting to regulate work breaks, even the time one had to go to the toilet, made it clear that this was no escape from the basic work environment of industrialisation. And traditionalism was not totally eliminated. A few women might rise to the position of office supervisor, but almost all female clerks worked for men whose jobs they could not aspire to attain; there was no open mobility ladder here. Although job satisfaction was still considerably higher than in the more traditional servile activities. Office rules were made to be broken. Clerks and secretaries always found the chance for informal socialising, for a somewhat self-determined pace of work, in contrast to the rhythm large factories had succeeded in imposing. Working under male supervision with limited mobility was no new experience. As always, clerks were protected by the belief that their work would be temporary; indeed the chance to make a 'good' marriage, perhaps even with the boss, was one of the attractions of the job, however imperfectly realised in fact.

It is not surprising, then, that as with female retailers, efforts at unionisation made only limited headway, though they were undertaken. A National Union of Clerks was formed in England around the turn of the century. In 1912 an Association of Shorthand Writers and Typists actually banned men from membership. But these organisations were small, and fragmentation further reduced their effectiveness. Interestingly, key demands focused on what we would call fringe benefits, insurance programmes and pensions, rather than basic conflicts over wages or hours.[50] This suggests not only that the latter were not regarded as unduly burdensome, but that some female clerks were taking a slightly longer-range interest in their jobs, to the extent that pensions, for example, might prove important. A minority of older women, including spinsters and widows but also some married women, did put many years into clerical work through the early decades of the twentieth century. This was a pattern of increasing importance during the economic uncertainties of the 1920s and 1930s, when many married women, even in the middle classes, needed income and respectable work. Yet the basic female work pattern was not yet broken, as the typical clerk was young, single and expecting to get out in due course, with little or no interest in formal organisations. Hence a smooth adjustment to a major new kind of work which easily fits the expectations women had developed about what a good job should be.

Focus on the processes of adjustment to new jobs, however, is not the whole story, either in the early industrial period or at the turn of the century. The gradual urbanisation of women's work brought about undeniable problems. Individual women could not take advantage of the jobs available. If the expectation of marriage was not met or if one's husband died or was disabled, an older woman was thrown into a labour market that valued speed and dexterity in female employees and was dominated by the young and single. Many found only the most miserable jobs or no jobs at all, though as noted white-collar work began to break this pattern somewhat. Even aside from the host of individual problems, it remains possible to view the work adjustments of the majority of women as unfortunate. After all, women failed to get top pay or top jobs. Yet we risk the application of irrelevant standards in stressing this too much. Most women did not seek the 'top' in work (many men in fact did not either). Work was designed to fulfil limited goals, and for many women it did so.

The Pioneering Professional

By the end of the nineteenth century a somewhat different world of work was developed for women, which involved quite a different job ethic and ultimately a more varied set of grievances. The rise of women professionals, almost entirely from middle-class backgrounds, was not revolutionary in terms of numbers. Few middle-class women were professionals even by the 1920s; only a small percentage of all women workers were professionals. But even small numbers could provide a challenge to the work values of other women and to the expectations men had of employed women.

It is difficult to generalise about professional women's work experiences. It has been said that when women entered an occupation in large numbers they tended to dilute its professional qualities. Whether this is true or not remains to be seen. It is common to deal with women professionals in terms of journalists, nurses, teachers, artists, novelists, actresses, lawyers and doctors. Yet it is obvious that the training and experience of the woman doctor are very different to that of the painter or even the nurse.[51] It has been suggested that professional status is achieved only when an occupation attains the following: a professional association which sets standards of training and entry *and* conveys any new knowledge which will keep the profession from competitors; insistence on regular, formal training followed by an entry examination; and, finally, strict licensing procedures. These then are the criteria applied generally to male professions. A profession differs from other occupations in its ability to control entry. Without question, the list of professions expanded with the maturation of industrial society. Not only doctors and lawyers but also architects, engineers, accountants and others made the grade by the 1920s. Other key groups such as teachers and nurses also moved toward professional status but never met the full set of requirements. Both teaching and nursing, indeed, established associations, but they did not directly control standards and could not completely restrict membership. Both have developed increasing standards for formal training and examinations with licensing required in many instances. However many enter the ranks without fulfilling the established set of requirements. The teaching and nursing professions have been able to enforce their own standards, and therefore to control entry, effectively. In England and France, for example, the bulk of the teachers, particularly females, were uncertified − not licensed − and not graduates of formal teacher-training schools, well into the twentieth century. Fields such as nursing and teaching achieved only semi-professional status; whether this was a direct result of women's entry is a point of consideration.[52]

By the twentieth century there were outright women professionals. A handful of women served as doctors and lawyers; far fewer entered the newer professions such as engineering or accounting. But the bulk of women aspiring to something more than factory or clerical work were to be found in teaching and nursing. Their inability to reach full professional status resulted from two factors. Men, who ran school systems and hospitals and who, as politicians, set licensing procedures, did not view women as potential professionals. They might seek them as teachers, where their skills were vitally needed in an expanding occupation, where their vaunted maternal abilities seemed particularly applicable, and where their lower pay scales relieved many a school budget. But without doubt they would discourage them from professional aspirations. By the same token most women, possessed of a set of values not incomparable with that of the mass of women workers, did not develop the permanent job commitment necessary to achieve professional status. Perhaps the most important requirement for professional status that is more or less assumed is the difference between job-orientation and career-orientation. For the woman professional this is a crucial difference. A profession depends as much or more so on the individual's full self-identification with the job than the prerequisites noted earlier. In very simple terms, the job is one's life: I am my profession. This remains the most critical stage for self-development in the women's growing-up process as we will see in the discussion of women's contemporary economic struggles. For now it is important to emphasise the facts: most women workers were confined by a job-orientation mentality rather than a career orientation. Even in teaching and nursing the commitment was limited. A teaching job was, more often than not, a temporary experience, to be dropped after the main goal, marriage, was achieved. Which came first in this situation can be endlessly debated: women's work values were obviously reinforced by job discrimination, while this in turn was partly based on the work values that were well established by the late nineteenth century.

Yet, important as the failure to achieve full professional status is (even males in primary school teaching, where women soon predominated, shared in this failure), it should not obscure the important gains involved in massive female entry into teaching and virtual monopolisation of nursing. Never had so many women found jobs based on extensive training. If a health role was not entirely new — midwives, usually untrained, provided some precedent for women in nursing — the teaching role had been traditionally if not exclusively male.

Female nurses existed in the early nineteenth century, mainly as untrained menials in hospital wards, scrubbing floors, making beds and washing linen and bandages. Some cooked for and fed the patients as well.[53] Typically, these nurses came from poor families and devoted their lives to a religious order, as in France where the *Soeurs de Charité* worked as nurses while vowing poverty.[54] Faith in God, however, was not enough to meet the expectations of an increasingly health-conscious society, and this is where both new jobs and new training came in.

Florence Nightingale is rightly hailed as making the nursing profession scientific and respectable — and most definitely female.[55] Earlier efforts were made; for example, in Germany, Theodor Fleidner organised groups of deaconnesses to study under him for five years before becoming nurses. Inspired by this example Elizabeth Fry organised the first English institution to train nurses. The religious orientation remained strong, as Florence Nightingale discovered; to modify this, Nightingale set up a school requiring a year of close training and seeking to attract better-educated candidates in the first place. Classes and regular examinations became integral aspects of a nurse's preparation. The hold of religious communities delayed comparable developments in France. Among the pioneers for change was Anna Hamilton whose book on nursing encouraged the formation of schools first in Bordeaux and then in other cities including Paris.

The result of such efforts in all industrial countries during the second half of the nineteenth century considerably upgraded nursing. With new respectability and growing need, numbers expanded rapidly, growing in England by 210 per cent. Nurses' associations were formed from the 1870s onward, attempting to require registration of all qualified nurses. But it was not until 1919 that state licensing was provided in England and Wales, with a General Nursing Council established to supervise the operation.

Nursing had come a long way from the dark alleys surrounding the city hospitals of the early nineteenth century. But while it was now respectable, nursing had not shaken off all the implications of a charitable calling, which prevented even trained and highly motivated nurses from some logical rewards, such as reasonable hours of work or sustaining salaries. On the continent religious orders continued to compete with the newer secular organisations of nurses, leaving the latter at a distinct disadvantage in bargaining, and in approaching formal professional status. In England, the supply of nurses quickly exceeded demand, adding greatly to the problem of professionalisation. Hospitals spread rapidly, but not as fast as the number of women seeking respectable work and an outlet for their rising level of education. Hence despite vigorous organisational struggles to professionalise, less than a third of all nurses were certified by 1901.[56] Even after licensing was required, the material conditions of nursing remained meagre. And despite their legitimate claim to scientific knowledge, nurses worked under doctors; unlike a true professional they were not in ultimate command of their field.

Even so many women found new opportunities in nursing. Working-class girls used, and continue to use, nursing as an avenue for social mobility, an access to the middle-class world. Precisely because requirements concerning training, examining and licensing were completely formulated, many women could take advantage of the opportunity to enter an eminently respectable occupation. For despite special training, nursing retained obvious ties with the larger world of women's work. It recruited heavily from groups such as domestic servants, for the work was not entirely different. As usual, mobility was not simply occupational; many women found or sought in nursing the chance of a good marriage. This in turn meant that many nurses lacked a professional mentality, i.e. a long-term devotion to the job. A 1913 study in England showed that the average length of service for a nurse was four years; this was a 'meantime' occupation between school and marriage.[57] Here was one reason that, until compelled to do so, many girls found it neither desirable nor sensible to spend the time and money required for certification, while hospitals in their turn, pressed for funds, tried to hire whomever they could.

Nursing and teaching prove surprisingly akin to other forms of women's work. Both produced articulate demands for better conditions and equality of opportunity with men. Female primary school teachers could be found pushing these demands in France as early as the Revolution of 1848. However both occupations accommodated, particularly venturesome women from a wide social spectrum: the daughters or urban artisans, who could acquire a bit more education than usual; daughters of middle-class families. A minority, by necessity or design, made a career of it. The two new aspiring occupations fit within the general pattern of an upgrading of female skills without a revolution in work values.

The case of women in the so-called traditional professions and to an extent in the arts was far different. Here was a decidedly atypical female experience, accessible and relevant mainly to women in the upper-middle classes. Here also was the key ingredient missing in the new female professions of teaching and nursing: an unusual sense of job commitment. Professional women confronted overt sexual discrimination and severe economic liabilities head on. When the traditional barriers finally cracked women found that institutions such as law schools and medical schools cost money that few could afford; even a wealthy family hesitated giving funds of this magnitude to a mere daughter, for a son more logically fitted the bill and guaranteed surer rewards.

Among the male professional strongholds some proved more difficult than others to penetrate; for example, law proved most difficult while medicine was the first to lower its discriminating barriers. This no doubt was due in part to the influence of nurses who proved themselves quite capable. Neither profession can be regarded as friendly, however. Women doctors made more rapid progress in countries like France and Sweden than in England. A noted French doctor, Mme Kergomard, was nominated to the *Conseil Supérieur de l'Institut publique* in the latter nineteenth century; by 1900 French women doctors had their own publication, *La Revue de Médicine et de Chirugerie féminines.* In England, pioneering women had to work around the centuries-old walls of prejudices. They had to resort to finding loopholes in admission procedures to the medical profession. Elizabeth Blackwell, trained in America, was the first woman doctor recognised in England.[58] Elizabeth Garrett Anderson, another noted physician, came in through a back door by passing the examinations for the Society of Apothecaries.[59] Excluded from obtaining the necessary training in hospitals and dissecting rooms in England, it was almost impossible for women to pass the medical qualifying examinations. It finally took an act of parliament to require medical schools and hospitals to open their doors to women. And even then the battle was just begun; Sophia Jex-Blake faced constant harassment from male colleagues in Edinburgh, although she withstood the siege to become the first woman in Britain to obtain her medical certificate through the traditional male channels. But before World War II there were only a tiny handful of women doctors in England.

Individual women were pioneers in the legal profession also. In France the first female lawyer, Mme Jeanne Chauvin, fought vigorously for the rights of women to enter the profession. But the fight was arduous, especially in England, for as late as 1902 there were only twenty women barristers in England.

As individuals, women made their mark in the universities, engineering and architecture. Mme Marie Curie demonstrated women's potential in science, winning two Nobel prizes in the early twentieth century. Women made a greater impact on the arts, although not to the extent of preventing recurrent questions such as 'Why are there no great women painters?' The struggles of women art students resembled that of the medical pioneers, as they were barred from particular classes when human models were used. Despite the lack of public sympathy, women of the nineteenth century were making their mark in the profession: Rosa Bonhaur, by way of an example, gained a reputation in French painting during the 1860s. As literary artists women excelled. Literary women blossomed in the nineteenth century (with precedents even earlier such as Mme de Lafayette who is credited with writing the first novel, at the end of the seventeenth century). Mme de Staël, George Eliot, Georges Sand, Harriet Martineau, the Brontë sisters – the list here is long. Early in the twentieth century Selma Lagerlöf won the Nobel Prize for Literature. The theatre provided women with another field of expression, and from music halls to grand opera and the Shakespearian stage women 'artistes' made a profound mark on modern culture.

With the partial exception of work in popular theatres, the history of women artists and professionals is clearly a history of enterprising women. Openings were created which were to prove more significant after World War II, though women have yet to gain a significant share of positions as doctors and lawyers in the Western countries and lingering cultural inhibitions keep most of them out of training efforts for professions such as engineering.[60] We can legitimately hail the pioneers, who combined perseverance with family backgrounds that provided enough influence and income to support not only a long training period but a long battle for acceptance. By the same token, we must note the distinction between these women and the world of work for the masses of women. Professional women, whether married or single, had to devote their lives to work, the only area of female employment where this was typically the case save out of necessity.

Thus the struggle here for women was fought on many fronts. The strongest front proved to be tradition: women were simply not fit to work alongside the chosen few. Institutions of higher learning built walls around them not to create an environment for learning but to keep out the unwanted and for centuries this included women. The other fronts were more subtle and therefore most pervasive. On the personal front women had to battle with their own families' preconceptions of their destiny; sons were professionals, daughters were not. When women were able to break open a small crack in these fronts they faced yet another: costs. As we have seen women were beginning to succeed in their challenge to the traditional front and the family's preconceptions. However the battle was not carried forth immediately becuase of the lack of funds. One of the saddest commentaries of the female experience as it struggled in the nineteenth century and pushed forward in the twentieth century is the failure of women financially to support a key channel in their growing-up process – higher education. The laments of Virginia Woolf in 1928 told the story of the past in her very moving essay *A Room of One's Own*. Her realisation that the inferiority of women's higher education was in part due to the fact that women did not take care of themselves first. Dismayed at 'the reprehensible poverty of our sex' Virginia Woolf lashed out at her foremothers:

What had our mothers been doing then that they had no wealth to leave us? Powdering their noses? Looking in at shop windows? Flaunting in the sun at Monte Carlo? If only. . .her mother and her mother before her had learnt the great art of making money and had left their money, like their fathers and their grandfathers before them to found fellowships and lectureships and prizes and scholarships appropriated to the use of their own sex. . .our mothers had mismanaged their affairs gravely.[61]

The point was well made, for many middle-class women raised funds — did and still do — but rarely for themselves. They have spent many hours knitting and sewing clothes, making foods, soliciting funds for one cause after another; homeless children, alcoholics. But comparatively little time and effort went into taking care of themselves and their own daughters.

Yet while we separate the true professionals from the masses we risk returning to a familiar confusion. Professional women are typically hailed as the finest examples of women's modernisation. Those whose work experience did not measure up are easily regarded as missing something, missing a crucial aspect of self-identity. Without playing down the importance of the professional experience, however, it does not make sense to measure the whole of women's work history by what a handful of women did. This is the barest transposing of measurement by male standards, and male upper-class standards at that.

Women made contributions and won rewards at semi- and sub-professional levels. Their adaptability at the turn of the century, in entering white-collar jobs and, a step above, teaching and nursing jobs, easily compensated for the decline in traditional roles in domestic service, agriculture and textile manufacture whether at home or in the factories. The wave of the future had been established without a total disruption in work values. Women were going to type, teach, sell and nurse, as they retreated from traditional service functions and, in terms of the proportion of employed women involved, from production as well.

And here we can return to another vital problem, while waiting for the discussion of the evolution of women's work roles in the most recent decades. Women did retreat from production. In pre-industrial society they had supplemented producers, though already with a heavy leaven of service functions in urban artisanal households or in peasant cottages. The typical woman, married or single, did some productive labour, by raising vegetables and tending domestic animals. In the reaction to the first onslaught of economic change a substantial minority of women moved entirely into the service sector, but most women who worked at all were still involved with production, in agriculture, domestic manufacturing, and to a lesser extent in factories. By the end of the nineteenth century the commitment to service was becoming marked. From the pioneers in the formal professions to the lowly shop assistant, women were serving, not making. They won jobs, they confirmed their overall work ethic. But had they been excluded from the economic mainstream?

Women's Work and the Great War

The question can be posed precisely in terms of the history of women's work in World War I. Many historians have seen modern war as the only time in which women could display the full range of work roles, then to be shoved back to economic inferiority immediately on the war's end. While there is some validity in this view, at least in terms of certain problems of postwar adjustments, it is basically faulty. Modern war tended to speed up the processes of female work adjustment, not thwart them. Through this we can essay a final evaluation of the pre-contempoary work adjustments of women.

World War I created a serious labour shortage which women were called upon to meet. It is easy to claim that only now were women given full economic expression, having been held back in all prior stages of industrialisation from fulfilling their natural desire for identification through work. The war proved, in this view, that women could do a man's job as soon as men stopped blocking their way. And then, as suggested above, the male conspiracy returned; as soon as the troops returned, women found themselves forced out to pasture again.

Women did take on factory jobs in World War I. This was not totally new, however, for women were entering metalwork and other 'male' industries earlier; but the pace was vastly stepped up. In armaments manufacture a few women won highly paid factory jobs. Yet the majority of women took these jobs not because they were now free for self-expression but because self-expression was denied them by war itself. With men at the front marriage rates plummeted, and with them the sought-after goal. Married women, deprived of their man (and often widowed) felt the direct threat of economic misery; new work was the only recourse. The deterioration in the civilian standard of living — the lack of adequate food and clothing — affected women severely. Citation of a few women in high-wage jobs may cloud the facts; they were few in number, and high wages brought scant improvement in living conditions in the best of circumstances in those embattled years.

The war accelerated the decline of traditional female work sectors. Domestic service was particularly hard hit, though it was far from dead; over a million and a half female servants continued working in Germany. Domestic service had been dying of female volition already; the wartime jolt was not great. Women manufacturing workers in the luxury trades were harder pressed; production in dressmaking and millinery was drastically reduced by declining demand and lack of raw materials. Branches of food processing, such as confectionary, were hard hit. The war exacerbated the previous crisis in the traditional sectors of women's manufacturing. Thus the net gain of women in essential wartime industries, such as metals and munitions, did not constitute a massive increase of women in manufacturing overall. There was an increase of factory as opposed to shop employment and a change in skills. But even in the new areas women rarely performed the same tasks as men, as assembly line techniques and automatic equipment subdivided skilled jobs. Enterprising manufacturers used this opportunity wisely to introduce new machines. Women proved quite adaptable to new equipment and willing to reap the small rewards from the new, semi-skilled positions.

However, the principal contribution of women to the war effort was, predictably, outside the industrial sector, as jobs in government and business offices proliferated. The hundreds of thousands of women filling office jobs and operating communications centres easily outnumbered the few thousand women filling new factory roles. Women involved in transport work, for example, increased immensely. But few worked in repair shops or in running vehicles. Most worked in offices, ticket selling, and of course cleaning interiors of ships or trains.[62]

Hence in England the growth rate of women in the industrial sector from 1911 to 1917 was just 18.7 per cent, not a dramatic annual increase over earlier levels; absolute numbers rose from 2,275,000 to 2,702,000 women. The total number of women replacing men in the factories amounted to at most 376,000.[63] Industry brought some shifting of women, along lines already suggested; it brought relatively few new women (except youngsters reaching job age who probably would have sought manufacturing jobs anway) into industry. Most new employment was concentrated in already growing white collar service sectors. Yet even here, one must be careful to place new numbers of women on the job in the proper context; delayed marriage, with men off at the front meant delayed departure from jobs, but not a permanent disruption of women's work goals.

Women, particularly in manufacturng, were displaced by men at the end of the war. The marriage rate soared (as it always does after a major war). Some women were undoubtedly disgruntled at displacement, having tasted new work and independent earnings. Perhaps more women than before found it desirable, if not always possible, to combine work with marriage. There was in fact an increase in the percentage of married women working in the 1920s. They were mainly from working-class families, as economic pressures could not be handled without more wage earners, while reduced family size cut the income from older children at work. But the over-riding impression remains one of continuity tempered by gradual evolution; the war created neither radically new work patterns nor demonstrably higher levels of female disgruntlement when some opportunities were closed off. In belatedly achieving marriage women continued to find the logical conclusion to formal work. The steady increase of women in white-collar jobs in the postwar years confirmed that the war had operated within the evolutionary context of women's work. Legislation in several countries, as in England in 1917, raised the school-leaving age to fourteen and maintained some school requirements up to eighteen. This naturally worked to curtail the absolute number of women working *and* their percentage *vis-à-vis* men, for women had long concentrated their work experience in their teen years. But improved schooling correspondingly opened the way for ever-increasing numbers of women to claim the abilities necessary for white collar work.

Twentieth-century industrial society is a service oriented society. Outright production jobs command an increasingly small percentage of the total labour force. This at least suggests an answer to the problem already raised. In so far as women moved more rapidly than men from production to service work they were seizing on the leading economic trends of a maturing economy. They might not yet grasp the summit. They made inroads into the formal professions, themselves in the service category, but they were in no sense feminised. Service work at lower levels proved compatible with women's work goals and constituted a highly viable economic adaptation. Through this ongoing adaptation women would weather mini-crises prompting employment shifts and wartime economic disruption without losing sight of what they wanted out of work.

Of course the story is not over. One must test every stage of women's work history for an understanding of what was expected from work and what was gained. This test becomes increasingly imperative in recent decades and indeed in projecting future trends. But during the initial phases of economic change, stretching to nearly two centuries, female adaptability was high. Women concentrated in jobs judged particularly suitable but were able to broaden the definition of suitability as the service sector modernised and expanded. Where they could not find suitable employment they held out in the majority of cases, preferring the intense but unpaid work of the housewife. Their job reactions allowed them to bear the pressures of industrialisation more successfully than male workers.

They were perforce exposed to change, and managed at their own pace. They consistently, save in the recondite professional sphere, refused to make their primary identification with work. This explains relatively low levels of protest; it explains acceptance of distinctive conditions. The evolution of women's work and work ethic requires a broad context, for women themselves placed it in a wider view of life. Long seeing their work as part of a family economy, existing or to be formed, long seeing the family as the antedote to an unacceptable work commitment, women essentially modernised their work as the family itself evolved. Given their primary focus, women were inevitably prime movers in the shape the family took.

Notes

1. G.D.H. Cole and Raymond Postgate, *The British Common People* (1961).
2. See for example, the work of Ester Boserup, *Women and Economic Modernization* (1970); Shelia Rowbotham, *Hidden From History; Rediscovering Women in History from the 17th Century to the Present* (1975) and Betty Shield, *Women in Norway; Their Position in Family Life, Employment and Society* (1970). Women's work role has been downgraded further by the growing belief that with industrialisation women were forced out of the labour market and that therefore their economic contribution was truncated. Quite apart from the solid economic contributions provided by the work of housewives, a vital aspect of women's family history, this view is misguided. One of the persistent myths pervading women's work history is that at some point in the past there was that 'golden age' when women worked as equals to men, when women's influence was as important as that of men if indeed women did not dominate because of their vital production role. Exactly when the golden age existed is usually, and deliberately, left vague. Some find the golden age in Western Europe around 1750-90, the peak years of the domestic manufacturing system. But, aside from the brevity of the period which suggests that women were kicked out of Eden almost as quickly as in Biblical times, this was already a period of change and it was really the beginning of the modern evolution, not to be abruptly terminated with the advent of modernisation. Other historians have more logically placed women's golden age earlier. Germanic women, tending garden plots and caring for domestic animals while their men hunted and fought, perhaps had more important roles than did their counterparts in

medieval Europe, where both men and women worked at agriculture but with
women now in a definitely subsidiary position. The equation can be turned
around, however, with an argument that women had their best shot at work
equality in a purely agricultural society.

3. The work of Emmanuel LeRoy Ladurie, *The Peasants of Languedoc,* trans.
John Day (1974) and that of Hufton, *The Poor of Eighteenth Century France*
both describe the inferior work roles for women in pre-modern times.
4. *P.P. Report on Employment of Women and Children in Agriculture,* (1843),
p.109.
5. *Publications of the Board of Agriculture:* H. Holland, *Cheshire* (1808), p.282.
6. Hufton, *The Poor of Eighteenth Century France.*
7. Pinchbeck, *Women Workers,* p.282.
8. Hufton, *The Poor of Eighteenth Century France,* p.317.
9. For a good discussion of prostitution and working-class girls see Judith R. and
Daniel J. Walkowitz, 'We are not beasts of the Field: Prostitution and the Poor
in Plymouth and Southampton under the Contagious Diseases Act', in Mary
Hartman and Lois W. Banner, *Clio's Consciousness Raised* (1974), pp.192-225.
10. Hufton, *The Poor of Eighteenth Century France,* p.210.
11. For a discussion of the importance of this new work for women's sense of
emancipation see Edward Shorter, 'Female Emancipation, Birth Control and
Fertility in European History', *American Historical Review,* 78 (1973),
pp.605-40.
12. Pinchbeck, *Women Workers,* pp.27-52.
13. Slicken Van Barth, *Work in the Agricultural Revolution* (xxx), p.xx.
14. *PP Report on Employment of Women and Children in Agriculture,* (1843),
XII, p.7.
15. Peter N. Stearns, *Lives of Labor; Work in Maturing Industrial Societies* (1975),
p.396.
16. E. Lipson, *The History of the Woolen and Worsted Industries* (1921), p.6.
17. Pinchbeck, *Women Workers,* p.134.
18. Ministère de l'agriculture et du commerce, *Statistique de la France:* Industrie.
LV 1847-1852.
19. Arthur Young, *The Farmer's Tour through the East of England* II (1771),
p.75.
20. G. Lipscomb, *Journey into Cornwall* (1799), p.144.
21. Robert Bezucha, *The Lyons Revolts of 1834* (1974), p.8.
22. Ibid., p.25.
23. For a good discussion of women's work roles in the family see Joan Scott and
Louise Tilly, 'Woman's Work and the Family in Nineteenth Century Europe',
in Charles E. Rosenberg, ed. *The Family in History* (1975), pp.145-78. On
budgets, Maurice Halbwadis, *L'Evolution des besoins* (1933) and *La Classe
ouvrière et le niveau de vie* (1913).
24. For an excellent study of domestic service in England and France for the
nineteenth century for which I am greatly indebted see the work of Theresa
McBride, *The Domestic Revolution* (1976) and 'Social Mobility for the Lower
Classes: Domestic Servants in France', *Journal of Social History* (1975),
pp.63-78. Generally it has been assumed that domestic manufacturing and
agriculture rapidly declined (itself an over-statement) and women either
vegetated or rushed off to factories along with the men. Yet even in England
the number of women in the factories was insignificant through the first half
of the nineteenth century. In 1841 there were 8,787 women in factories
compared to 712,493 in domestic service (*Parliamentary Papers;* Abstract of
the Answers and Returns. . .Population of Great Britain: *Occupation Abstract,*
1844, XXVII). Factory labour existed and it would expand steadily but it
never commanded the attention of most women workers, for even when

domestic service began to fade out women sought other alternatives.

25. For a controversial discussion of governesses and their lot see M. Jeanne Peterson, 'The Victorian Governess; Status Incongruence in Family and Society', in Martha Vicinus, *Suffer and be Still: Women in the Victorian Age* (1972), pp.3-19.

26. Isabella Beeton, *The Book of Household Management* (1861), p.8.

27. McBride, *The Domestic Revolution,* Chapter 2.

28. Ibid., pp.37-39.

29. Jane Ellen Frith Panton, *Leaves from a Housekeeper's Book* (1914), p.24.

30. George H. Wood, 'Real Wages and the Standard of Comfort Since 1850', *Journal of the Royal Statistical Society* 72 (1909), p.21.

31. *The Servant's Practical Guide: A Handbook of Duties and Rules* (London, 1880), p.169.

32. For the 1871 figures for England see *Census of England and Wales,* 1871, Summary Tables, Table XIX, p.xliv; Table IVII, p.xxxvi.

33. For a discussion of family work roles and factory settings see William M. Reddy, 'Family and Factory: French Linen Weavers in Belle Epoque', *Journal of Social History* (1975), pp.120-22.

34. Esther Boserup, *Women and Economic Modernization,* (1970), p.xx.

35. On the rise in female wages see Ministère du travail et de la prévoyance sociale, *Salaires et coût de l'existence à diverses époques, jusqu'en 1910* (1912).

36. There is very little work done to date on female Luddism. Available information is vague as to the nature of the rioters. It is never clear if women were involved directly; for example, Pinchbeck in *Women Workers* notes brief hostility to the spinning machine in the late eighteenth century and some machine breaking. At this time it seems that women were more active in inciting and supporting male rioters than the actual attacks, but even here the evidence is very scant; see B.L. Hutchins, *Women in Modern Industry* (1915), p.270 (and here only one occasion of female inciters was found in Leicester in 1788): Rowbotham, *Hidden from History,* notes. New findings of M. Perrot indicate minor incidents of female Luddism in France also.

37. *Factory Commissioners' Supplementary Report,* Part 1, XIX, p.38.

38. See the work of Margaret Hewitt, *Wives and Mothers in Victorian Industry* (1958).

39. Elizabeth Leigh Hutchins in *Labour Laws for Women in France* (1907), is one example of the ambiguity that was felt.

40. Parliamentary Papers, *Factories Inquiry Commission,* First Report (1833) XX, p.1.

41. For a thorough discussion of working conditions in industry at the end of the century see Stearns, *Lives of Labor,* passim.

42. Royal Commission on Labour, *The Employment of Women* (London, 1893), Cd.6894, p.36; Heinrich Herkner, *Probleme der Arbeiter-psychologie* (1912).

43. Louise Tilly, Joan Scott and R. Burr Litchfield imply this type of major crisis in women's work in their unpublished manuscript, 'Married Women and Work in Nineteenth Century France and England', (paper presented at the Second Berkshire Conference on Women's History, Oct. 1974).

44. *Census of England and Wales, 1871* and *1891.*

45. *Census of England and Wales, 1891;* and *1911; Kaiserliches Statitisches Amt, Berufsstatistik,* 1895 and 1907; Belgain censuses were decennial and can usefully be compared from 1890-1910.

46. Fédération française des travailleurs du livre, *Dixième Congrès National* (1910), p.53.

47. Information derived from the respective national censuses in the years cited.

48. For a brief but thorough discussion of the shop assistants' struggle for better

job conditions see Lee Holcombe, *Victorian Ladies at Work* (1973), pp.103-40.

49. *Censuses of England and Wales, 1861, 1871, 1911.*

50. For a discussion of female clerical workers the following are useful: Fred Hughes, *By Hand and Brain: The Story of the Clerical and Administrative Workers' Union* (1953), II; F.D. Klingender, *The Condition of Clerical Labour in Britain* (1935); David Lockwood, *The Blackcoated Worker: A Study in Class Consciousness* (1958); B.V. Humphreys, *Clerical Unions in the Civil Service* (1958); Hilda Martindale, *Women Servants of the State, 1870-1938* (1938); Dorothy Evans, *Women and the Civil Service* (1934).

51. Edith J. Morley, ed., *Women Workers in Seven Professions: A Survey of Their Economic Conditions and Prospects* (1914) is a thoughtful contemporary look at women professionals.

52. Another example can be found with librarians; see Dee Garrison, 'The Tender Technicians: The Feminization of Public Librarianship, 1876-1905', *Journal of Social History* (1972-73), pp.131-59.

53. For a study of nursing see M. Adelaide Nutting and Lavinia L. Dock, *A History of Nursing: From the Earliest Times to the Present Day*, 4 vols. (1907-12); Brian Able-Smith, *A Short History of Nursing*, Minnie Goodnow, *Nursing History* 9th ed. (1953).

54. Agnes Pavey, *The Story of the Growth of Nursing as an Art, a Vocation, and a Profession*, 4th ed. (1953); Mary Stanley, *Hospitals and Sisterhoods* (1855).

55. For a biography of Florence Nightingale see Cecil Woodham-Smith's account in *Florence Nightingale, 1820-1910* (1951).

56. Report from the Select Committee on registration of Nurses, *Parliamentary Papers*, 1905 VLL, p.102.

57. Pensions for Hospital Officers and Staffs. *Report of a Subcommittee of King Edward's Hospital Fund for London* (1900), p.21.

58. For a recent biography of the first woman doctor see Dorothy C. Wilson, *Lone Woman; The Story of Elizabeth Blackwell, The First Woman Doctor* (1970).

59. For a study of Elizabeth Garrett Anderson see Jo Manton, *Elizabeth Garrett Anderson* (1965).

60. See Dr Ingrid Sonnerhorn, *Women's Careers: Experience from East and West Germany* (1970) for a discussion of the low level of attendance by females at universities (p.115).

61. Virginia Woolf, *A Room of One's Own* (New York, 1929), pp.21-23.

62. See Maureen Greenwald, 'Women Workers and World War I: The American Railroad Industry, A Case Study', in *Journal of Social History* (Winter 1975), pp.154-77.

63. Figures on England can be found in Irene O. Andress and Margaret Hobbs, *Economic Effects of War Upon Women and Children in Great Britain* (1918).

3

A WOMAN'S PLACE

Everyone is familiar with the cliché that a woman's place is in the home. But the cliché is trite and undermines the significance of women's functions in the home. There is no one family role. Women have served as wife, mother, consumer, housekeeper, health director, educator, recreation coordinator, counsellor and financial manager, often all at the same time. This complex role needs to be carefully studied for us to grasp how women really functioned and may function in the future.[1]

Women's family role proved to be the most dynamic source of her changing mentality. Their position in the family has provided and continues to provide them with their foremost means of identification. Indeed, in the modern period this identification gained importance, as more and more women married and managed households. But at all stages of life, even in pre-industrial society, most women, married or unmarried, have been closely tied to a family. The position we want to examine particularly concerns the married woman, in her key role as wife and mother, the status of which modern women have been most successful in upgrading.

With the nineteenth century married women gained a new and respected position in society, which is one reason why marriage proved increasingly popular. A vital measure of their new status was the rise of their legal standing in the community. For centuries married women had been virtual nonentities before the law, but the nineteenth century saw strong attacks upon the old inequalities. It is no accident that the most successful and enduring changes in the law concerned women's position within marriage. Among the most important gains were the right to custody over children, the right to divorce, and the right to own and transfer property. Married women were beginning to be recognised as responsible individuals. In some instances, they were able to move from a position of inferiority to one of superiority, as in the case of child custody. The legal gains were not easily acquired, but they ultimately did mark women's new position in the family,[2] and they also won backing from a number of men, essential for legislation in a male-controlled political world, but also a clear sign of the changing roles.

Marriage has always been of prime importance for women in Western culture. Modern society saw more women able to attain this goal than ever before, as the percentage of women marrying rose over 90 per cent by the mid-twentieth century, in contrast to the 50 per cent characteristic of Europe in 1700. Not only were more women marrying but they were doing so earlier. There has been a drop of almost six years in the average marriage age in most western countries. Thus marriage involves most of the life of the majority of contemporary women, from their late teens onward. This is why the history of modern women must, to a large extent be the history of married women and their adaptation to industrialisation and urbanisation, which facilitated marriage by increasing prosperity and social contacts but also placed new stresses on the family.

Partly because of new pressures, the family served as the major vehicle for women's growing-up process. Alterations in its structure and functions help define women's existence and also mark crucial changes in their outlook. The modernisation of women within the family was subtle and complex, with patterns and rhythms varying from one class to another and from one country to another. But the general point remains: it is within the context of the family that the most intimate aspects of a woman's life are revealed, her physical and psychic well-being, her fundamental sense of purpose.

Women and the Family in Early Modern Europe

Marriage in pre-industrial society was almost literally a matter of life and death for women. In the countryside women of twenty who never married could expect to live nine years less than their married sisters. This may have reflected lack of emotional fulfilment but above all it followed from meagre living standards. For, as crude and unromantic as it may seem to us, the basis of marriage was economics, and without a spouse women, even more than men, suffered from insufficient material support. All social and to a great extent political and religious functions had their foundations in the family, and even friends and work were derived through family connections. In an unpredictable agricultural economy the family as an economic unit provided the basic necessities of life: food, clothing and shelter.

Peasant society was extremely hostile to the venturesome individual, suspicious of anyone who was not part of a familial unit, and few women could even contemplate this role. Except for a minority, mainly of course in Catholic countries, who escaped to convents, the unmarried woman found herself locked in a family, but in a subordinate position precisely because there was no viable alternative outside.

Whether working for neighbours or, more commonly, for her own kin she held the most menial position, totally dependent on a male relation — father, brother or uncle — and often the scorn of that man's own wife. We have no precise way of knowing what life was like for her, for her subordination prevented any independent records. One presumes that she was expected to perform the most arduous tasks, receiving the smallest portion of food, the first to sacrifice in times of bad harvests. It was no wonder that marriage and the chance to form one's own household loomed so large in the pre-modern woman's expectations. Yet almost half of all women were never able to fulfil this goal. The tenuous economics of peasant society, where there was not enough property to go round, made it very difficult for a man and woman to set up a separate household and form a family. In England 30 per cent and in France 50 per cent of all women could not afford to marry and therefore endured the lowly position assigned to the spinster for their entire lives.[3]

The economic basis of marriage and the family cannot be stressed enough. Only those women fortunate enough to provide a satisfactory dowry would achieve marriage while the amount of the dowry largely determined the social and economic level of the mate selected by her parents, sometimes with the aid of a village matchmaker. A woman married a man not from a sense of fondness for his person but from the need for access to property for the future, since her parents' land would go to her brothers. Likewise the man chose his wife not for her physical charms but rather the size of her pig or cow, the common form of dowry offered.[4] Sometimes a woman was contracted by her parents to marry a man she did not even know. Given the small scale of peasant society, however, some familiarity was probable, though it could produce a very limited choice. Within a community of 300, the typical village size, the number of marriageable individuals would be less than 25, and this included older widowers as well as men nearer the woman's age.

When she could marry was also inevitably related to property and economics. Relatively late marriage age, between 25 and 28, prevailed in western Europe for several reasons. At the top of the list was the parents' need for enough time to accumulate a suitable dowry and their desire to get some good years of work from a healthy adult daughter before she left. An eldest daughter had a good chance for marriage at the proper age, but the youngest daughter saw her opportunities diminished considerably, as the family's resources were severely reduced by older siblings' needs. Also parents who were now usually over 50 (in pre-industrial society the youngest child was often born when the mother was over 40) could not be expected to produce the extra income needed for a dowry and might require the daughter's care as their needs increased with age. Hence the old story of the younger daughter who remained at home. Economic need and available property sealed her fate here too.

Finally, it was because the economic role of the family was so vital that marriage choice could not be left to a 'girl' of 25. She might know her suiter, but formal courtship might consist of a private talk of only half an hour, after which the parents came in, cursorily determined if the girl was willing to proceed, and then settled down to complex negotiations to make sure the son-in-law would have the right prospects or property and to determine the amount of dowry needed. Marriage, if contracted, was by no means the end of the story, but it had hardly been made in heaven even though a girl might well count herself lucky to marry at all. If her fate was better than a spinster's, however, and her status higher and her functions more diverse, she paid her own price for a marriage that brought emotional satisfactions only by accident, a price in terms of toil and a toll on her physical being.

A woman's function in the family depended heavily on the family structure. Essentially there were two types of family structure, the extended and the nuclear.[5] In an extended family multi-generations lived together under one roof or in close proximity — grandparents, parents, sometimes an aunt, and of course children. Recent work shows that there were variants on this theme. In Austria for example one typical family form, called the stem family, consisted of grandparents, first son and his wife and children, as long as the grandparents remained alive.[6]

The nuclear family included only father, mother and their children (although occasionally a brother or sister of the married couple, usually of the husband, might live in). Both types of family structure could also include one or more servants, who served as all-purpose labourers for a farmer with a bit of extra property. The average pre-industrial family was of the nuclear type but we must hasten to add that averages are rather misleading. Marrying at quite a late age, a couple whose children followed suit had their first grandchild when over 50. They would usually live only about five years more, inevitably producing at their death a nuclear family. But apart from exceptions when a grandparent lived well beyond the average, even five years of overlap in an extended family could aid a newly married couple by increasing the mother's ability to work while babies were cared for by her husband's parents and could shape a child's formative years as well. Yet the extended family was not typical and applied mainly to the new familial unit formed by the eldest son. For a woman the typical arrangements meant that, whether involved at first in a stem or extended family, or in a nuclear family, she left her own parents' home and went to live with her husband and possibly his family.

It is particularly important to try to establish the most common family structure since this directly affected a woman's activities. In an extended family there might be two or possibly more females to perform domestic chores. This could prove advantageous for the newly married woman as the work load would theoretically be shared and the older woman could offer her wisdom and experience to the novice. At childbirth this might be especially comforting to the new mother. Even afterwards child care services might be provided by the paternal grandparent, thereby allowing the wife more time and energy to devote to other family related tasks. In the more common nuclear family, in contrast, domestic responsibility was borne by only one woman (unless a servant could be afforded), until the first daughter approached adulthood (and even then many a household, overburdened with children, sent such a daughter into servanthood to relieve the burden on their resources). There was no assistance with the first children, no guidance save by village tradition and neighbours' advice. Yet we need not necessarily bemoan the limited durability or availability of grandparents, for the nuclear family had at least one potential advantage: the absence of overbearing mothers-in-law — for we must not assume that relations with the husband's mother were any sweeter than they are today. If not overbearing, grandparents could require care on their own account, which a new wife might be pleased to avoid.

Early Modern Motherhood: Nasty, Brutish and Far From Short

No matter what the internal arrangements, however, there were certain tasks that all women were expected to perform, and these tasks were arduous. The first and foremost duty of the married woman was to provide children, which was long held to be the *raison d'être* for marriage. To be sure, the west European family limited childbirth somewhat by late marriage, and this may have been a conscious decision to protect property from too many heirs; elsewhere in Europe marriage came earlier and more children were born (though more died as well). Everywhere, however, once marriage occurred children were urgently desired. They were seen as contributing to the family's economic resources, as the family's potential labour supply, and in a society when they started to work in the fields around the age of five this was literally true. Obviously the peasant family remained aware that a cautious balance had to be maintained in this regard. Too many children could destroy a family; too many young children simply could not be provided for. Regulation of family size was maintained partly by design and partly by natural forces working against undue expansion. We know that birth control was practised by some peasant families, as primitive contraceptive devices made of animal bladders were used as condoms. We know also that peasant women nursed each child for an extended period, often up to two years, mainly to save on limited food supplies but also to prevent pregnancy. However, the major determinants of the number of children born to peasant women were biological factors which were beyond their control and even unknown to them.

On the average, the peasant woman gave birth within a year after marriage and every two years thereafter until menopause. This meant six to eight children born, and at least fifteen years of life devoted to carrying and bearing children and recovering from childbirth. Among the most important considerations in explaining the size of a peasant family was female fertility. Given the rather long spacing between births combined with limited knowledge about formal birth control, one can assume that the peasant woman's fertility level was low. Poor nutrition undoubtedly contributed to this. Recent studies have shown that the onset and maintenance of regular menstrual function in women are both dependent on the maintenance of a minimum weight for height (for example, in America today the necessary ratio for menstruation for a fourteen year old girl 5'5" in height is 96 lbs).[7] Even without exact knowledge of peasant diets we can assume from the incidence of diseases and causes of death that much of the population was underweight for their height and/or suffered from nutritional dificiencies of other sorts. Late onset of puberty, about 18 for peasant women, also reflected inadequate nutrition. Given the high levels of physical exertion required of peasant women and the poor food intake it seems highly likely that many also suffered ammenorrhea, that, is, cessation of the menses even after puberty. Under-nutrition was undoubtedly most severe in times of economic depression and crops failure, and it became an acute danger for women during pregnancy and lactation. The peasant woman knew that she did not conceive during her period of nursing but she did not know why. Lactation required an enormous amount of additional calories but she was generally unable to take in the necessary additional food and had to rely upon her own support system. This drain on her fat ratio prevented her from returning to the necessary weight for renewal of menstruation. Peasant culture reflected some awareness of all this as it encouraged a pregnant women to eat more, for now she was 'eating for two'. Indeed peasant myths surrounding pregnancy and birth control were long held even after they had ceased to be effective or wise, as we will shortly see. Many women in the lower classes still believe that nursing prevents conception and, well into the twentieth century, they continued to nurse their children for long periods of time in this hope. By then, however, their nutritional intake was so superior to that of the seventeenth- or eighteenth-century peasant that their fertility level was quickly restored and the old wisdom no longer applied. Similarly, promptings to eat heartily, began to prove dangerous to pregnant women in societies rich enough to afford regular overeating.

One further aspect of the life cycle must be considered to understand the peasant woman's reproductive span – the onset of menopause. Menopause occurred earlier than in modern society, again because of undernutrition and physical exertion. This was a significant factor in the combination of causes, nutritional at base, that explain why the peasant woman's fecundity was shorter and also more erratic than that of her modern counterpart.

A final dimension of the biological forces regulating family size related to sexual impulse. Peasant society provided only limited scope for sexual stimuli. Hunger, exhaustion and extremities of weather in the meagre cottage inhibited sexual drives. The peasant woman who had barely enough to eat and had to spend twelve to fourteen hours daily in hard physical labour, who suffered great pain and the chance of death with each pregnancy, had little time, energy or interest in sex. Enjoyable and frequent sex is largely a modern luxury, as we will see, save for the upper classes who might indulge more freely even in pre-industrial times.

Even so, most married women were burdened with many pregnancies. This did not, however, produce extraordinarily large families on the average. For family size was also regulated by the high rate of infant mortality and a large number of stillbirths. Even when pregnant the woman was often unable to provide the extra body weight needed to ensure that the infant would itself be the proper weight at birth. The heavier the mother, the higher the birth weight of the infant and the better its chance of survival. Many infants died before or at birth due to pelvic disorders of the mother, most

commonly caused by rickets, which made delivery almost impossible
in some cases. The result was that about 50 per cent of all children born
alive died before the age of two, mostly in their very first months of
life.

Peasant culture conditioned women not to expect all their
pregnancies to be successful. Death was an ever present reality to be
accepted as natural, and rituals such as funerals helped ease the pain.
This is not to say that mothers did not suffer disappointment and grief,
but the pre-industrial woman could not afford a modern level of
emotional attachment to an infant. Indeed peasant families burdened
with too many children might kill a new born child, usually by exposing
it to bad weather.

Pregnancies took a heavy toll on the woman's health. The process of
child delivery was primitive, left to the fortunes of nature for the most
part. Women delivered their babies at home, with some sort of midwife
in attendance and without pretence at privacy or concern for
sanitation. Very little could be expected from the midwife whose only
qualification for her position was that she had borne a child herself and
was probably recommended by the parish priest. Many a midwife
turned to this line of work when too old to be lucratively employed –
not a very strong guarantee of quality. The midwife prepared the
lying-in bed and observed the stages of labour. Her major function
seemed to be to regale the suffering women with tales of woe of other
women who had gone through the process. She rarely interfered with a
normal labour except to break the woman's water sac. When the child
was delivered her duty was to cut the umbilical cord and prepare the
infant. Some midwives believed that the infant had to be totally
immersed in cold water, while others doused only the top of the head.
Still others recommended that the head be splashed with brandy. While
all this was being done, to the infant's possible harm, the woman was
left essentially on her own to proceed with the afterbirth. The
importance of this stage of delivery to women's health was not
recognised even by medical researchers until the eighteenth century,
and it long remained ignored in practice. Many a woman suffered the
pain of infection and some even died because of the failure to deliver
the afterbirth completely.

Small wonder that pregnancy was surrounded by superstitions.
Religious ceremonies might help but pagan practices were even more
common, whether overlaid with Christianity or not. Pregnant women
in Ireland sometimes took mud from long ditches called 'Priests'
Beds' to avoid a painful labour, while many ritualistic precautions were

developed to insure newborn infants against bad fortune and evil spirits. Midwives often purveyed more superstitions than medical aid, bringing as much fear as comfort. If scared by a spider your child would have a corresponding birthmark; children of a breechbirth would be evil; a third child would not turn out well — the list of dangers was almost endless.

In this way motherhood began with complications and fears. Immense physical and emotional strain of each new pregnancy marked most of married life. The horrors of pregnancy itself were most vivid for those victims of complicated deliveries, stillbirths or breechbirths. The village midwife tried to assist as best she could but such complications were well beyond her range, and the result was almost certain death for the child and often the same fate for the mother. Dreadful stories are told of midwives' blunders in trying to remove a dead foetus from the womb, while tales of infanticide and child swapping complete the primitive picture of the whole procedure.[8]

It is difficult to generalise about post-natal care. It has often been assumed that women rose immediately after delivery to go about their chores. But doctors even at the time were suggesting that at least in principle they should not rise or even sit up for at least two weeks. Peasant women could not afford this indulgence and erred in the opposite direction, but the wealthier who followed medical advice invited infection which was the largest killer of women shortly after delivery. Here was an early example of damned if you do, damned if you don't; neither normal practice nor new medical advice assured any security. Most women were left to nature, which too often showed its contempt for human life.

After each successful childbirth, whatever her physical and emotional state, the woman encountered her next major family responsibility, the care of the infant. This was never considered to be a full-time task, for in few other respects was the peasant woman's role so different from that of her modern counterpart. Again, the economic nature of familial relationships explains much of the distinctiveness. To a working economic unit children were correctly viewed as economic liabilities until the age of five, when they were expected to contribute to the family's resources. The demands on the peasant mother's time and energy were such that she could afford little attention, indeed little love, for a new baby. Infant feeding provides an obvious case in point. The folksy image of the peasant woman as Mother Earth with her full breasts, her rosy cheeks and her fat baby contentedly sucking is idyllic but not accurate. The picture should reflect a worn and haggard woman with a scrawny baby, who was nursed overlong despite the poor quality of the milk, in order to save on food and prevent a new pregnancy. The child was nursed when time permitted, for the mother had to attend to her other duties outside the house; demand feeding was impossible. Peasant culture supported this practice, for the infant was regarded not only as a nuisance but also as an animal-like creature whose will had to be broken to become human. The infant's needs were secondary, its demands almost purposefully ignored.

Lacking a concept of motherhood it is not surprising that women used other feeding means when available. Nursing required considerable sacrifice on the part of the mother in terms of physical strain as well as time. Those women who had economic means, particularly but not solely in the cities, chose to avoid even this aspect of mothering by hiring wet nurses. In France a significant minority of women from the larger cities commonly sent their children out to baby farms to be nursed. In eighteenth-century Paris 21 out of 30 babies[9] were wet nursed according to one estimate, suggesting that even most lower-class women engaged in the practice. Yet it was well known that infant mortality rates for babies who were farmed out were well above the 50 per cent average. The English did not rely as much on sending babies out to nurse, for it was more common to bring the nurse into the home. By the late eighteenth century wet nursing in any form began to wane with a change in attitude toward children and the development of the concept of modern motherhood, but this merely accents the distinctive traditions of the pre-industrial centuries.

For the peasant women who could not afford a wet nurse yet did not want to nurse or could not do so, other methods were employed. Frequently babies were fed artificially, either directly with a spoon or by means of a sack that was soaked with a gruel mixture. Both methods proved extremely harmful for the infant's delicate digestive system and many of the babies so nourished died. In France, if one was affluent enough to have an animal who had just given birth this might also be employed. The legs of a goat or ass were bound and the infant was to suck directly at the animal's teat. The goat was found to be far more cooperative than the ass in this venture.[10] It is impossible to say how widely any one feeding method was employed, even as to the animals involved; it has been claimed that whole villages in Bavaria used animals exclusively as early as the sixteenth century.[11]

Whatever the method employed, be it nursing, handfeeding or use of animals, and whatever the social class, the setting urban or rural, feeding took a minimal amount of time, and very deliberately so. Yet feeding provided virtually the only time the mother spent directly with her child. Generally infants were bound in swaddling clothes and hung up on a peg while the mother went about her main domestic chores which consumed most of her energy. Her efforts at mothering were minimal. There was no attempt even at toilet training since by the time the child could be trained there was likely to be another child hung on the peg. So children waited until they were unswaddled and could be told what to do, often again around the magic age of five when they became economically useful and therefore human beings. We get the impression that the toddler picked up the family's ways at its own pace. If this proved to be too slow or even too fast for the family the child was severely disciplined. As little beasts with wills to be broken, children's corporal punishment was rigorous. Life was hard and demanded toughness and obedience from both men and women, and the sooner this could be learned the better one was able to relate to peasant society.

Childhood thus was scarcely a developed concept, and so mother-hood remained minimal in terms of emotional involvement or prestige of role.[12] When available, older children, primarily girls, performed many of the maternal functions described above, and of course by the time a child was five it was expected to begin to behave as an adult anyway. Between the years of five and nine children performed any number of household and farm tasks suited to the level of development. By their early teens children were sent out to service or, in the cities, apprentice-ship, and the mother's responsibility ended altogether.

In the peasant family, it was far more essential that the woman fulfil her role as producer and housekeeper and devote herself to those working actively than to act as mother to infants. Mothering was a risky investment and the returns were low, given the high rate of child mortality and the whole set of concepts by which early childhood was judged. Especially if others in the family were hampered, it was not economically sound to devote too much time to a baby that had a fifty-fifty chance of survival. Frequent pregnancies further complicated attention to any one infant, particularly as they passed the age of two when their mortality rate finally did decline.

Thus the functions that most readily spring to mind when discussing women in the family apply only partially to the pre-industrial setting. Becoming a mother was a vital duty, consuming much of married life; being a mother meant far less. Apart from begetting children a wife's main family function involved the long list of domestic chores which were the life supports of the family. It is true that her economic role was inseparable from the family's existence; even having children was part of this role. All of her duties as producer, from making clothing to caring for livestock, defined her family existence, forming it into an intensively demanding physical experience when combined with repeated pregnancies.

All of this describes a fairly common lot, before about 1800. We have focused on peasant women, as they comprised at least 80 per cent of the female population, but, as indicated with nursing, the basic outlines of the family role apply to urban settings as well. There remains an obvious variable: the husband. Chosen for economic reasons, usually with the wife-to-be possessed at most of a right of refusal, what the husband would turn out to be was almost an accident. There were two major aspects to this, the emotional and the economic. Peasant economic fortunes varied widely; a relatively large landed holding might, through bad luck or mismanagement, yield to poverty within a generation. Much depended on the husband's skill and strength, yet these were hard to calculate at the beginning a marriage.

Emotional satisfaction might develop even though it was not seriously considered in forming the marriage; but deep hostility might just as easily arise, if the husband proved brutal and insensitive. Lack of privacy in a small cottage or urban apartment crowded with children and even animals created great strain. Two outlets the pre-industrial woman, particularly the peasant woman, did *not* have in modern form. One was frequent or enjoyable sexual activity. There is every indication that peasant sex was a largely male performance, a quick foray with little chance for female orgasm. Lack of frequent sexual activity followed, as we have seen, from poor nutrition, enervating work, and, ironically, the fact that the peasant woman was so often pregnant. One key sign of this was the pre-industrial conception cycle. Far more babies were conceived in May and June than at any other time. Spring fever, greater privacy when children could be sent outside the peasants' cramped cottage, help to account for this; more important was the economic result, for with children most commonly born in February and March the woman's vital household and farm work was least seriously interrupted — she would still be available for planting and harvest. But with rare use of artificial birth control devices (which were in turn highly fallible at best), one supposes that peasants commonly refrained from sex during much of the rest of the year. So emotional bonds might be formed as husband and wife shared work and a common existence, but they would rarely be cemented by sexual pleasure.

Second, the woman lacked the possibility of ending an undesirable marriage. A man might desert, finding employment in a city, but a married woman would be economically bereft and the object of intense community disapproval if she tried to leave. Divorce was unknown save to the very rich. The woman in fact did not contemplate alternatives to her lot, for her whole culture insisted that marriage was for life. Even widowhood was disadvantageous. Few widows could remarry — villagers often ridiculed those who did — yet they could hardly maintain their economic status by themselves. Luckiest were those with an adult son to take them in; at the other extreme was the old crone of the village, an object of fear in her black garb who was suspect because she was no longer part of an economic unit.

Marriage, then, remained the best possible state, but it was chancy and fraught with risks and hardship. Variety there was, to be sure. We have stressed rural conditions, and it must be admitted that urban women, with broader social contacts, had certain advantages. They began to menstruate earlier, for example, and were more certain of marriage. But normally marriage was still based on property considerations; childbirth and the basic concepts of childrearing differed little, as the eagerness even of city workers to send their infants out to unknown rural wet nurses indicates.

In city as in countryside, if one isolates the work of the married woman one can stress its vital familial context and construct an argument about the harmony of pre-industrial life, the clear identity given to the married woman. But when one examines the whole familial context, any image of a golden age in the past must disappear. Childbirth, infant mortality, the risks of an unsatisfactory husband were added to strenuous physical labour. A lack of alternatives and sense of resignation instilled in childhood and reinforced by religious preaching, which might offer some solace with the prospect of a better after life while sternly stressing women's inferiority on earth, sustained these women. But this gave no indication of what women might seek if new alternatives were presented. For this a new social and economic framework was required. Such a framework was on its way by the mid-eighteenth century, but in the meantime the world of women was largely confined to the world of four walls, a thatched roof and an earthen floor, leavened only rarely by contacts even with the broader village community.

The Sexual Revolution: The Female Experience

Eighteenth-century Europe was wrought with upheaval as it embraced its multi-dimensional revolution. In the throes of modernisation political, social and economic structures were transformed. Urbanisation, industrialisation and the population explosion altered the way people lived, worked and played. These forces of change were pervasive, touching every level of society. Big cities, new work roles and more babies made for a very different set of family relationships. Women's role was to expand significantly as the family modernised.

Women were the primary agents in the development of the modern family. Their impact on changes in the family during the initial phases of modernisation is only beginning to be recognised. Historians and demographers have long been so obsessed by the sheer weight of numbers that they have ignored the human dimensions involved. One is given to believe that population expanded by the frenzied efforts of a demographer's stork, variously called medical advances, the advent of the potato, or the impact of industrialisation. But we know that babies are not brought by the stork; human decisions as well as human actions are involved. In the case of the population revolution the major impetus for change came from women. In the eighteenth century women suddenly began to become pregnant more often and to see more of their children survive. How this came about and what its impact was on women's history form the key question we must try to answer.

The population revolution resulted from a combination of a decline in mortality and an increase in births. Various explanations have been set forth to account for this sudden switch in demographic trends. Improved sanitary measures, the decline of periodic plagues and famines and agricultural transformations are among the most important, with changes in agriculture heading the list as they affected that mass of people whose nutritional levels hung in such precarious balance. Increased food production was the basic ingredient that sustained massive population growth. Agricultural breakthroughs such as the introduction of the potato and other root crops enabled the majority of people to raise their standard of living above the pre-industrial subsistence level. Among the most important benefits of the agricultural innovations were improved diets which were both regular and more nutritious. Nutritional changes altered the female's life cycle markedly. They produced a decline in the age of female puberty from 18-20 years in 1750 to about 14-16 years in 1850. The implications of this biological alteration are manifold. Obviously lower ages of puberty meant that women were fertile for long periods; in fact, menopause began to occur slightly later as well, again as a result of better nutrition. In all, approximately ten years were added to the period of women's fertility, within merely a century.[13] What the personal aspects of this development were involve far greater interpretive problems. The psychological effects of earlier puberty and later menopause have not been fully investigated. Was the young girl of sixteen or less as ready to cope with menstruation as the eighteen or twenty year old, particularly in a society unprepared for such precocity? Were tensions created within the family by this development, as for example mothers having to deal with daughters who were menstruating earlier than they had? We know that nineteenth-century mothers expressed concern about the early age of sexual maturity.[14] And judging from the phenomenal increase in illegitimacy rates from a traditional and fairly stable two per cent of all births, in Western Europe, to upwards of eleven per cent from about 1780 to 1870,[15] one assumes that family relationships were indeed strained by women's new life cycle. More and more girls, particularly in the lower classes, were defying the traditional norms of community and society. The actual process of menstruation was slow to gain new attention, despite the falling age of puberty, which can only have complicated the phenomenon for the girls experiencing it. This was not a subject openly discussed until the mid-nineteenth century, even in terms of personal hygiene. Women relied upon traditional devices, which generally consisted of a diaper protector, the fabric of which depended on one's social class, with those in the upper classes indulging in linen protectors. Whatever the situation women seemed to bear their newly prolonged burden with little comment. Here is but one vital area of the female experience in which understanding and handling of natural processes did not keep pace with change in the century of transition to an industrial society.

The female lifestyle was affected most dramatically by the increase in fertility. More women than ever before found themselves pregnant and more often than ever before. Perhaps of greater importance than the longer period of fertility (which for each generation amounted to several months at most) was the regularisation of women's ovulation. Better nutrition made for a more stable menstrual cycle and shortened amenorrhea after pregnancy; both enhanced the probability of more frequent pregnancy.

Rural lifestyle and outlook were even more dramatically transformed by greater contact with the outside world. Throughout most of the seventeenth and eighteenth centuries the typical village was very nearly self-sustained, an isolated unit of a few hundred people (half of them young children at any given time). Intrusions into this little world were rare and unwelcome. However, by the second half of the eighteenth century village gates admitted more and more people, some natives and some strangers, as industrial life began to penetrate the village economy. Merchant representatives, the putters-out, with their city ways went into the countryside to recruit labour. Peasant women, as we have seen, found their economic worth enhanced even in their teens, as they could now contract their labour for money wages. The more one worked, the greater the return. Gradually the seeds of a market mentality, bent on maximising self-interest, were planted. This new sense of economic worth promoted new behaviour and eventually a sense of individual identity. Add to this the example of city folk and the contact with a much wider array of people, and a change in basic outlook was bound to come.[16]

The first signs of change were small and too many have scarcely seemed worth mentioning, but their significance was real for they pointed to a new pattern of behaviour for women. With their extra money, women workers could buy new products. Processed foods, mainly bread and milk products and often tea, coffee and sugar, made their way to the peasant's table. Observers by 1800 were bemoaning the intrusion into simple rural ways of the city's market mentality, particularly the interest in new goods as a form of enjoyment and self-expression. Yet women themselves seem to have welcomed the change, and for good reason. The ability to buy bread freed them from hours of baking and allowed them to pursue other functions. Again, a small beginning but easily expanded. Ordinary women were launched on a career as consumers, that is, purchasing agents for the family, which eased some traditional work burdens and provided new functions, possibly new interests. Manufactured clothing, particularly cottons with their varied styles and bright colours, soon joined the list of goods for purchase. Their use offended traditionalists even more, for peasants should look like peasants, but by the same token they served even more clearly as a means of self-expression, of individuality. Increasing numbers of women ventured from the village to the city, whether forced by lack of customary rural jobs or lured by the presumed excitement of urban life. Rapid urbanisation began after 1800 and by 1850 half of England's people lived in cities, most of them immigrants from countryside. The majority of the women involved were young and particularly open to new ways. The impact of the market mentality was obviously more sudden and profound for the new city dwellers as they encountered a wider variety of people and suffered a more dramatic uprooting from traditional controls.

Human behaviour altered even more fundamentally. There was a change in sexual appetites; indeed some have called it a sexual revolution. More and more women were engaging in sexual activity, which was a key reason for the enormous increase in the number of births within and outside of marriage. For the ordinary woman, sex was becoming an integral part of life, of self-identification. This was a gradual process, one that is far from complete even today. Women's new sexual awareness was also to have ambiguous results. A young woman might be lured by sex into situations where, abandoned, she had to have an illegitimate child or simply accept a premature marriage in which she would be overburdened with children. But sex, not only in its new frequency but in its expression of a personal desire for pleasure, could provide a new outlet, and the beginnings of modern mentality. One cannot exclude the possibility of sexual pleasures prior to the sexual revolution of the late eighteenth century. For the most part however, tales, such as those of Boccaccio, portray a small segment of society, the upper class or the urban bourgeoisie. Given the dreary existence of the common woman one would be surprised if she had the energy or even the desire to indulge in sensual delights. In her period of greatest energy, young adulthood, the woman was carefully supervised to preserve virginity, for peasant society was prudish, as the low rate of illegitimate births and conceptions before marriage indicates. For the woman married at last but burdened with domestic chores and childbearing, sex could not serve as a focal point in her life. But by the second half of the eighteenth century sex became more openly discussed and practised. More time could be given to sexual pleasure and new techniques were developed to heighten both partners' enjoyment of the relationship. Slowly books and pamphlets began to appear giving advice on how to improve one's sex life. The outspoken work, *Aristotle's Complete Master-Piece*,[17] though condemned by moralists, was perhaps the first in what has become an increasingly lucrative market, the eighteenth century counterpart of Alex Comfort's *The Joy of Sex* or David Reuben's *Everything You Wanted to Know About Sex*.[18] Even in a semi-literate society its message spread widely, by word of mouth as well as direct reading even into the early twentieth century, when the working class still turned to it for lessons.

It was growing industrialisation and growing population which brought this new sexual world into being. A youth who could earn money, in domestic manufacturing, or who had to go to the city because local resources would not suffice, could not be expected to maintain customary deference to parents or village elders. Indeed many women and men were glad to escape the repressiveness of the old ways. Young girls moved further from home and out of the watchful eye of parents or employer-neighbours, and were able to meet young men in similar circumstances. Soaring marriage rates were the result. More and more women were reaching the traditional goal, but they were also beginning to demand more and marriage started to change in character more than its rate.

Increasingly marriages were founded on that elusive emotional tie which we call 'love', rather than economics, although the latter remained a primary consideration, especially when the parents had property. Population pressure created a growing property-less group, for whom dowries and detailed marriage agreements were irrelevant. These people could marry for what they thought was love, even though the subsequent family remained a significant economic unit. Their freedom from property concerns showed not only in more frequent marriages but also, particularly for women, in the beginnings of the modern trend toward lower marriage age. But at almost any level of the economic spectrum, the family and its ties remained strong. Even if many young girls were theoretically free to marry as they chose, parental sanction was still commonly sought and the larger family still provided emotional support. But the parental stranglehold was loosened and family bonds began to be those of the household one formed oneself, through individual choice.

The new marriages were not necessarily more successful than the old, partly because the standards for measuring success were changing. Still far from being made in heaven they were more and more often made in bed, which might not provide a durable base. Some women's historians have argued that the increase in marriage rates was merely a sign of the increasing desperation of women at this time, a refuge from strangeness and isolation with the undermining of their economic position as the locus of work shifted from home to factory. Their only hope for survival was to give up and marry.[19] It is in fact impossible to determine whether positive or negative motivation was the greater. It has yet to be proved that millions of women yearly sought marriage out of desperation alone. Rising rates and earlier ages of marriage might just as well reflect some joy at the prospect or the new search for pleasure.

One result of the sexual revolution was a dramatic rise in the illegitimacy rate. Here was a clear indication of the new pleasure-seeking mentality, produced by the sexual stimuli of wider social contacts and a new sense of self and self-indulgence. Some women bore their bastards gaily, not fully realising how new their behaviour was.[20] No doubt others were victimised by men, believing that marriage would follow their yielding and not necessarily desiring new pleasure from the sexual act at all. Some might end as prostitutes, for want of support for their children. On the whole, however, illegitimate births were tolerated, even accepted by the property-less classes, showing that attitudes were changing substantially, and marriage frequently resulted after a bastard or two had been born (often sired by the man ultimately married). For many, by the early nineteenth century, this new behaviour had become the norm, to the horror of traditional moralists. A study of Bavaria shows that almost half the women married were pregnant or had given birth previously. A Bavarian girl expressed her new sense of morality when asked why she kept having illegitimate children: 'It's okay to have babies, the king has okayed it.'[21]

Marriage itself provided new sexual outlets. The rise in legitimate birth rates indicated that sexual interests continued after marriage (or, for the propertied classes, were first expressed there). A clear sign of increased sexual activity within marriage was the regulation of the conception-birth cycle. With better nutrition women became more consistently fertile, and the availability of manufacturing or other work at home reduced the economic necessity of the traditional conception cycle. In rural areas, conceptions were spread out more evenly through the year as sexual intercourse became more frequent and regular.

The sexual revolution, however, was not without its disadvantages. The normal lot of the married woman became more burdensome, and we cannot tell, for this early period, whether new pleasure even partially compensated. For the fruit of more frequent intercourse was more children, yet infant death rates were lower than ever before. More women endured more pregnancies, in all the major social classes throughout this age of transition. Evidence of this was the recurrence of epidemics of puerperal fever in the late eighteenth century, a major killer of women in the few weeks after giving birth. Many a woman's health was impaired by frequent pregnancy even if there were no direct complications, and more living children involved more care.

There were two obvious limitations to the new freedom. The most complete revolution touched only half the populace – the lower classes, those without property in city or countryside. Illegitimacy increased not at all in the propertied group which strongly suggests celibacy during early adulthood, particularly for women, even though with better nutrition the age of puberty declined faster here than in the lower classes (reaching 14, in one mid-nineteenth century English city, while the average working-class girl was beginning menstruation only at 16).[22]

Second, the sexual revolution was often a brief fling for women, confined to a few years before the burdens of motherhood became too great. It was easy to be exploited, easy to indulge in new pleasure without thought to the consequences. Some women may not have realised they were doing anything new as they indulged in premarital sex. Many, for example, continued to profess ardent religious belief and showed no signs of a modern outlook, but more commonly, the new sex did follow from new ways of thinking. It was most freely expressed in the first few years of indulgence, not only before marriage, for many in the lower classes, but within marriage for elements of all social groups.

To grasp the essential lifestyle of the adult woman we must look at the role which sex played in marriage, for all classes and through the whole of wedded life. It could serve as a base for new compatibility, new emotional links between husband and wife, just as it played an obvious role in changing the criteria for choosing a mate, from primacy of economics to primacy of romantic attraction. Marriages might still fail emotionally but their emotional importance was heightened. This, rather than sex alone, was the real revolution. From 1750 onwards we can begin to talk of a more general transformation of women's familial role. For the emergence of the modern wife, mother and homemaker, not the modern sexpot, was the main event of this stage of women's history.

The Emergence of Modern Family Life: A New View of Marriage

In nineteenth-century Europe women made major strides in their own modernisation process through their family roles, for their responsibilities steadily increased, giving them new dignity in the home. Every aspect of a woman's life was affected, but the time and form of change depended to a great extent on her social position and perhaps her country. Working-class women responded very slowly to a modern life style, despite their leading role in new sexual behaviour in their teens and early twenties. Middle-class women, with the same dynamism their class displayed in other activities, sought innovation often for the sake of innovation. This was particularly the case in

England and Germany. In France the class differences were not so distinct. The middle-class French woman was not as quick to adapt to new ways as her sister across the channel. Quite generally, however, woman's changing position brought her new importance and respect both within the family and in society beyond.

It also introduced a new tension into marriage when the new spirit of self-assertion came into conflict with the accepted subordinate role. Efforts to find a new balance began early in the nineteenth century, first in the middle classes, with a search for a new answer to the old question of whom and when to marry. Now that young women themselves were asking this question, it became more important than ever to come up with the right answer and make the correct choice. 'No deliberation or circumspection can be too great in a transaction of such importance as the choice of a partner for life. An error here leads to the most serious consequences. It is fatal and irreversible.'[23]

Both the novelty and the significance of marriage were reflected in the rapid rise of guidance literature. Young girls sought advice in the new marriage manuals which began to flood the market in the early nineteenth century; thousands were published all over Europe, though particularly in England and America, stressing the importance of marriage and its growing complexities in modern society. The evolution of the manuals mirrored the changes in marriage itself. Early in the century young girls were advised that the most important consideration in choosing a mate was his moral character. This generally referred to a man's religious qualifications. A manual of the 1830s, entitled a *Guide to Domestic Happiness,* made the point

> You ask, Melissa, whether in forming a matrimonial connection, it be absolutely your duty to give your hand to the man whom you have reason to consider as a true Christian, or whether, without incurring Divine displeasure, it may not be given to one who is nominally such provided his character and his conduct, in other respects, be fair and respectable? . . . that a woman who receive of her husband a person of whose moral and religious character she knows no more than that it is outwardly decent, stakes her welfare upon a very hazardous experiment.[24]

This religious tone was soon dropped in favour of a more secular outlook. The new stress was on compatibility: 'congeniality of sentiment, temper and character constitute the first essential of wedded life. Before you irrevocably engage yourselves, let it be with a decided persuasion that your characters, after diligent investigation, assimilate.'[25] The manuals were also filled with fearsome stories of women who chose their mates solely for economic reasons. The moral was clear: 'all who enter into the marriage state from mercenary motives, though they may enlarge their possessions and increase their fortunes, live in splendid misery, and find that they have bartered happiness for wealth'.[26]

Another aspect of the modernisation of marriage was the rising influence of doctors, whose comments, widely disseminated particularly after 1850, represented the views of science as against the traditional spokesmen for the religious community. From the doctors women learned that a mate's physical health outweighed his religious qualities. With health given new value, medical practitioners throughout Europe became key intermediaries in the marriage market. Their influence was and continues to be substantial in setting the tone for discussions of marriage. As against even material concerns, women were advised to look into a man's health history, rather than his bank book. The bridegroom should be neither consumptive nor an alcoholic; he must not have a family history of insanity. Age similarity was heavily stressed, again a new point, as well as avoidance of any blood relationship. Dr Allbutt's advice to a woman doubtful about the health of her husband was typical of the growing emphasis on the topic: 'She should be sure that he is free from any contagious disease which can be communicated through sexual intercourse. I should like to see it the custom for women or their parents to demand a recent medical certificate of freedom from syphilis from all men.'[27] In France doctors worried about how their oath of professional secrecy should affect their attitude when they knew of impending marriage; should they reveal that one of their patients was 'afflicted with syphilis?'[28] All of this expanded the idea of compatibility to cover physical as well as personal harmony, even if it reflected an expectation that males might have had prior sexual experience. A French doctor tried to link health and compatibility according to a rather simple notion of the physical basis of personality, believing that harmony was best obtained with a marriage between persons of differing temperaments: 'The bilious should marry the lymphatic, the sanguine should unite with the nervous'.[29]

Marriage manuals did not penetrate all classes equally, and even by 1900 they were far from unanimous. But the need for advice of some sort almost inevitably followed from general social change. Young women and often their parents were confused by the new range of contacts and the fact that marriages could be contracted with virtual strangers. Hence the search for guidance, first largely from older authorities writing in news media, then from newer kinds of experts. But how much innovation was there in actual selection of mates? We can say with some assurance that the manuals helped to create a new trend, for they were widely read and respected. But we can also assume that many groups and individuals clung to the traditional manner of selection.

Custom was best observed in the rituals which followed the choice of partner, as when couples asked formal permission to marry. In Holland variation on the 'peace pipe' ritual held sway in cities as well as countryside. A young man presented himself at his fiancee's door, asking for a light for his cigar, which she would oblige; a second visit, with the same routine, alerted parents that a decision had to be made, as both parties were serious. If on a third visit the door was closed the suitor knew that his suit had been disapproved; but if it was open, his cigar was lit, and, to complete his bliss, his fiancée offered him another when he had finished the first, everything was all set.[30] But the gradual decline of this sort of ritual should not deceive us; we do not know that young men or women took a closed door with customary seriousness. And commonly traditions themselves began to change. In Bavaria, for example, the custom of *Heimgarten* gave way to new freedom for the young couple. *Heimgarten* was the peasant tradition by which a suitor gained about half an hour with his prospective bride, after which the parents came in to see how the couple got on and took charge of all further arrangements. From the early nineteenth century *Heimgarten* became increasingly informal, as couples met in meadows or even haystacks before reporting what was often a *fait accompli* to their parents.[31] Arranged marriages, which the upper class found it particularly important to maintain, persisted to a certain extent. A large dowry could save an old patrician family struggling to keep its place in a society where money counted for so much, while good connections could push the family of a new industrialist towards the top of the social ladder. But for the most part people began to exercise personal choice, even though it might sometimes involve a compromise to accommodate parental wishes.

Greater choice did not, however, necessarily involve the kind of disavowal of older standards of selection that the more progressive advice literature suggested. Economic considerations were not forgotten. In France far more than in England, dowries were vital to propertied groups in city and countryside and even in the twentieth century one observer called marriage the most important financial decision a bourgeois would make in his or her life.[32] Cementing the dowry was a marriage contract, with four parts. First, conditions for the administration and disposal of the couple's fortune (for which any number of arrangements might be made, ranging from control by husband alone to the more common provision that the wife would maintain hold over the property she brought to the marriage); second, enumeration of goods of all nature brought into the marriage; third, the allocations made to the couple by the parents; and fourth, a will stipulating what was to go to the survivor. Even at the end of this first hundred years of change the contract applied to almost 50 per cent of all marriages, which suggests how important the custom was even to people with modest economic prospects. By 1856-80, however, only 39 per cent of all marriages were by contract and by 1900 the figure had fallen to 26 per cent. Clearly, increasing numbers of couples were taking health and compatibility as well as property into account; for some, dowries and contracts became positively suspect, for they might create tensions and even hostility.[33]

We can see the continuing interest in the financial aspect of marriage if we look at the many advertisements for partners in family journals and newspapers. *L'Alliance des familles,* devoted solely to listing marriage offers, featured many like the following: 'Young man, 26 years old, 170,000 francs, excellent home, desires young girl with similar position'. 'Young girl, distinguished, pretty and musical, -- years old, dowry of 10,000 francs wishes to meet a man with similar economic background and interests.'[34] But advertisement itself was something new, a sign that even customary ties could no longer be formed easily in a mobile society. Unexpectedly, girls advertised almost as often as men. Young women were becoming progressively bolder in their courting procedures generally. Traditionalists shook their heads in dismay at girls who approached dancing partners or sought advice on how to set up a flirtation. Moralists tried to warn of the distinctions between love and passion and the dangers of an unconsidered marriage, but it was the newer manuals, advising compatibility and even sexual attraction, which reflected the trend in actual behaviour. The manuals also increasingly advised against unduly long engagements, the traditional pattern in the upper classes (and lower down the social scale, as couples needed time to build up capital). Even in the early nineteenth century individuals demanded that the age of consent for women be lowered so that there be no unnecessary delay for 'two people uniting themselves, when they were really suited, as came about when there was conformity of character'.[35]

With the new kind of marriage a woman won new rights, however informal, in relation to her husband. Marriages based, or thought to be based, on love, which ideally embraced the new factors of passion and personal compatibility, required mutual esteem and respect. With the new rationale happiness had to include the woman, whose position was emotionally as important as that of the man.

This was faithfully reflected in the manuals, as they turned to discuss the nature of marriage on this new basis. Reciprocity was the key; as the *Family Economist* put it around 1850,

> What is fair for one is fair for the other. In the married state there should be the strictest equality. The husband must come down from the position of master, not that his place may be taken by the woman . . . but that she may be the sharer of his pleasures, hopes and joys, as she has ever been the partaker of his pains, fears and sorrows..[36]

The clear implication was that women were to gain new rights and pleasures in what was now a concomitant relationship. Women had the right to partake in decision-making: 'In every undertaking the husband should consult the wife, and he should engage in no important enterprise without her advice and approbation, because their interests are identical; courtesy, if not necessity, demands consultation . . .'[37] The wife had a right to her husband's secrets: 'There ought to be no separate interests, no mysteries, no secret purposes, no concealments, all should be fair, clear, and open as the light of day; as in water face answers to face, so should the aims, pursuits, and pleasures of married people to one another.'[38] Mutual confidence, it was everywhere held, alone made a marriage work.[39]

One of the most important of all the new rights was that of sexual fulfilment, now recognised and strongly supported for the wife. One of the earliest spokesmen for the right of women to sexual satisfaction was Richard Carlisle, whose highly popular manual *Every Woman's Book; Or, What Is Love?* appeared in the 1820s. Carlisle's philosophy was that

> Equality and the right to make advances, in all the affairs of genuine love, are claimed for the female. The hypocrisy, the cruelty that would stifle or disguise a passion, whether in the male or in the female, is wicked, and should be exposed, reprobated, and detested. Young Women! Assume an equality, plead your passion when you

feel it . . .[40]

Equality was to be carried through to the most intimate relationship between husband and wife, their sex life. This was most explicit in Dr Michael Ryan's discussion of marriage obligation — in another popular marriage manual typical of medical advice — in which he noted that 'to preserve conjugal fidelity . . . requires two things: First, that the debt should be paid by one spouse to the other; and secondly that it should be paid to this person alone'.[41] Similar sentiments were being advocated in France at the same time. Gustave Droz, in his bestseller of 1866, proposed to convert women from the passive sex role. He wrote that

> It is nice being an angel, but, believe me, it is either too much or not enough . . . A Husband who is stately and a little bald is all right, but a young husband who loves you and drinks out of your glass without ceremony is better. Let him, if he ruffles your dress a little and places a little kiss on your neck as he passes. Let him, if he undresses you after the ball, laughing like a fool. You have fine spiritual qualities, it is true, but your little body is not bad either and when one loves, one loves completely. Behind these follies lies happiness. Thank heaven if in marriage which is presented to you as a career you find a side that yields laughter and joy; if in your husband you find a beloved reader of the nice novel you keep in your pocket; if in your husband you find a. . . But if I say the word you will cry Scandal![42]

Rights of consultation, compatibility and sexual enjoyment were among the most innovatory aspects in the nineteenth-century modernisation of marriage. Obviously the philosophy of marriage based on an equal relationship between husband and wife, one of love and equality, continues to be evoked as the ideal to the present day. But the ideal for whom? Not every married woman modernised in this way. The evolution of criteria for choosing a mate was roughly common to all social classes. The lower classes might not read the manuals, but they too married increasingly for love. France moved more slowly than England but in the same direction. Nevertheless when it came to the more important question of the nature of marriage itself social classes parted company in every country.

For the most part only middle-class women sought to modernise their roles in marriage along the lines sketched in the marriage literature.

This does not mean that lower-class women were changeless, they moved in a different pattern, adapting more elements of the old along with adopting some new ones. In the lower-class modernisation pattern the new included the steadily declining age at marriage. By the late nineteenth century girls born in factory and mining families were marrying between the ages of twenty-one and twenty-two. The increasing rate of marriage and new sexual attractions, resulting in a rising number of pre-bridal pregnancies into the late nineteenth century, were other new developments. So, however, were new economic roles and new extended family relationships, but changes here, just as clearly, differentiated working-class women from their middle-class counterparts.

The crux of the difference between the two class patterns lay in the relationship to the husband after the honeymoon was over. Working-class women were bound to the more traditional concept of marriage in which the husband assumed the leading role, with wife and children expected to sacrifice their needs in order that his be met. There was and continues to be a strict segregation of roles in the working-class family, with no pretence at equality until the last few decades if then. The concomitant relationship was strictly a middle-class innovation.

Yet it is not at all clear which pattern of adaptation was best, the radical one of the middle class or the conservative one of the workers. Time was a crucial factor. Even though change was gradual for both classes, the middle-class pattern involved relatively rapid transformation from one generation to the next. This might be beneficial in some cases, as old problems were resolved, but it could also be traumatic. It was largely beneficial in the case of health improvements, for example, but proved quite upsetting in the case of child-rearing. With slower change, working-class women had an easier familial adjustment, even though more restricted living standards created demonstrable material problems. The ability of the working-class women to maintain links with tradition could have provided them with a greater sense of security. But if innovation provided initial shock for the middle class, traditionalism proved increasingly limiting for working-class women over time.

In our attempt to establish an overall pattern we should be careful not to regard Anglo-American developments as wholly representative. French families, be they middle- or working-class, have not been studied as extensively as English or American. Sources themselves are hard to come by, which suggests a different kind of evolution (one demanding fewer advice manuals, for example); particularly notable is the absence of the female press which was well established by the mid-nineteenth century in England and America. It was not until after World War I that a mass market developed for such a press in France. The very absence of a market earlier might suggest a slower rate of female modernisation. There may have been more potential market than entrepreneurs realised, for the sources available indicate that there was change in middle-class outlook and behaviour in France quite similar to the English pattern. We have already seen similarities in advice on lovemaking and shared decision-making power.[43] The difference seems to be that the French evolution took place more slowly and so caused less insecurity. Urbanisation was more gradual and ties to agriculture were strong until well into the twentieth century, which helps explain many disparities in behaviour.

All in all, then, we can posit a common evolution tied roughly to the overall pace of change in a society, but differentiated according to class. In order to flesh out this general scheme, we must turn to married life itself and women's role in absorbing and causing change in all aspects of family activities.

Middle-Class Homemaker: A Model for Women's Growing-up Process

The middle-class woman, the nineteenth-century pioneer in the making of a modern life-style, learned very quickly that the new rights she gained involved grave responsibilities. The right to partake in the decision-making process and even heightened sexual intimacies became a burden to her, and the cult of the 'perfect wife' and 'perfect mother' presented her with an unattainable goal. Historians have tended to under-estimate the importance of this new development, and it has often been assumed that the exaltation of woman was nothing more than putting her upon a pedestal to be admired or displayed as men wished.[44] On the contrary, the image of the woman as perfect wife and mother resulted from her growing stature in the family. Far from being idle symbols of purity, women found their familial roles becoming increasingly complicated. Now the family's manager, the housewife was the source of its health and happiness. Her sphere of activity was limited to the confines of the home, but the home itself gained a new importance as more time was spent there, with hours of work shortened and leisure time increased.

The role of perfect wife and mother involved enormous expenditures of energy, both physical and mental. It easily led to feelings of guilt, that new roles were imperfectly understood and fulfilled. Most women kept trying, nevertheless, and significant innovations resulted from their efforts.

The middle-class woman generally began her married life between the ages of twenty-three and twenty-five in England, more nearly twenty-five in France. Her husband was typically between one to two years older. Probably the middle-class marriage rate was even higher than rising national averages, as property considerations added to the newer emotional needs; the middle-class spinster existed but was a rarity, witness the difficulty of recruiting 'genteel' unmarried ladies for jobs such as governess of children too precious to be entrusted to lower-class care.[45]

Pending further research, for the structure of the middle-class family has received little attention, it appears that the nuclear form predominated from early married life onwards. Recent studies of middle-class communities such as Islington and Kensington in London give us some idea of the housing of the class in the nineteenth century.[46] The typical home in England was a narrow, three story terrace house, with kitchen, living room and dining room on the ground floor, three or four family bedrooms on the first floor and a servant's room along with a child's bedroom on the second. There was no space here for extended kin to live. In France, middle-class families lived in much smaller apartments, on a single floor; here, even more clearly than in England, available housing could not provide a middle-class standard of living for multi-generational families. Nor, apparently, did relatives live nearby, for a class that was quite mobile geographically; mother was rarely next door. Advice literature in England, directed to the middle-class housewife, suggests that mothers were not conveniently at hand, as the housewife was urged to seek aid from neighbours even in as important an event as childbirth. A common format for the advice literature was a letter from a newly-married daughter seeking maternal wisdom, which suggests that newlyweds, however brisk their correspondence, were forced to make urgent decisions on their own.[47] The long discussions that filled French and English household manuals indicated that middle-class women expected to move at least twice in married life, even after the displacement of marriage itself; the maxim, equally current in England, America and France was that three moves were equal to a house fire, in the strain placed on women.[48] Again, this points to nuclear families as the norm, as neither relatives nor parents would keep pace with this mobility. Correspondingly diaries and personal letters, though scanty, show that communications with family were normally conducted through letters, with occasional visits at holiday time and perhaps once a month the rest of the year.

Compared to the pre-industrial family and the working-class family of the day, the middle class put a premium on privacy; hence for example the desire to have separate bedrooms for parents and children.[49] This often stretched the family budget, and certainly added to the physical demands of cleaning for the woman, but the privacy gained thereby was sacrosanct. In the nuclear family, however, with no relatives to share the work load or simply to give advice, the middle-class woman could find herself alone and overburdened.

Before going further, we should consider what we know about the life style of middle-class families in the period. First, they had extra resources, which allowed them to maintain relatively extensive living quarters. If housing and furnishings were the typical middle-class indulgence, clothing and food reflected more than minimal standards. But the class was constantly tempted to higher material expectations and it was the woman who had to make a budget stretch if any of these were to be realised. Stretching, in turn, involved a host of household production activities — making clothes, bottling and preserving food in addition to the daily maintenance of several rooms and a large family. To ease this physical burden, as we all know, middle class families in the nineteenth century used some of their extra resources for paid help. The use of servants was not new, but few middle-class women were experienced in this responsibility, at least in an urban setting. Throughout most of the century, how a middle-class woman handled her servant, indeed how adequate the servant was in dealing with a demanding set of household chores, formed an important part of women's family experience.

The servant can be seen as a brief (two- or three-generation) substitute for extended family ties or the employment of a neighbour's child in the village. The higher one rose on the prosperity ladder in the middle class, the more servants one employed. At the bottom, in fact, were some families without a servant at all. And the middle-class family rarely managed to afford more than two servants. The typical English or French family employed but a single servant, the maid-of-all-work or the *bonne à tout faire*.

Historians have delighted in discussing the relationship of servants to the middle class. Conventionally the servant is viewed almost exclusively as a status symbol, indicating that the family had arrived socially. It is common to read that the main distinguishing characteristic between a middle-class and a lower-class woman was an attitude that demanded the keeping of at least one servant as an inferior who could be ordered about.[50] However, the relationship between housewife and her servant goes well beyond this attitude. Given traditional use of servants and the immense physical demands of keeping up a middle-class household it would have been odd *not* to employ servants. Indeed a single servant in no sense relieved the housewife from numerous physical chores. What dominates any reasoned judgement of the middle-class relationship with servants must be first, the overwhelming and continuous spate of complaints throughout the nineteenth century, pervading letters, and special features in women's magazines, that servants were performing badly; and second, that the urban middle-class experiment with servants tailed off within merely seventy years after the class itself began to grow.

The use of domestic servants was at best an intermediary step in the modernisation of the middle-class family, even though historians have claimed that the keeping of servants was the essence of the middle class. In fact one sees, in looking at the situation from the viewpoint of the middle-class woman, the employer, that the practice was heavily traditional, imitating either the aristocratic upper class or even village artisanal customs of hiring young people for menial tasks. Hence older sectors of the middle class, such as parish rectors or lawyers, insisted most strongly on maintaining servants. Families from traditional professional backgrounds, like that of Karl Marx (whose two servants were funded by Friedrich Engels) were more likely than newer business families of somewhat greater means to rely on servants. For the new middle-class family, the servant was a stranger in the home, coming often from the countryside into the new urban setting (unlike the rural servant of the eighteenth century who commonly went to work in the homes of relatives or neighbours). Contemporaries recognised this indirectly in their criticism of the middle-class mistress as snobbish and standoffish, unconcerned about her servant's well-being. In fact, much of this aloofness was due to her uneasiness with strangers, her desire for privacy.

Yet for a time the servant seemed indispensable, creating an ambiguous situation. Increased standards of living — not only a bigger home but also new emphasis on cleanliness and extensive child care — involved new demands on the time and energy of the household manager. The servant enabled the middle-class woman to meet the rising standards, or at least so she long thought despite the stream of complaints.

The theme here is familiar. With a servant the middle-class woman gained or retained an important role as employer. This power, more than any other, brought with it new headaches in the urban environment. Hence the century-long lament over the problems with domestic servants that filled household manuals and women's magazines with discussions of what was popularly called the 'servant question'. The difficulty was two-fold, in middle-class eyes: there were not enough servants and those available were not good enough.[51] The consensus of opinion in the advice literature was that the failure to find competent servants was largely the fault of the mistress, who was incapable of giving tactful orders or directing employees.[52] To some extent this criticism was valid. Most middle-class women were new to their position as the size of the class grew steadily in the nineteenth century. Many found the role of formal employer uncomfortable at the very least.[53] On the other hand the only servant most women could afford was the lowest in the domestic servant hierarchy, the unskilled general maid.[54] She came from extreme poverty, either from a labourer's cottage, where it was no longer possible to feed or clothe her, or from a peasant's home in France or from the wretched city slums in England. She had no idea of what the middle class considered the ordinary habits of civilised life, let alone the new refinements of cleanliness and sobriety. She was very young, generally under twenty years old. Hence a vicious circle, in which each party could easily misunderstand the other.

The relationship between servant and mistress was intense. The middle-class woman, unsure of her own new functions in the household, felt ill at ease with a rough young girl in her home, and often drifted into squabbles over who was to do what, and how. One gets the impression that servants may have won more battles than they lost. Middle-class women wrote that they could not get their girl to clean properly, that she often went out shopping and returned late, that she drank or stole, or more commonly just shouted at her mistress. Given the high rate of turnover one might assume that the middle-class woman finally took the initiative and fired the servant, but again the evidence suggests the contrary. In the first place many a housewife was too intimidated by the servant girl to fire her. More commonly the girl, fed up with one situation or looking to improve her position, left work within one to two years of service. The common lament by the middle-class mistress was that no sooner had she trained her servant than she left, burdening the employer with the chore of hiring and training another girl.

Problems began with the first step, as the middle-class woman set out to find a servant, no easy task since the number of servants, although more than doubling in the nineteenth century, never came near the number of middle-class families. The lack of numbers was overshadowed by the problem of quality. The importance of choosing the *proper* servant was heavily emphasised in the manuals; the mistress was to look for 'integrity, sobriety, cleanliness and general propriety in manner and dress and a knowledge of the duties of the prospective department of household management'.[55] To find such a paragon, women had to rely primarily on references from neighbours or leads from the local tradespeople. Some advertised in a newspaper, but generally this was for the more specialised servants such as governess or cook. Later in the century employment agencies were available, but their use was limited as they continued to offer bad servants. For the most part a middle-class woman had to accept the servant's own statement of qualifications for the job, which was not very helpful.

In return for service the servant was provided with a yearly wage plus room and board. In many homes the employer gave her used clothing to the girl, and in addition there were expected gifts such as the Christmas box. Housing was limited, as we have seen, particularly in France, but it still costs some money. In all cases servant and mistress worked close together and the servant was nearly omnipresent.

Despite the variety of conditions, the expense of a servant usually put substantial strain on the household budget. This conditioned life on both sides of the domestic fence. Middle-class women expected a substantial return for a rather minimal outlay. Servants could easily be or feel themselves to be mistreated when the household overextended itself. If economic pressures were too intense the servant was slighted as to food, accommodation or fuel for heat or lighting. These savings on the part of the mistress did not go unnoticed, for here too servants might hold their own in assertiveness. Servants complained often about the inadequate living quarters, the poor and insufficient food served to them, or the workload. This is not to imply that every servant-mistress relationship was sour. Undoubtedly there were a good many employers who went out of their way to help their servants and servants who did likewise for their mistresses. No matter how good the mistress's intentions, the relationship could turn into a nightmare. And if snobbish or pinch-penny employers could make life miserable for servants, the servant who rebelled by stealing, breaking household property or simply refusing to work well could make the housewife's lot unbearable, so great was her dependence on household help.

A key aspect of the middle-class woman's life, even with a competent servant, has been too often overlooked. The amount of daily menial labour involved in maintaining the home was overwhelming and physically exhausting even for two women, especially with the care of from three to five children added to basic housekeeping. This is why a servant seemed essential and why she often proved inadequate and left. This put the housewife back in the vicious circle of recruiting and training, while herself undertaking demanding household tasks.

For a transitional period, then, middle-class women's domestic management position included the role of employer. But because the results were unsatisfactory housewives began to make re-adjustments. The domestic servant was necessary particularly before the middle class curtailed its birth rate and before other, more modern means to run a household were developed. The problems involved in directing an unskilled, often sulky teenaged servant added seriously to the strain of household management and spurred middle-class women eventually to eliminate them on a full-time live-in basis.

By the end of the nineteenth century, indeed as early as the 1870s in France, middle-class women began to run their homes without the assistance of servants, a result of both internal and external forces. With smaller family size plus the introduction of labour-saving devices and the expansion of retail stores to cater for women's domestic needs many women found that it was more economical in terms of time and energy to do without the servant. At the same time servant girls were discovering that other opportunities were available and so the number of servants for hire stagnated or declined. The middle-class woman retained some help with her household up to World War I and indeed beyond, but this was common on a part-time basis by 'dailies' or 'chars' who came in once or twice a week only.

This transformation, rather than the transitional use of servants, really signalled the modernisation of the household and the new domestic role of the middle-class woman. The family finally attained privacy.[56] Though there was grumbling at the decline of servanthood the middle class did not seek new recruits by raising pay, a clear indication that the servant's value had diminished. When able to maintain the household through new organisation and new devices, the middle-class woman had come into her own.

It was essential, for example, to develop new procedures to ensure that income could be stretched to meet growing needs. The middle-class housewife resembled the businessman in her emphasis on careful accounting and planning. Traditional virtues of frugality helped here, but this was a class that wanted more than the spartan life. In advice manuals a whole new 'science' of rational domestic economy developed, beginning from careful purchasing on a large scale, to spreading expenses and keeping budget books. Simply to maintain middle-class standards French and English women busily pursued the art of domestic economy, which became a nineteenth century household catchword.[57] The rule for all was 'If you wish affluence, be economical...if you have affluence be more economical.'[58] The middle-class housewife turned scientist as she applied rational planning to her time and money.[59] The successful manager was one who ordered her every minute and every penny. Elaborate timetables were drawn up as models for women to follow. The general maxim was that the early riser was best as she was sure to be on top of things.[60] At the same time, observers, particularly in England, found women's efforts inadequate; some even claimed that housekeeping standards had declined, due to poor education.[61] What actually happened was that most women did take on a new, more rationalised approach but still found their resources strained; to be criticised in the literature that they turned to for guidance only added to their troubles.

Women, of course, consulted their husbands on financial matters. The middle-class wife expected to be fully informed of her husband's total earnings. She also expected to be the determiner of where his money should go. Since she was the one who set up the budget which included all household expenditures she did in fact assume the major role in financial decision-making. French manuals noted that large expenditures had traditionally been for husbands alone to allocate but that now it was the custom for the husband to defer to his wife's sage advice in such matters.[62] Women complained that they could not operate the family's finances without this cooperation on the part of their husbands, and we must assume that they increasingly got it.[63]

Here, then, was the new and vital economic role for women in the family, a novel division of labour that gave women enormous power in the family and even in the broader economy. The new power provided women, first in the middle class and gradually in the working class, with one of the key modern means of self-expression, consumerism. Middle-class women in the nineteenth century became the major supporters of a consumer-oriented economy. Many new industries were founded or expanded as a result of the new financial power of women in the family. Advertising boomed by playing on the woman as consumer. This was a peculiarly Anglo-American phenomenon for several decades, but large-scale advertising for women spread to France after World War I. It made women aware of the many new items available to them though it added frustration when the array of new products so temptingly offered was simply out of range.

Industries specialising in household appliances also prospered. One of the first major industries to cater for women was the sewing machine industry. From the 1860s onward in England, by 1900 in France the sewing machine was a basic necessity. It was expensive, consuming up to five per cent of annual middle-class income, but savings or purchase plans made it feasible to buy, and it could be used to save money as well as labour in the long run.[64] The list of household appliances could be expanded, including stoves, bathtubs and the like, almost all related to basic household functions.

Increasing consumerism put great strain on domestic finances, as rising prices and soon inflationary economics became constant concerns for the middle-class housewife. Rent and food remained the major monthly expenditures. The housewife was responsible for providing suitable housing and proper furnishings for her family in addition to food and clothing. But in England, rents alone doubled in the nineteenth century,[65] causing middle-class families to flee to the suburbs for relief; France had less suburban development but here too rising rents pressed the class, particularly after 1870. Middle-class women spent many hours a day, and often sleepless nights, worrying about balancing the budget, often with ill effects as reported in a comment on 'The Ill-Health of Women' which appeared in a popular English manual:

The problem of making both ends meet when the income is insufficient has a most pernicious effect upon women's health. The process is thoroughly disheartening and devitalizing. It gives an anxious, worn expression easy to recognize. Those who try so laboriously to save must, of necessity, spend themselves.[66]

Instalment plans provided at least stop-gap relief, and middle-class women increasingly turned to credit purchases in order to balance their budgets. At first there was a barrage of criticism against this type of financing.[67] French manuals insisted that 'Credits are the ruin of the home...'[68] But by the end of the century instalment buying became general practice, and the same domestic literature that blasted spending beyond one's means carried advertisements touting the possibility of buying a sewing machine for almost nothing down and twenty francs a month. Credit plans, however, postponed problems of budgeting; they did not solve them. Housewives never were able to achieve a position where money matters were not crucial to everyday concerns. But worry, sensibly directed, could pay off. In spite of rising costs, women did manage to provide their families with increasing material prosperity. Most kept their heads above water and gained increasing amenities, so that the material contents of the middle-class household by the early twentieth century differed substantially from those of fifty years before.

However difficult the achievement, something like a modern household had been created by this time. Extra resources were vital in this, but two changes in traditional mentality were equally significant. First was a new rationality in household direction and second was the *kind* of new purchases women grew interested in. Middle-class housewives began to mechanise their operations, and their zeal to find new ways to perform their household tasks, and to perform these tasks better was the very contradiction of Luddism. The desire for plumbing facilities, for example, has generally been viewed as part of the 'sanitary revolution', a new definition of household standards, but it also bears witness to a fascination with new devices and to women's growing concern about a new level of cleanliness in the home. Piped water, better drainage systems, bath tubs, eventually toilets and even washing machines mark the ever rising standard of cleanliness in the middle-class family. The stove, vacuum cleaner and sewing machine were all also improved.

Mechanisation did not fully remove the housewife's domestic burdens. It is true that piped water eliminated the heavy chore of carrying water up and down several flights of stairs each day, and improvements on the kitchen range were no small relief. But it was a long time before coal- and wood-burning stoves were replaced by new sources of energy such as gas or electricity; well into the twentieth cetury women still had to haul coal or wood for the stove. The washing machine not only saved work; it also created it, since with its arrival women did more washing. If one scans the domestic manuals over a period of time the trend is clear. Early in the nineteenth century washing was done weekly but linens were cleaned at most every two weeks. By the end of the century middle-class women were washing their linens every week, at least in England and America.

In France, the modernisation pattern developed by middle-class women was somewhat different. The household appliance craze which began at mid-century in England never took off in France. Specialised stores performed many of these tasks instead. The increase in small retail shops in the nineteenth and twentieth centuries shows what was happening. The French women relied more upon the *charcuterie* and *blanchisserie* to provide prepared food and clean clothes.[69] It was noted by one of the self-appointed authorities on domestic management in France that the failure of French women properly to handle their domestic chores turned to the great profit of the new stores.[70] But this may be unrealistic carping. The fact that French women did not increase their standards of cleanliness as rapidly as the Anglo-American model might mean that the physical work load was not as great. On the other hand, shopping itself might take up a woman's day, though at the same time, it afforded her an increased opportunity for socialising. It is difficult to evaluate these differences. Without question the French woman's health and that of her children remained inferior to the English, which suggests not just a difference but a slower or less adequate pattern of modernisation in housekeeping.

Eventually, even in France, new appliances as well as new services were adopted, forcing women to re-assess their housekeeping and to set themselves ever higher standards. A woman with time on her hands might have sat back to wonder if the treadmill was worth it. But the treadmill did not allow this introspection, and women pushed on with their new concern for rationality, mechanisation, privacy – and higher and higher criteria of self-evaluation as housewives. This modernisation of millions of households, though concealed behind curtained windows (carefully cleaned), was as radical as that which was going on in factories or corporate offices.

From the woman's perspective these new functions were fundamental to her new status, in spite of the criticisms launched against inadequate housekeeping: indeed many of the criticisms came from traditionalists who found women's eagerness for a sewing machine, for example, in lieu of the old time-consuming hand stitching almost immoral. The criticisms no doubt increased anxieties for women who were trying new methods but were unsure of their propriety; nothing else can explain why women continued to read articles that criticised practices, such as instalment buying, which they increasingly engaged in. Criticism remained a popular item in household magazines, though it is more often leavened with constructive suggestions, and has played its part in preventing many middle-class housewives from using their new found time for more diverse pursuits.

The middle-class wife was not manager alone. She was also mother, and here again, a traditional function was dramatically upgraded. Here too critics poured scorn on women for failing in their duties, compounding self-doubt with the anxieties connected with new roles, and the middle-class mother was besieged by outside comments, as she sought guidance. She, more than anyone, altered the nature of mother-hood, striking a new balance between having children and caring for them — just as she finally struck a new balance between intrusions on privacy and successful household management. But while woman as mistress of the household and woman as mother moved in similar directions, there is no question that motherhood received pride of place in the public eye. The burdened household manager was one and the same as the dutiful mother, but the latter role changed more dramatically in societal definition and had a more profound effect on the evolution of the family in general.

Modern Motherhood: The Vital Revolution

No other position in modern society has yielded such exclusive power to women as motherhood. The dynamics of being a mother and mothering were revolutionised by middle-class women in nineteenth-century Europe and America alike. Every aspect of the process underwent dramatic change, from giving birth to child-rearing and discipline. The conversion of woman as mother into wielder of power continues into the present. To some this may sound strange, for the decline of motherhood, its loss of functions, is widely discussed today. It is repeatedly claimed that modern society has stripped motherhood of its traditional importance, as encroachments of a bureaucratised state cut into maternal roles. At the tender age of five, for example, children are taken from their mothers' care and sent off to school, and mothers are left as nothing more than ancillary figures who dress their children and send them off to be moulded by others. Family planning has further undermined women's position. Now having fewer children, in a shorter period of time, women find their only function in society, their mother role, limited to a few years. The argument contends that traditionally, motherhood consumed the whole of married life, whereas now even ancillary functions take up only fifteen to eighteen years, at which point the female is put out to pasture with nothing to do but graze and gaze. There is some truth in this derogatory story of decline for many women. But the general conclusion that women's maternal power base has been eroded with modernisation does not follow. What hits home hardest in the critical argument, the sense of confusion and purposelessness when the children leave the nest, merely emphasises the importance of the years of childrearing, an importance which overrides even state education and lasts well into the child's adolescence. In order to understand the complexities involved in this development we need to look at the historical process, remembering that at our starting point in pre-industrial society, where birth was the only real maternal function, there was precious little to erode.

We can begin with the legal standing of the mother. Prior to the nineteenth century, women had no formal rights over their children. Fathers were considered the only legal guardians and officially took all the decisions about the children's upbringing. They had sole custody of children in any dispute. This power was not always exercised in actual practice but it reflected the theory of parental rights and it could be used brutally, when for example fathers removed their children from the home and prevented mothers from seeing them at all.[71] In less than a hundred years the whole situation was reversed. If anyone's position in the family became defunct it was the father's, at least as far as the law went. Mothers became the only parent fit to make decisions about their children, the natural custodians in cases of separation or divorce. One need only look at the records of the domestic court systems, especially in England and America, to measure the growing importance of the maternal role.

How did such changes occur? A number of factors were involved, the most important being the rise of the woman's status in the family. As the family moved from an economic unit to the modern unit, based on emotional ties of love, power positions changed. In pre-industrial society the father was granted the position of power as the most reliable economic provider. It was assumed that the father was the only parent who could care properly for the children in maintaining them (economically, that is) and, in the case of sons, training them to be providers in turn.

The modern family, founded on the premise of emotional commitment, on love, saw a revolution in familial hierarchy. The new basis of the modern family soon led to a recognition that the parent who provided the love was the most important. Here the father found himself in a very difficult position, for his role in the family did not modernise as quickly as the woman's. Legally, in fact, his role to this day continues to be defined in the traditional and limiting terms of economic provider; hence his continuing responsibility for monetary child support even when he has lost contact with his children, on grounds that the woman is the essential emotional provider.

Changing economics further undermined the paternal role. Working now far from home, a father's contact with his children was severely restricted. Often when he returned home he found that he and they were too tired for pleasant interaction. For a brief period children worked beside their fathers in the new factories not only on

machines but in business offices. But both machinery and business structures soon became too complex for this and to protect or educate their children, families withdrew them from early work.[72] With advancing technology, fathers could no longer pretend to offer training to their sons, and technical or secondary schools took over this
- function. In his stead was the mother, who provided love, the essential new family ingredient. As such she assumed the power position, recognised not only by law but by most fathers, by other women, and at least into their rebellious teens by most children themselves.

The change in the concept of motherhood from the woman's point of view, following from new personal values, was quickly touted in the public press, particularly of course in childrearing manuals (for here too a new literature developed to fill the need for guidance in a new situation). Women everywhere came to realise the increasing importance of their maternal role. But far more than sentimental soliloquies were involved; actual practice changed and really provided the basis for the new claims. Women's initiative in modernising traditional ways was more pronounced in their role as mother than in any other function, inside or outside the home. And their personal achievements were greatest in this area as they tackled age-old problems such as death in childbirth and infant mortality. Early in the nineteenth century middle-class women began to challenge the traditional concept that it was in the grand design of nature or the deity that innocent women and more often babies should die in childbirth. With the rejection of traditional fatalism, the modern mentality began to take form.

Yet success was slow in coming and could prove painful. For most middle-class women anticipations of improvement outstripped reality. For many, the problems encountered as they adopted the modern concept of motherhood far outweighed a feeling of enhanced power. As was typical of almost all the new roles, increased status brought increased responsibilities.

The most dramatic changes in motherhood occurred in England and America beginning early in the nineteenth century. On the continent women were to change at a slower tempo and less completely.

As with household management, science invaded the art of mothering. One sign of its growing influence can be seen in the number of books, periodicals and pamphlets which flooded the Anglo-American market in the century, all proclaiming scientific prowess in varying degrees.[73] Science's influence was felt most directly with the development of family medicine, starting with obstetrics, later pediatric medicine and ultimately child psychology. The nature of the growing relationship between doctors and women has only recently been recognised. Women did not play a passive role but, desirous of new health care, actively sought help from doctors who responded, sometimes belatedly, to this new concern.[74] Again the interaction was most pronounced in England and America as more and more women sought a doctor's aid whether in the form of the many volumes of advice literature authored by physicians or through direct consultation. In France developments in family medicine were slower and never reached the level that prevailed in England. Nevertheless change occurred, and in the same basic direction. As early as 1845 it was recommended that the first thing a woman should do after marriage was to choose a doctor, the most important choice for her life after choosing a husband.[75]

We have noted the common assertion, offered particularly by sociologists, that pre-modern women spent more of their time mothering than do modern women. This reflects ignorance of any real historical trend. We know that the pre-modern woman conceived about every two years, so given the fact that she married in her later twenties she could expect to be pregnant every other year from the age of 27 to 39 and possibly at 41 though fertility sharply declined after 38. Of the seven or eight children born only half would survive. Further, the chances that the first born would not survive were greater than average, meaning that motherhood might not begin until nearly age 30. If the first born lived and the mother had a final child at 41, motherhood might extend for twenty years, taking into account that any active care ceased by the time a child reached 5 or 7. Also to be remembered is the considerable part played by older daughters in caring for smaller children.

There is no need to minimise the efforts of the pre-industrial mother; we have described how much she had to do to maintain her family. Obviously material conditions improved dramatically with industrialisation, and particularly in the rising middle class. But improved conditions did not mean that motherhood was necessarily made less time consuming. By the twentieth century many girls were marrying by the age of 21 and having their first baby at 23 and might have their last at 30. At the same time, relatively few infants would die; infant mortality overall was down 20 per cent. But this is not the main point, as few women were bearing all the children biologically possible; the middle class, marrying later in the first place, pioneered the new trend which sees most women completing families by their late twenties, that is, within a few years of marriage.

But the end of repeated pregnancies did not mean the end of motherhood and here is the key difference from the pre-industrial situation. Quite unlike the traditional mother, the modern woman's responsibility for the child covers an unusually long period up to the age of eighteen at least and demands the active provision of physical care and overall guidance. If we assume, as we could not with pre-modern woman, that the first pregnancy is successful but that the final child is born within five years of the first, the woman of the early twentieth century was also spending at least twenty years in mothering. Motherhood as consumer of time has changed slightly; if anything it has inched upwards while its nature has been transformed from pregnancies every two years to caring for the individual child more than twice as long as pre-modern women would have found necessary or possible. So change there was, but not the kind that put motherhood out of business. Again the parallels with women's domestic standards are striking, for just as women reacted to new household devices by expanding their definition of cleanliness to take up the slack, so too new techniques alleviating some aspects of mothering brought about a redefinition of emphasis which added other duties. We may again criticise this tendency to fill time with old goals that had roots in tradition even if dramatically updated in practice, rather than brand new functions, but this is what happened.

The new attention to motherhood was to begin right away, within the first few months of pregnancy. Unlike her great grandmother, who paid very little attention to pregnancy until delivery, the nineteenth century middle-class woman grew very concerned about the whole process, for being a good mother began almost with conception. No other function so completely involved the woman both physically and emotionally. The majority of middle-class women would be pregnant at least once in their lives and most, until late in the century, between three and five times, so a reassessment of pregnancy inevitably commanded wide attention.

Pregnancy was for the first time seriously and openly discussed in the early decades of the nineteenth century. New manuals, written mainly by doctors, depicted explicitly the physical phenomenon including childbirth itself. This was a significant advance over earlier comments which referred to pregnancy only in the most shrouded and metaphorical sense, treating childbirth only in terms of women's fulfilment of a natural destiny. Middle-class women found these spiritual discussions less meaningful by the 1800s. Many came to believe that pregnancy was far from natural. Some were frightened by the pains associated with delivery. More were fearful of the real threat of death, for thousands of women died annually in childbirth in both Britain and France. If childbirth was natural, then nature had to be improved upon. In their efforts to improve their personal well-being as well as that of their family, in their new desire for self-control, women sought the aid of science, at least through doctors' writings, which promised to provide solutions to the traditional problems of childbirth.

Anxiety increased as pregnancies were more likely to occur given the more regular fertility and heightened sexual interests of nineteenth century women. The chances of having as many as fifteen children were far from remote. But repeated pregnancies and hordes of children were not in tune with the new middle-class woman's vision of herself, and the first step in modern mothering involved new handling of pregnancy itself. First, women demand to know about their condition as soon as possible. The new manuals provided detailed information on the signs of pregnancy: cessation of the menses known as 'ceasing to be well' in England; swelling of the breasts; nausea and vomiting for the first few months (one French doctor insisted that vomiting occurred immediately on conception),[76] the quickening movement of the foetus between the twentieth and twenty-second week; and finally increased size and weight gain. In addition one suffered from toothaches, drowsiness and excess saliva. In France doctors were also performing internal examinations, called *'le toucher'*, to determine not only the fact of pregnancy but to be sure that there were no complications. In England this examination was not generally performed until labour was well underway, precisely because it involved internal probing of the woman; English doctors debated the moral implications of the *toucher* throughout the century and it was not until about 1900 that prudery was overcome and the examination became normal procedure.

Eventually more precise methods were introduced to determine pregnancy early. The vaginal speculum, although not new, was being used by the 1830s to determine the size of the vagina, which grew larger after conception. The speculum also allowed a close examination of the uterus, which changed colour with pregnancy. The application of a stethoscope to the woman's belly to listen to the foetal heartbeat was another important development in the nineteenth century. One other innovation, which France again pioneered, was the testing of urine for chemical changes due to pregnancy.[77]

Thus the importance of pre-natal care was beginning to be recognised. Growing specialisation in obstetrics and increasing concern by women themselves overcame traditional hesitation, as some of the new examinations provided quicker and more reliable identification of pregnancy, a crucial first step. Following this, the health of the mother-to-be demanded new attention as much depended upon it, including the health of the baby and the ease of the delivery itself. In order to prepare properly, women were advised to seek a doctor as soon as they thought they might be pregnant. Regulated diets, moderate exercise and suitable clothing which would allow support and freedom of movement were the general guidelines set forth by doctors. By the twentieth century blood and urine tests, and blood pressure examinations, along with attention to dental care were routine aspects of pre-natal procedure for middle-class women.

By this time the full impact of the advances made in prenatal care saved many mothers' lives and eased undue fear and anxiety for many more. One of the important early services performed by doctors, even before medical advances were widely applied to actual treatment, was to dispel traditional ignorance and with it many needless fears and some harmful practices. From the early nineteenth century, doctors assured women that birthmarks on babies were not due to traumas during pregnancy. Doctors vigorously urged that superstitious practices be abandoned in favour of sound hygiene; doubling food intake, based on the belief that the pregnant mother was eating for two, for example, was harmful, and moderation in diet was urged.

In abandoning traditional beliefs in favour of radically new medical procedures, women were showing a new sense of self – a genuinely new mentality. The trend was general, within the middle class, but the extent of change can be measured by key comparative differentials. In France, despite the innovative work in obstetric techniques, women well into the twentieth century continued to use midwives rather than doctors for deliveries. Part of the explanation may have been the internal examination, which French doctors were more often willing to employ. It is clear that women were reluctant to undergo the *toucher*. In one French manual the doctor went to some length to explain that during this test a woman must think of the examiner only as a physician, not a man.[78] The fact that English doctors long delayed this examination may have made it more acceptable, for medical advance could not exceed patients' adaptation to it. French women were probably prompted to shun doctors by their unbelievable backwardness in many other areas, for there was an immense gap between the pioneering researchers and ordinary practitioners. Many French doctors as late as 1858 were still bleeding women in their fourth month of pregnancy.[79] In contrast, bleeding had been almost completely eliminated as part of general medical practice in England before 1800. Finally, French midwives received formal training in medical schools and were licensed after being tested by a doctor, an immense improvement over election of an influential village widow or selection by the parish priest. Dr William Farr, the English Registrar General, wrote in 1856 that French midwives were 'more receptive' to innovation than their English counterparts. In England, partly due to doctors' own desire for a greater role, training was not required and licensing was a farce; the English midwife offered no assurance of qualifications and middle-class women recognised this, turning to doctors in growing numbers. This difference, perfectly understandable from the point of view of a nineteenth-century woman, had important effects, as the English conversion to scientific practice was more abrupt and complete.

Despite this difference in medical personnel the main point is that for the first time the middle-class woman had readily available information on what had been traditionally conveyed by word of mouth, whether through manuals written by educated doctors, trained midwives in France, or direct consultation of doctors.

Along with the new information on pre-natal care the nineteenth century saw dramatic advances in the actual child delivery process as well. Middle-class women, using the new methods of science to gain some control over their physical destiny, were vitally concerned about this crucial event. The major innovation in child delivery was the use of trained personnel, the most important being the obstetrician. Obstetrics as a medical specialisation began in the late eighteenth century. In France, Dr Baudelocque is often credited as founder of the practice in the late eighteenth century, while Dr Charles Gordon holds similar fame for his work in obstetrics in England. Well into the nineteenth century this new field commanded the interest only of a few pioneering men and women. England was one of the earliest countries to initiate some obstetric training for all doctors, as by the 1860s most of the leading universities granting a medical degree required a minimum of three months of training. In line with this England also produced the earliest obsteric society, in 1858; in contrast, its French counterpart was not founded until the late 1880s, the organisational lag reflecting the overall hesitation in the use of doctors over midwives in France. The pattern increasingly taking shape in France was a combination of doctor/midwife at childbirth, with the trained midwife acting mainly as assistant. As a result maternal and infant mortality rates did decline. However, the more extensive innovation in England seemed to produce substantially better results and by the end of the nineteenth century infant and maternal rates dropped significantly below that of France.

In England women chose doctors over midwives in the belief that they offered several advantages: superior training, knowledge of the newest techniques in obstetric care, and an impressive array of instruments such as improved forceps, the curette and the dilator, all of which facilitated complicated deliveries such as breech births or still births. Adoption of doctors' care or even the use of trained midwives dramatically altered the delivery process by the second half of the nineteenth century. No longer did the expectant mother prepare her own bed for lying-in or have to listen to an untrained midwife tell lugubrious stories while in labour (doctors constantly urged against saying anything that would heighten anxiety at this time for the woman). With any complications the middle-class woman was increasingly sure of doctors' care; even in France midwives had to summon a doctor when the delivery presented problems, for it was against the law for them to use forceps or administer drugs. Of greater improvement was the fact that the woman was no longer ignored in the afterbirth process.

Perhaps the greatest benefit which the nineteenth-century doctor provided for the new middle-class woman was relief from the traditional pains of childbirth. With the introduction of anaesthesia, provided by ether or chloroform, not only pain but anxiety were greatly alleviated. Here, women's own initiative proved crucial, particularly in England (French doctors in this area offered few objections to anaesthetics, showing more sympathy for the woman in labour). The first major breakthrough in painless childbirth was the development of chloroform in England by Dr James Simpson in the 1840s. A debate quickly arose as to the safety of the new chemical. Many doctors were reluctant at first, and refused to introduce it on the grounds that pain was natural to childbirth and persisted usually no more than a few hours; therefore one should not risk unknown complication, perhaps even death as a result of overdose – a reasonable position if the chance of overdose were high. But Simpson along with others proved that this was not a real danger in obstetric cases. More important, women were adamant and insisted on the new solace, until doctors were gradually forced to yield.

Throughout most of the nineteenth and early twentieth centuries most women were still delivered at home. Specialised lying-in hospitals were established in England, France and Germany but they had only a few hundred patients. Middle-class women shunned them entirely and so did most lower-class women. Hospitals retained their reputation as places where the very poor went to die amid impersonal surroundings; in fact maternal mortality rates were far higher than average in the new hospitals, for the danger of puerperal infection was particularly great. Conditions varied from one place to another, and sterilisation was not practised either at home or in the hospital. It gained ground only slowly despite the knowledge developed around mid-century by Semmelweis in Austria and Pasteur in France, that it was vital to prevent infection. Women everywhere suffered from a critical lag between medical knowledge and practice into the late nineteenth century, and deaths from puerperal fever remained high. Attention to the importance of sanitary measures, particularly in post-natal care, was most neglected in France, where in addition women were urged to stay in bed from 10-14 days after delivery.[80] Bathing was not recommended until eight days after delivery, thus encouraging a breeding ground for putrefaction. Here again, medical knowledge could only be as good as women's new expectations to produce full results. By the mid-nineteenth century, the fatalities of childbirth were widely condemned, in letter after letter to the women's magazines, and with constant prodding, things began to change. Patients who were now impatient had at least as much to do with medical advances in this area as ordinary practitioners themselves, particularly when they could read of a new research discovery and insist that it be applied.

By the twentieth century the switch to science and medical personnel was beginning to pay off. To anaesthetics and more skilled care in complicated deliveries was added careful sanitary precautions: open and well ventilated rooms, clean bed linens. In England women were now urged to get out of bed within twenty-four hours, and to initiate daily vaginal cleansing after delivery. As a result deaths due to puerperal fever were down to 0.15 per cent of all deliveries in England between 1915 and 1925 and, with somewhat slower developments along the same lines, to 0.18 per cent in France. Overall, in this decade, the rate of maternal deaths due to accidents in childbirth was 0.04 per cent of all births in England, 2 per cent in France where the inferior medical care now showed clearly. In both countries also, though again with England in the lead, infant mortality began to plummet.

If the application of formal science showed most clearly in childbirth, the modernisation of motherhood only began there. It was increasingly recognised that the first four weeks in the life of a the child were crucial to health, though it was not until the twentieth century that major medical advances were made to cope with this period. Until then the most radical changes designed to improve the well-being of infants and children consisted of basics such as clothing, feeding and love. Swaddling, for example, disappeared, and with it most of the philosophy behind it. Children should be watched and cared for so that swaddling was not needed for their own protection; for, most radical of all, the infant was no longer seen as a beast to be tamed. Swaddling began to meet intense criticism in the eighteenth century and it had been abandoned by middle-class mothers by the early 1800s.

With the realisation that the infant was a tiny human with special needs, a 'baby boom' business soon developed. One of the first items to head what continues to be a growing list of infant needs was clothing. The new magazines for mothers were flooded with articles, queries and advertisements for the baby's layette. Comfort and cleanliness were stressed in the new clothing; all coverings should be soft to the touch and allow maximum freedom of movement. The baby's hygiene received top priority. Babies were to be bathed frequently and their clothing, especially nappies (diapers) — another nineteenth century production — changed frequently. The result of all this was good for the baby, but for the mother it involved increased work. With the baby free to move one had to be constantly alert in order to protect the child. Perhaps the most lucrative market to develop, most clearly reflecting a new emotional awareness of the child's needs, was in toys. Toys were needed not only to occupy the infant, but amuse him also. Rattles became highly popular. Contentment was the key to the new attitude toward children, and the baby's happiness became the most important concern of the middle-class mother.

Contentment involved more than clothes and toys; feeding was still more important as it involved mother as well as child. Changes in feeding methods and patterns in the middle class were just as radical as those in dress but the motivations went beyond the child's well-being to include the middle-class woman's growing interest in greater personal comfort. The traditional use of wet nurses and certainly the use of animals for feeding declined quickly among English middle-class families. France, remaining largely rural during the nineteenth century, relied more on these two methods, yet here too middle-class women by 1850 were relying as fully on their own nursing or artificial feeding as were their English sisters. The hallowed tradition of sending city babies out to be wet nursed had become a minority phenomenon even in the 1820s in Paris, and middle-class mothers, if they used wet nurses at all, increasingly brought them to their own homes where they could be supervised. And this was merely a short-lived stage towards general abandonment of wet nursing in any form.[81]

In England a vigorous campaign was conducted against the use of wet nurses. The line of argument captures the growing desire for an intimate and vital link between mother and child. One could not rely on wet nurses first because they rarely provided proper nutrition for the infant. It was noted, accurately, that the milk of wet nurses was generally old and of inferior quality. According to the women's magazines and manuals a wet nurse might be used if the mother were unable to nurse herself, but the criteria set were impossibly high: the nurse should be young, with well-developed breasts (neither too small nor too large), with a good complexion and teeth and sweet breath and preferably brown hair (for redheads and blondes were believed to produce inferior milk) and of course she should be free from disease and of high moral character.[82] As it was impossible to find such a paragon this early advice merely confirmed the growing antipathy to the whole practice of wet nursing. Wet nurses along with midwives were accused of being the main causes of the high rate of infant mortality. Lacking the vital emotional tie which now was supposed to link mother and child the wet nurse often neglected the child. This was the point that struck the deepest chord: only the mother could provide for the well-being of her child, and so mother's milk was the only milk for the baby.

Middle-class mothers, therefore, increasingly decided not to employ wet nurses less because they were found harmful than because they roused resentment in the mother. Just as general servants were proving to be strangers in the private world of middle-class women, the intrusion of a wet nurse in the intimate relationship with a child was most traumatic. French observers specifically noted the jealousy stirred in the mother as she watched her baby's love turn from her to a stranger.[83] Add to all this the growing cost of wet nursing,[84] particularly when room and board had to be provided in the home, and we have the gamut of good reasons to drop the practice. The upper classes kept on a bit longer, but here too wet nursing began to die out.

Within the middle class, then, it seems clear that most women nursed their infants, a particularly dramatic change in France. Certainly the manuals and magazines were filled with praise of the joys of breast feeding. This was not only the best method of feeding for the infant but, more to the point, it was most beneficial to the mother. It was pleasant, it provided her with a restful moment with her baby, away from the chaos of domestic chores. It helped her recover her shape after pregnancy and it was still seen as an effective means of birth control. Nothing was as beautiful as a nursing mother, or so the advice literature proclaimed.[85] The appeal of nursing reflected the growing self-awareness among middle-class women; it was not sold as best for the baby alone.

Yet even with all the propaganda, many middle-class women still did not buy the argument. They agreed with the attack on traditional methods but not necessarily with breast feeding as the only alternative. Breast feeding was time-consuming and an economic use of time became an increasingly important element in the middle-class family. Furthermore the new concern with an infant's contentment brought a demanding change in the feeding schedule. In both England and France babies were to be fed every two or three hours during the day. The only relief from this schedule was the concomitant advice that the child be weaned by the ninth month as the mother's milk declined in quality; a major departure from tradition. But until this point a conscientious mother was urged to breast feed with unprecedented frequency, just as her household chores were becoming more burdensome. More significant than demands on time, however, was the fact that breast feeding proved to be for many women physically uncomfortable. Every household manual noted the pains of breast feeding and offered remedies for the many problems such as engorged breasts, cracked nipples and milk fever. There were many laments by the more conservative elements that the modern woman was refusing to fulfil her sacred duty because of these drawbacks.[86]

Middle-class women faced something of a dilemma here. They wanted on the one hand to provide their children with the best care which they believed they alone could furnish. Yet at the same time they were beleaguered by the discomfort and the time involved in feeding, and sought alternatives, defying doctors' advice and conservative critics alike. They chose to innovate with artificial feeding methods. Before the nineteenth century, if breast milk was lacking, mothers were often forced to rely upon artificial feeding methods, generally termed bringing up by hand. The methods involved either spoon feeding or feeding through a cloth soaked in a gruel mixture. This last method could prove disastrous for the infant. However, by the second half of the nineteenth century important advances were made which facilitated effective artifical feeding. The biggest improvement was in the vulcanisation of rubber which was used to make teats and many varieties were soon flooding the market.[87] In France, Darbo was considered one of the better makes as it was light and agreeable to the baby.[88] Glass bottles were soon being preferred to metal containers. At the same time formula mixtures were being developed especially for the newborn. With the popularisation of the nutrient value and pasteurisation of milk, bottle feeding became even more popular. By the last quarter of the nineteenth century artificial feeding was becoming widespread in France and England.[89] Although women had a choice and breast feeding was by no means abandoned, more and more found that artificial feeding offered an answer to the dilemma of providing an intimate method of feeding far more convenient than the 'natural' method. The mother did not have to stop her other activities in order to care for the baby; she provided it with a warm bottle. In addition women were enthusiastic about the new freedom. They could go out of the home more freely than if confined to breast feeding alone. Also the new method allowed the mother to follow the growing interest in demand feeding. Bottle feeding eliminated many of the discomforts that long plagued nursing mothers while in no way jeopardising the baby's safety. Again a concrete illustration of the modernisation process: nature could be improved upon in self-interest.

While bottle feeding provided a solution to many traditional problems it was not perfect. There was one particular danger in the new method that reflected the lingering hold of tradition even when innovation was utilised: it was perilously easy to overfeed. From the early nineteenth century the decline in the number of deaths due to atrophy and the increase in those stemming from overfeeding is a telling aspect of modernisation. Middle-class mothers, in their efforts to provide the best for their babies every time they cried, tended to overfeed. Warnings in the manuals suggest that many fed their babies every time they cried. Then finding their babies colicky, they dosed them with harsh purgatives to relieve the excess resulting in diarrhoea that proved fatal to thousands of babies every year. As in other areas it took time for women to strike a healthy balance between the new methods and the desire to please the child.

A healthy balance proved to be a futile and frustrated goal for most mothers in the nineteenth century, for traditional infant illnesses were loaded against the improvements. In the absence of specific medicines or medical care for infants, mothers were left with only the grisly statistics on infant mortality. Ignorance was the major killer of thousands of babies every year. Mothers dismissed early signs of illness as normal stages of an infant's life; colds were often neglected as symptoms of teething, resulting in thousands of infant deaths due to pneumonia as complications inevitably set in. There was a new problem, arising from the immense desire to intervene, when mothers went to the other extreme and over-medicated their babies, for drug excesses killed many babies as well.[90] Paediatric care was just beginning to be established by the end of the nineteenth century; it would be a decade or more before its influence was felt.[91]

Physical needs commanded only part of the attention of the new mother. A healthy child should be not only well clothed and fed but emotionally content as well. The new trend in middle-class child-rearing patterns to indulge the child was theoretically designed to make its deepest impression in the child's psychic development. The hundreds of childcare manuals which began to flood the market by the mid-nineteenth century (in England and America primarily) show the beginnings of modern child psychology, perhaps appropriately well before its formal birth. The new outlook saw children as innocent beings who were all goodness and, if given proper care and love, guaranteed to emerge as perfect adults. The mother bore the prime responsibility to adapt to the individual personality of her baby and meet the particular needs of each child at every stage of development.[92]

With these new attitudes came the upgrading of the woman's position in relation to her children and the increase of her status in the family. It was the middle-class woman herself who initiated the changes, desiring a deeper, more intimate relationship with each child and convinced that this would provide her with a more rewarding life. Beyond this, the philosophy ultimately developed that the woman was not only a mother to her child but also a friend. Perhaps unduly naive middle-class women believed that with their personal care the child's future happiness was secure. The new attitude was partly the product of new needs. With a loss of some economic functions through industrialisation the woman sought to maintain her sense of purpose, her vital place in the family network, by dominating child care, although this selfish reason was not predominant. Middle-class women, gaining a new sense of self, expressed this in part in the direction of each individual child. That middle-class women found themselves trapped or victimised into the new motherhood role does not seem likely, most of the new ways were self-selected. For years the task of each mother was to make the child happy, for her sake and that of the future adult. Only through careful observation of her baby's every move could the mother appreciate the child's particular temperament, capabilities and personal needs. Now each child was held to be endowed with his or her own psyche, learning pattern, even sense of humour, that required individual attention from the mother. The old maxim that children were to be seen and not heard was severely criticised by the childrearing philosophy of the new middle class. Instead, children were now encouraged to be as free and open as possible in front of their mothers (whether this was to apply to fathers is doubtful since there is no direct mention of it). This was a dramatic change from the pre-modern view of children as economic entities who were expected to work as soon as their little hands and feet permitted. Now children were to be entertained and educated by the *mother* (though they were expected to be circumspect in front of the more authoritarian father), as well as provided with material sustenance.

A new dilemma presented itself to the middle-class mother, as the child grew older. How was one to ensure or instil obedience while providing the new level of love and emotional commitment? In the seventeenth and eighteenth centuries corporal punishment served as the main disciplinary means. But in the nineteenth century, in France, England and elsewhere, this was quickly modified in favour of what was called positive childrearing. Most now considered that corporal punishment and fear caused more harm than good, creating trauma for the child and destroying the vital emotional link. It is also possible that these means declined as a result of the diminution of the father's role in discipline, as mothers had never been prime agents in the direct corporal punishment though they were not above threat. Now even threat was gone. The nineteenth-century child was to learn through reward rather than punishment; if touching a forbidden object, for example, the child should be given instead an object that it liked while the other was removed from its reach.

Discipline and new emotional ties helped to create a fundamentally new problem in family evolution: adolescence. The recognition of adolescence as a distinctive period of life that had special needs and required special attention from the mother was as revolutionary as the development of the individual child concept. Pre-modern society had no need to consider adolescence as a special period since more often than not teenagers were sent away from home to work. Another important change was the extension of what is now called the adolescent period as the age of attaining puberty decreased while years spent in education increased. This not only kept the teenager dependent on parents but also commonly provided him or her with an education superior to the parental level, another potential source of friction. The middle class, eager to keep at least daughters virginal until the age of 23 to 25, when they could marry, had to impose more durable restraints than pre-industrial families had maintained, restraints that would cover

a minimum of nine years of pubescence rather than seven and amid far
looser general community controls.

It is obviously difficult to generalise about new tensions between
adolescent child and mother, but there is no question that middle-class
mothers in the nineteenth century became articulate about the
problem, which indicates its growing importance. The very fact that
mothers had lavished so much affection on their children, expecting
grateful, loving friends in return, guaranteed new friction at this stage
of life. Pre-industrial women expected less and so had fewer tensions
with children, who were trained to be more docile anyway. It is clear
from the letters written to women's magazines that middle-class
mothers were having problems controlling their daughters' growing
feeling of independence as early as 1850.[93] The stress on daughters
might reflect a lingering belief that they should be particularly submissive, which clashed with the modern mentality calling for self-
expression being exercised actively by married women. In addition, in
the nineteenth century middle-class girls had fewer outlets for independence than their male counterparts. The boy was sent off to school
in many cases, relieving that tension for the mother. If secondary
education was not financially possible he would be off training for
work. Boys were also permitted to socialise more freely outside the
home than girls. The adolescent girl found herself confined to the
home or, when at a dance, carefully chaperoned. This all heightened the
mother's responsibility for managing the sexual development of the
adolescent. The steadily declining age of puberty left many a mother
confused; she appealed for guidance about how much she should tell
her daughter about sex, and how early. Yet, inevitably, too many
mothers failed to educate their daughters properly, especially to face
the onset of puberty.

One sign that middle-class mothers were having a difficult time with
the sexual maturation of their children was seen in the frenzied discussion about masturbation. The horrors of masturbation were vividly
portrayed to both mother and child through the many manuals on
sexual behaviour published in the nineteenth century.[94] The argument
shows the increasingly explicit attitude of the Victorians. Masturbation
was prohibited not because it was sinful but because it was
'scientifically' proven to be harmful. Any number of diseases
supposedly were results of indulging in this sexual experience. Young
girls were warned that in addition to probable debility, indeed
premature ageing, their sexual pleasures would be cut off. The middle-
class mother was hard put to deal with a sexually active girl from the

age of fourteen until marriage at, say, twenty-four. The only solution was constant and anxious attention. The mother was to keep a careful eye on her daughter's behaviour to check against the masturbatory menace.

From babyhood to adolescence, the responsibilities of the mother were increased with modernisation. Recognition of adolescence was the key reason that the years spent mothering actually increased. The task of providing sustenance for the child steadily expanded to include new definitions of adequacy; to food and clothing (which the mother generally made herself at considerable expense of time and energy), were added the new items, both tangible and intangible: toys, entertainment and above all motherly love. A modern mother was successful if her child grew to maturity healthy, educated, happy and successful. If a daughter failed to marry or to make a marriage work a mother could feel a great sense of failure as she was held primarily responsible for not having prepared the girl properly. The same was true with regard to a boy's later career in life.

For the middle-class mother this was a never ending problem, for at all stages of childhood commitment outstripped new means of coping. Toys or bottle feeding were all very well, but there was scant innovation in children's medicine, little but guesswork to handle adolescence. Small wonder that special problems, such as the persistently high rate of child mortality, caused such anxiety into the twentieth century. The facts in this case were not new but the emotional involvement, the personal identification were, which turned fact into tragedy when, as would occur on the average at least once in a middle-class family, an infant died.

The importance of the new concept of motherhood undeniably increased steadily even when its demands could not be fully met. New institutions outside the family could not challenge the new maternal status. Schools, for example, which took the child physically away from 'mama' did not diminish the maternal influence. The fact was that the mother controlled the crucial first years of life. When the child did enter school she remained responsible for moral supervision and indeed for supplementing formal education itself, checking homework, answering questions and trying to determine why the child failed to progress well, in proper middle-class achiever fashion, where this was the case. The spread of education and the extension of time spent in schools relieved some problems, as in releasing hours for care for the home, but created others. For some mothers who were determined to maintain full responsibility for the child could suffer real frustration when forced by the new school requirements to share their control.

What strikes us most about the new concept of motherhood is the sense, sometimes cloying, of commitment and responsibility. By the end of the nineteenth century, physical burdens were gradually diminishing, but the emotional burdens increased and show no signs of reversal. Inevitably there were built-in tensions: could the new, self-sacrificing mother be compatible with the modern woman and her need for self-expression? For some twentieth-century women the answer would prove negative, and the modernisation of motherhood begun in the nineteenth century may turn out to be a transitional phenomenon. But the process has not yet been abandoned and the nineteenth century did produce one final innovation which helped make the incompatible compatible.

The nineteenth century middle-class woman thus far had new skills, new importance, but immense new duties as household manager and mother. Her lot could easily seem impossible, and indeed it was for some. Alcoholism and drug-taking (opiates being freely purchasable in pharmacies until the early 1900s) alone kept some women going. But further relief was soon provided.

The new demands of motherhood could not be fulfilled if combined with a continuation of the traditional birth rate. Furthermore the woman had broader considerations of self, including sexual enjoyment, to take into account. Her response was characteristically innovative and prompt. The most dramatic expression of the new outlook of the middle-class woman was the general acceptance of birth control as basic to a woman's growing-up process. By limiting the number of children she bore she was able successfully to implement the new designs in household management, in childrearing, while attending to her need for personal expression as an individual. She quickly realised the impossibility of giving the individual attention now deemed necessary to each of the traditional eight children born to the family. The same applied to her role as mistress of the house, for she could not manage the family's budgetary problems while raising the material level and standard of cleanliness and still take care of eight children. Preservation of her own self-interest, her own health and mental balance, required that she exercise full control of her body.

Birth control also served as the nineteenth-century woman's only successful means of coping with the horrors of infant and maternal mortality. The absence of pediatric medicine made it difficult to cut further into the high rate of infant mortality, and while advances in

obstetrics were more substantial the lag between innovation and imple-
mentation kept maternal mortality rates at high levels at least until the
1880s in England and the 1900s in France. Birth control reduced both
risks of death considerably. The woman who was not physically
exhausted from repeated pregnancies would be more capable of
sustaining child delivery and potential hazards such as puerperal fever;
and she simply exposed herself to risk less often. Also the better the
condition of the mother, the better the child's chances of survival
would be and certainly, with fewer children, the better the care for
them could be. Doctors recognised this and encouraged artificial birth
control, except in France, where they were hindered by religious or
legal limitations. Perfection of birth control techniques was essential to
women's emancipation but so was the mental conditioning which
prepared the way for them to be used and indeed actively sought after.
In both respects birth control was integrally tied to women's
modernisation.

By the mid-nineteenth century middle-class women were having only
five children at most, in France even fewer. By the end of the century
the typical middle-class family in England had three children, in France
two. Birth control was obviously practiced within a generation or two
of the creation of the new urban middle class and then steadily
increased in use. It not only facilitated the woman's job as housekeeper
and mother and gradually improved her health on the average, but also
allowed her to be freer sexually.

The introduction of birth control techniques in the early nineteenth
century constituted the second stage of the sexual revolution. The first
stage, beginning in the late eighteenth century, had been marked by an
increase in the birth rate, both legitimate and illegitimate, and it most
obviously touched the lower classes. With the new birth control techniques, however, the middle-class woman took the lead in sexual activity,
within the framework of marriage. The second stage of the sexual
activity allowed women not only to increase their sexual activity but
also to increase their enjoyment by reducing the fear of unwanted
pregnancies. Here, finally, was a benign circle in which relative freedom
from worry enhanced pleasure, which could be indulged in with
growing frequency and imagination.

The varied needs of the modern woman and modern family
prompted a technical revolution in birth control. The biggest breakthroughs came in contraceptive devices, particularly those that appealed
to women as the prime decision-makers in initiating birth control.[95]
The first major advance in nineteenth-century contraceptives came

early, with the popularisation of the sponge — a simple and convenient device. All that one needed was a piece of sponge of suitable size for insertion into the vagina attached by a piece of ribbon for removal after coitus. As early as the 1820s the sponge was noted as the best birth control device available and of particular benefit to women, preserving their health by preventing repeated pregnancies and enhancing their sex life by freeing them from fears of unwanted children.

By the 1840s the douche was developed, which destroyed sperm immediately after coitus through vaginal injections of liquid solutions. Many different syringes were soon manufactured along with an impressive list of douching solutions, the effectiveness of which was varied. An assortment of pessaries and early forms of diaphragms, was also available. The most common in England was the Check pessary which worked along the same lines as the sponge in that it was inserted into the vaginal tract to block the sperm. Contraceptive suppositories of spermicides were manufactured also. By the end of the nineteenth century the array of contraceptive devices was truly formidable, and each came in a host of sizes and qualities. This variety, the rapidly declining birth rates in the middle class, and the advice literature for women which urged smaller families make it unquestionable that most middle-class women used one or more of the new techniques throughout most of the nineteenth century. And of course the trend was carried forward into the present century. The development of the contraceptive pill and intra-uterine devices improved the effectiveness of contraception, with no intrusion into the pleasures of the sex act. These essentially continued what was by now a well-established trend, for motives equally well-established.

There was of course a male contraceptive as well, improved though not entirely new — the condom. The vulcanisation of rubber did as much to improve the quality of condoms as it did for female diaphragms. But the condom had several disadvantages for women (and for men). It generally required interruption of the sex act for placement. It was considered by some, primarily men, to lessen sensual pleasures, and there was a certain reluctance to use it. More important was the fact that as a male device it inherently required the co-operation of males, leaving the woman dependent on another's initiative. Since gaining control over her destiny was the middle-class woman's overriding motivation in adopting birth control practices she preferred female contraceptives as giving her the greatest sense of independence as well as interfering least with sexual enjoyment. Some devices were in fact explicitly advertised as usable without the husband's knowledge,[96] though in most cases we can assume some mutual understanding in the adoption of birth control within the family.

Birth control became an integral part of the middle-class woman's life. It fitted the general pattern of innovation and openness to scientific advance. It was basic to the other modern functions assumed in the family. It provided self-expression as well, expressing the new desire for pleasure and personal control. We are accustomed to see the Victorian middle-class world as prudish; many historians have erred in dating the rise of birth control and thought that abstinence was the only method used.[97] Not so. The changes which the middle-class woman underwent led her to seek sexual enjoyment. Pleasure-seeking became more explicit after about 1870, as middle-class women took to sports such as tennis and bicycle riding and adopted less restricting dress. But this merely brought into general view an interest developed at least a generation before. In sex, as in family size, health and household functions, the modern family had been essentially outlined in both France and England before 1900. And with this the nature of the modern women herself had been shaped, for changes in family structure and function had been adapted to a host of new purposes.

The Working-Class Woman's Dilemma

Ironically, given the great popularity among social historians for study of the working class, we know very little about the working-class family beyond what the vital statistics tell us. The role of the woman in the working-class family remains a particular mystery until illuminated by sociological research dealing with the last two decades. Even more than her middle-class counterpart she remains, once married, locked inside her home. Lack of material from magazines and manuals compounds the problem of grasping her role and outlook, for literature was rarely directed to working-class women with their lack of funds and general reluctance or inability to read. Perhaps, indeed, she needed less guidance from outside experts anyway. For we are beginning to understand that working-class women made their own family adaptations and may be judged remarkably successful in dealing with change.

The role of the working-class woman in the family certainly underwent significant alteration in the nineteenth century as a result of the forces of modern living. By the end of the century the working-class family seemed to be adopting many aspects of middle-class culture and behaviour patterns, most particularly as it too began to limit family size after 1870-90. However, the working-class family's forging of a modern life style involved far more complexities and subtleties than mere imitation of the middle-class model. Even shared behaviour could result from different causes, and much behaviour was not shared at all, for the role of the working-class woman was and remains substantially different from that of her middle-class sisters. Birth control, a possible case of imitation in that it followed middle-class adoption chronologically and was indeed the subject of intense middle-class propaganda (as reformers saw benefits to the well-being of the poor if there were fewer mouths to feed), was part of a distinctive adaptation to the new forces of urban and industrial life. The physical health of the working-class woman was obviously to benefit from fewer pregnancies, but this does not seem to have been as important in the decision to cut births as it was in the middle-class family since there was little or no effort to improve the woman's pre-natal and child delivery care until much later than the advent of family planning. In fact it seems possible that women in working-class families were not really emotionally prepared for birth control. For many women the decline in children was viewed as a deterioration in their importance in the family. Recent polls indicate that the working-class still views numerous children as a sign of family success far more commonly than does the middle class. This is not to downgrade the importance of birth control in the class; by 1900 the rate of decline was as rapid as that of the middle class although, starting later, the working class continued to have larger families. However, the process here was not simply middle-class culture taken with a slight time lag. In the working class, economics was the primary factor in the decision to limit births. The economics of a large family became a definite burden by the late nineteenth century with the extension and strict enforcement of laws limiting child labour and requiring school attendence.

To appreciate the adjustment of the working-class woman we must begin with marriage itself. Greater variety of jobs and steadier employment meant that most working-class girls spent some part of their lives, about ten years on the average, actively earning a living. What impact this work experience had on their marriage is not entirely clear. It enhanced the opportunity for marriage by providing social contacts and some savings that could help start a household, and this opportunity represented a vital goal in the culture of working-class women, mothers and daughters alike. At the same time, working-class girls were getting married earlier in the nineteenth century than in pre-modern times and one to three years earlier than middle-class girls in industrial society itself. In England the mean age at marriage for young women dropped from 27 in pre-modern times, reflecting peasant patterns, to about 24 in the mid-nineteenth century to twenty in the twentieth century. Marriage ages declined more slowly in France as agriculture remained far more dominant, yet there was a drop from between twenty-eight and thirty in the seventeenth and eighteenth centuries to between twenty-five and twenty-seven in the nineteenth century as the working class gained ground.

Along with some economic independence through separate earnings, the new skills and values gained at work might make a girl a more attractive marriage partner. Her work experience might aid her in her lifetime job as household manager. She gained experience handling money, for example, sooner than her middle-class counterpart, and this could give her an advantage in dealing with financial matters in marriage. Those who had worked as servants might acquire house-keeping and childrearing skills.

With increasing urbanisation the basis for many working-class marriages continued to evolve; love relationships steadily replaced purely economic unions as social contacts and economic self-sufficiency increased. Working-class courtship patterns also modernised, becoming shorter and more informal as parental consent became less essential. More important, working-class girls found themselves freer from parental chaperonage than middle-class girls. There was far more mixing of the sexes in these early years. Nightly visits to the pub after work, Saturday night dances or attendance at the music halls, and Sunday afternoon excursions through the park enabled many working-class girls to meet men. No doubt some became victimised in these strange surroundings without family around to provide traditional guidance and protection. The high rates of illegitimacy are only one indicator of the potential problems the young girl encountered during her work years.

For the first half of the nineteenth century premarital sex among the working class remained an accepted aspect of the culture, as it had been developing in the late eighteenth century. We must stress, as against some common impressions, that this culture had rural origins and predated factory experience; a German worker, noting high rates of illegitimacy, said that they hardly rivalled those she had left behind in the countryside. For some, illegitimacy formed part of a pattern of promiscuity that could drive girls to ruin. Factory girls in Rheims in the 1830s often served as prostitutes in their scant spare time, calling this their 'fifth quarter of the day'.[98] Increasingly, however, premarital sex led to marriage; indeed pregnancy became an accepted way to convince the man of the values of matrimony. And some men wanted to be sure a future wife was fertile, like German automobile workers in the 1890s who said they 'didn't want to buy a pig in a poke'.[99] A working-class novel described a common pattern in England: a girl courted a co-worker for almost two years, the boy being in 'no hurry to marry until he could not honourably delay'.[100]

After about 1870, in fact, outright illegitimacy began to stabilise, even fall slightly, as working-class culture took more definite form. It is possible that pre-bridal pregnancies declined as well; certainly they were now usually followed by marriage, as responsibility was expected by girls and accepted by boys. Some believe this change was due to increased use of birth control techniques by the working class,[101] which cut illegitimacy without necessarily changing premarital behaviour or outlook. Others have argued, more persuasively, that there was a changing culture in the working class which frowned upon sexual promiscuity. There may in fact have been some imitation of the middle-class value of the virgin bride. But this was not a middle-class culture overall. Illegitimacy rates, for example, continued to be well above both pre-modern and middle-class levels, which shows that premarital sex was still common. We know also that many working-class women, married or unmarried, had to resort to abortion to achieve what birth control there was; 25 per cent of all working-class wives in one Berlin survey in 1900 had had at least one abortion, often before marriage.[102] Some women thus preserved premarital 'purity' only by resort to illicit dangerous practices. At the same time we must give the stabilisation of working-class families its due. Some parental control and a good sense of self-interest caused most working-class girls to avoid sexual promiscuity and premature pregnancy, as the differential between the age of puberty and the age of marriage was long, at least eight to ten years. And personal choice was commonly involved when premarital sex was accepted. It was not just a titillating part of courtship but an accepted means of converting courtship into marriage.

With marriage the working-class woman's experience remained dissimilar to that of the middle class in a number of important respects. The relationship between husband and wife was different, in some ways more traditional than the new middle-class relationship. In the working-class marriage the husband remained the major decision-maker in principle, the wife submissive to his will. There was to be a strict segregation of roles. Undoubtedly the lines were less clear in practice and there was much variation according to individual personalities. Nevertheless there was no pretence within the working class to the new concomitant relationship of the middle-class husband and wife. The concept of sharing in marriage remained rudimentary. We need only a few key examples. The social spheres of the husband and wife were distinct; the working man's world was a man's world.[103] The husband now went off to work away from the home, but in contrast to middle-class patterns his limited leisure was also spent away from home, with his male companions. Pub visits and soccer games were the male preserve. The wife was expected to socialise with her own set of friends, apart from her husband, except perhaps for a family walk on Sunday afternoon.

Of more consequence was the handling of the family's finances. Like her middle-class counterpart the working-class woman was solely responsible for accounting for the family's domestic needs such as rent, medical expenses, food and clothing. Even the husband's insurance fees were her responsibility, since she would get the benefit if he died. But there were several major differences between middle-class and working-class household management. The first resulted from earlier marriage age. The young wife was often unprepared for financial and housekeeping duties, even with some work experience. Lack of resources forced many new couples to live with parents for a time, which created strains of its own. Many working-class observers judged that early marriage set a bad tone for the relationship even later in life. Working-class culture, expressed for example in the music halls, picked up the emotional side of this: courtship was great fun for both parties but then the woman wanted marriage which could turn into mutual hostility or, more commonly, apathy. Related to emotional strain were the materal problems that resulted from lack of training. As we shall see working-class childrearing patterns involved relatively little attention to children, and often only the most rudimentary concern for a daughter's household skills; so the pattern was easily perpetuated, for habits picked up catch-as-catch-can when a girl married early could easily persist.

Constant economic deprivation strongly influence the husband-wife relationship in the working class, for even if a family's income rose above the strictest poverty line the wife received only a fixed allowance from the husband. Seldom did she even know how much her husband made, and almost always the husband kept a portion of his earnings for the new, male-centred recreations of sports and betting as well as the local bar. The only relief for the woman was that in some families the husband was expected to provide his own lunch from his pocket money, as was common among those French labourers who worked far from home and lunched in the local cafés on work days.[104] Even with this the housewife's budget was tight, sometimes needlessly so, as the husband expected the household to be provided for out of a fixed sum regardless of rising costs.

The lack of consultation between working-class husband and wife went even further. Wives were theoretically never to burden their husbands with the financial problems of the family. The were expected to make do with what they were given, no matter how meagre. No doubt many a wife complained about the return she received but many even failed to report major purchases, taking the cost out of their personal upkeep and that of their children, for they accepted the notion that balancing the budget was their job. Working-class wives quickly learned that in order to accommodate the family's needs her needs were to be sacrificed generally. Thus many a woman went without adequate food and clothing in order to provide for her family.[105] What seems like total male chauvinism made good sense during much of the nineteenth century, given the fact that the husband was the major breadwinner and that without him the family could not survive. The facts of life are not always equitable: the husband had to receive a greater share of calories simply to get through the work day, and required such small pleasures as a piece of meat or a glass of beer to motivate him to work at an exhausting job. The tragedy of the situation is that the attitude long outlasted the days of impoverishment early in the industrial revolution; women's lack of complaint over the principles of family income distribution perpetuated her subordination, though it might give her a continuing sense that she was playing a vital family role, as indeed her self-sacrifice was.

Life under such severe restraints made household management a unique and unenviable experience for the working-class woman. Unlike the middle-class housewife she did very little in the way of long-range planning. Household management was on a day-to-day basis, at best week-to-week. Some working-class wives tried to put some money away for savings in case of emergency, but this proved extremely difficult and was only meant for dire necessity such as illness or injury to the husband. Most working-class wives took in work such as washing, ironing or sewing to supplement their weekly allowances. As we have noted, a third of all working wives in England in the late nineteenth century were taking in lodgers to add to family revenues. But any extra work, certainly a chore such as caring for a lodger, meant that the working-class wife could not devote her full energies to managing the household as her middle-class counterpart did. For the working-class woman, household management also involved supplementing the family income — in 1907, French wives provided an average of 10 per cent of the household income — and the strain which this placed upon the woman affected all other aspects of the life style we now see as distinctive of the modern working class.[106]

It is not surprising that the task of managing the home was far more difficult for the working-class woman than it was in the middle-class. Material differences were stark, and there were cultural differences too. One wonders why the working-class woman's role in the family never brought her the same prestige (especially in view of her economic support) as the middle-class woman achieved. After all the working-class wife was also home-centred, urged not to work outside. She too served as consumer agent, in the new specialisation of labour that added to the woman's new economic functions. Yet she never found praise because in many ways she was doomed to fail. For the working-class woman, outside forces were such that she was rarely able to maintain any sense of control even in the late nineteenth century. Women and their husbands alike found it difficult to believe that the housekeeping was being done properly. Crowded housing and meagre diets made rational management of domestic chores impossible. The problem was compounded by the fact that there was little precedent in traditional rural society for the domestic skills needed in the new urban centres and we have seen experience hardly improved the situation, particularly as the steadily declining age at marriage plunged more and more ill-prepared adolescents into the responsibility of running a household.

The many complaints about the decline of the art of housekeeping in nineteenth-century England were more easily levelled at the working-class than at the middle-class woman. Whatever hard times came, depression or inflation, she was, indirectly at least, held responsible. A husband, noting that provisions had deteriorated as prices rose after 1900, summed up many a household battle: 'I never interfere about anything, because I think it's your part to attend to the house, but it seems to me you don't manage things properly'.[107] Such judgements could only lead the housewife to doubt her own worth. With the combination of emotional and material stress, the working-class wife could rarely develop a new sense of self, and without a positive self-image it was difficult for her to challenge old ways, but was bound to fail in her attempt to maintain traditional values in an increasingly modern environment. Thus she created her own vicious circle. We know, for example, that there was growing indignation over infant mortality in nineteenth-century England. By the end of the century working-class women were begainning to make an emotional investment in the child. But even after 1904 half the women in one factory town were judged resigned to a child's death, so long as they could provide a proper funeral, And even the women newly anguished over a child's death, which most would experience at least once, took scant measures to ensure against it. Suspicion of strangers as well as poverty kept women away from doctors even for childbirth. Health problems were the concern of the local herbalist or quack, who was known in the neighbourhood, or in the final analysis of God or fate; there was little positive action to be taken. Whether we are prepared to accept statistics in such emotional matters or not, it strikes us that both groups stood to lose. The traditionalists avoided sorrow but failed to gain the emotional support of real attachment to the majority of children who did live, in the urban environment. The cautious innovators failed to go far enough to protect themselves from grief by demanding the medical care which was at last available.

The situation on the Continent was less traumatic than that in England. More working-class families lived outside big cities, the husband commuting to work by rail. France had far fewer massive agglomerations and the French working class cut its birth rate earliest, providing another relief for the wife. But German as well as French housewives were judged to manage better than the English, keeping closer to customary ways. They were less trapped between tradition and novelty, less likely for example to mourn a child's death with new intensity. They were also held to a less rigorous material standard. Differences in eating habits made it easier for the Frenchwoman than for her English counterpart. Meat early became an essential in the working man's diet in England, to be served at least once a day; as this was the most expensive item in the working-class woman's budget this break from traditional diets pressed household resources. Women were also unskilled in preparing meat meals, which caused waste and, perhaps, the notoriously poor level of English cooking; there were complaints that working-class women either bought pre-cooked meat and served it cold, at needless expense, or squandered it by cooking it too rapidly.[108] Of necessity they had to buy the poorest quality of meat as well. French diets were not as radically changed as the English. The growing emphasis on meat was found only in areas of heavy industry such as mining and metallurgy, and many French workers took a main meal at restaurants. Still, French working-class wives were scarcely able to plan ahead any better than their English sisters, and housekeeping difficulties were common in the class generally.

Even the protest movements that developed by the end of the century could complicate the housewives' lot. Rising strike rates in all the industrial countries created new uncertainties about income and budgeting. Women might well support the cause, but housewives often pressed their husbands to return to work and were long known as 'the chief enemy of the labour movement'. The reason was not contentment but the arduous material responsibilities of the working-class wife and, possibly, her lack of rapport and communication with her husband. Material problems also curtailed outlets for direct self-expression. Labour-saving devices remained too expensive. A bit of new clothing might enliven a women's life — one source of the criticism of English housewives was their addiction to fancy clothes, and Polish peasant women who moved to mining towns in the Ruhr with their husbands took to buying new ribbons and hats. But in fact only unmarried working girls had the money for much indulgence in this area. It was in England, well after 1900, that a woman expressed her wounded pride in professing that she did not need new shoes, which she could not afford anyway, because 'there was no necessity for her to go out if the weather was not fine'.[109]

Added to dreary unrelieved household duties was the burden of motherhood. Again the hand of tradition remained strong here and little new prestige accrued to the working-class woman as mother. Workers were slow to cut their birth rate, long seeing children as economic assets and ignorant of the methods that might best be employed. New male workers often had no knowledge of condoms and some delighted in expressing their masculinity by siring large families. Women's views were ambiguous. Frequent pregnancies were customary and expected, but as children stopped being economic contributors, barred from work by factory laws and school requirements, they added to the problems of budget management. Some women lamented when most of their children lived, expecting the traditional 50 per cent mortality rate to ease their lot. A German wife with six children berated her husband, shouting 'Why don't they die?' Yet there were no new methods adopted, no eager receptiveness to innovation, to provide relief through birth control, which reached large segments of the class only after 1890. Even afterwards the average family had two children more than the middle-class model. Furthermore, working-class control methods more commonly involved abortions, condoms or sexual abstinence; there is no sign of sexual pleasure or imaginativeness in marriage, as initiative had clearly passed to the middle class.[110] Another potential outlet for expression and enjoyment remained unchanged.

Even after birth control began to limit family size, repeated pregnancies and the anxiety of providing material sustenance for the family proved an all-consuming task for the working woman; there was precious little time for new emotional support or new emotional enjoyment of the mothering process. While middle-class mothers strove to provide their children with toys and close personal attention and entertainment, the working-class woman took in washing or sewing or even went out to char in order to put food on the table and shoes on her husband and children.

Mothering thus remained fairly traditional. In both England and France, working-class women had their babies at home with the attendance of a midwife of mediocre quality. A few women went to the new hospitals but doctors were rarely consulted in pregnancy or afterwards. Patent medicine and traditional folk remedies were heavily relied upon. Feeding methods also remained traditional. Breast feeding lasted for up to two years, primarily to save on food but also as a means of birth control.

With crowded accommodation which allowed no privacy for the woman, children always underfoot, and household chores and work from the outside, the working-class woman could not allow her children to be free before her. There was consequently more reliance on traditional disciplinary techniques, including physical beatings. The picture was not totally unchanged from the pre-industrial past. Women paid new attention to toilet training, a virtual necessity in cramped urban apartments, and children were not swaddled. Working-class children responded by at least fond memories of their mother, against the image of a seldom-seen, authoritarian father.

Often more than memories were involved. Working-class women, whose situation was so unenviable in many ways, inventively developed a key twist to one older tradition. They built ties to an extended family, but around their own relatives, not their husband's. Marrying earlier, with slightly improved longevity, it was more common to have one's mother available for many years, and this link gave practical and emotional support to housewife and grandmother alike. From extended family contacts focused on the wife, workers derived economic support; a relative who was ill or unemployed could find a loan or an arrangement for a job through this network.[111] New emotional significance was involved as well; here is where affection most clearly influenced the life of the mature working-class woman. In both respects, frequent contacts with relatives, who typically lived nearby (particularly in the case of a young housewife's mother), provided a major means of coping with the new urban environment. This smoothed adjustments in many respects, compared to the isolation of the middle-class woman. At the same time it discouraged further innovation, as mothers tended to urge married daughters to retain old ways.

Commonly the mother provided the daughter with regular assistance with household chores. This assistance was far more economical and reliable than the hiring of a maid-of-all-work, which was out of the question on a worker's budget anyway. The mother's chief contribution lay in caring for the grandchildren while the daughter attended to her other domestic responsibilities or, in a minority of cases, went out to work.

What impact grandmother had on childrearing in the working-class family needs careful consideration. Her direct influence might have served to maintain traditional practices. On the other hand recent psychological studies have shown that the relationship between grandparents and grandchildren is generally easier and more open that that between parents and children. It is possible that in the working-class family it was the grandmother who functioned as something like the equivalent of the middle-class mother in giving new and close attention to the child and even indulging it.[112]

The mother/married daughter relationship went much deeper than provision of babysitting services. As soon as a working-class family had been in a city for a generation or two and could form the new extended ties, the maternal network provided the key social contacts for the wife. Relations with the neighbours were often strained. The necessity of sharing toilets and sometimes kitchens promoted bickering. Many families developed rivalries, checking each other's clothes lines, for example, to see which was doing better.[113] Cut off from her husband's social world, the working-class wife readily turned to her own relatives. The image of a man coming home from his job to find the house swarming with in-laws became a music hall stock in trade. The man reacted by hurrying off to a bar, thus reinforcing the woman's new and vital social domain.

Mothers also provided advice and this had extraordinarily durable implications. The omnipresence of the mother could easily contribute to the lack of self-image on the part of the working-class woman, as she commonly deferred to her mother's way of doing things at least for many early years of marriage. It was more difficult to innovate when the mother was there to criticise or question. It might have been the result of listening to her mother that the working-class woman continued to breast feed rather than use artificial methods. The mother might also discourage new methods of birth control as dangerous or immoral, and grandma herself had some stake in a number of grand-children to care for. Housekeeping methods and even the acceptance of continued subordination to the husband could reflect the mother's presence, next door or even under the same roof when the father died. But problems at home or with husband were also cushioned by mother's presence, maybe not even felt as problems when mother was there to say that they were normal parts of life.

The working-class women had thus developed a viable lifestyle shortly after the advent of industrialisaton, albeit a very different one from that of the middle class. Vital elements still persist precisely because of their early success. The extended family continues. Expectations for children remain limited – in the working class in contrast to the compulsive promotion of children which bears so heavily on middle-class mothers. A host of problems were long avoided by working-class attitudes. Adolescence was not a major issue until well into the twentieth century as workers went to work earlier, could marry relatively soon and were freer from cloying parental supervision. Mothers bowed out earlier from claims to complete control, and this may have been a key to smooth relations with adult children later.

Outside factors might even be mediated to preserve the now traditional working-class family. State education was initially resented as an expense, but its compulsion could not be avoided. Mothering, however, did not normally include careful attention to the child's progress or encouragement to go beyond the required years of schooling. So few working-class children even now advance beyond secondary levels despite significant efforts by the welfare state to facilitate their advance. Only craftsmen, close to middle-class patterns in care and high expectations for children, including birth control, provide a general exception within the broad working class.

Changes developed of necessity within the working class, such as birth control, preserved a vital traditional element. As the nuclear family remained more of an economic unit after courtship, than an emotional one, we can see why economics had to be the prime motivation for this class. The depression of the later 1870s brought many to the realisation that the cost of children could no longer be indulged in to the extent of a traditional number of births. What the working class did was in effect to cut births back so that the number of *surviving* children matched pre-industrial levels. Methods were, as we have noted, even less innovative than goals. If abstention or condoms did not suffice, women commonly chose to take their chances with an illegal abortion. Contraceptives for women themselves were unnatural, an attitude that applies as much to twentieth-century pills as to nineteenth century vaginal devices. Nature could not be tampered with, a continuing contrast to the middle-class woman's desire to bring nature under her control.

The working-class woman remained highly vulnerable to change, for her approach stressed the most gradual adaptations of tradition. Even birth control brought confusion and may have been encouraged primarily by the husband (whose co-operation was vital in all the methods used save abortion) on economic grounds. Family limitations came along with the rapid decline of domestic manufacturing and left many women confused about what role they had. A response was to continue to have more children than the middle-class, to fulfil the woman's more traditional expectations, and to encourage the children to stay within class boundaries so that, in her own later age, conventional kinship networks would be preserved. Only after World War II was there a sign of a new loosening of the culture of working-class wives, beyond grudging and limited adaptation to the necessities of a rapidly-changing society. And even now we must ask how much the world of the working-class woman has enlarged.

Conclusion: An Evaluation

For all their differences family roles remained the primary means of identification for both middle- and working-class women. There is no need to repeat the immense and surprisingly persistant distinctions in the nature of adaptation to change on the part of these two key urban classes. We can stress instead an underlying similarity: the growing dependence on emotional ties and satisfactions in the family. This did not displace economic functions, increasingly directed to consumption roles. The middle-class woman, exposed to tremendous novelty and on the whole attempting new methods to deal with her family activities, sought anchor in new relationships to children and husband. The working-class woman married for love as well, and might easily continue to find it. Increased attention to children, if not in the middle-class style, might bring new satisfactions. But neither of these relationships changed as predictably or extensively as in the middle class. The vital supplement was the extended family. Here was a broader combination, if weaker in any single link, than the middle-class formula. It, too, made the family the crucial focus in a changing world.

If one believes that woman's true liberation lies in freedom from the family role, these choices must seem unfortunate. The middle-class pattern, allowing more sense of self, might be preferable – not surprisingly most advocates of familyless freedom are middle-class products – but it was not emancipation from motherhood or wifehood.

A more relevant concern is whether women invested too much in the new emotional involvement with family. One possible test provides ambiguous results. Early marriage with a man a few years older, combined with the fact that from the mid-nineteenth century women's longevity increased more rapidly than men's, produced a growing percentage of widows in the adult female population. This was unprepared for; few people of either sex think of old age when marrying, yet by 1931 half of all Frenchwomen over 65 were widows, a total of over 5 per cent of all women in France. Yet, while widows died earlier than married women (single women dying earlier still), they survived death of spouse much better than men did, for the gap in health between married men and widowers was exceptionally great. As we have seen for the working class particularly, continued ties with children kept the emotional content of family alive for older women. But the family also involved chores of household routine, and there was no retirement from these. The varied if often prosaic aspects of the family gave women a purpose, indeed a variety of roles, that men might envy.

As with adjustments in work roles we need further tests for women's family modernisation, some of which only the future can provide. Middle-class innovative developments deserve comparison with the gradualist approach of workers, but the middle-class pattern looms ever larger as the class dominates in numbers and in culture by the late twentieth century. Can the working class maintain their distinctive modernisation pattern surrounded by another, dominant model? Can middle-class women continue to combine the family anchor with individual self-expression? Recent twentieth-century developments need consideration here, but so, even earlier, does the final aspect of the general process of female modernisation. Women, as individuals at least, progressively branched out into the broader society. Some abetted family modernisation in the process. Others turned against the family, at least in its current forms. In both respects this final general role provides a test for the quality and durability of women's basic familial focus.

Notes

1. Women's roles in the family have for too long been over-generalised,
understated or simply ignored. Until recently most historians have found the
family unworthy of investigation, assuming that it has been constant, that is,
without a history. A new spate of family study has done a fair amount towards
remedying this but the historians involved have paid little attention to women,
their primary concern being children and fathers (see for example Philip
Greven, Jr., *Four Generations: Population, Land and Family in Colonial
Andover, Massachusetts* [1971]); one noted family historian puts the women in
the home, save for churchgoing, and then merrily writes several chapters on the
pre-industrial family without further mention of the female (Peter Laslett,
The World We Have Lost [1965]). As we will see the family has undergone
significant changes in size, structure and functions. More specifically, in the
last two centuries many crucial changes were wrought by women in their
efforts to modernise. This is why, even for overall family history, we must
rescue women from their passive background role and attend to the evolution
they have undergone. We need more than the concern for structural analysis
that has preoccupied family historians, prompting them to play down human
dimensions that mould the structure. But it is not only family historians
who have left our picture incomplete. Women's historians have also not
realised the full implications of the role of wife and mother. Most historians
of women play down the familial role of women as being insignificant and
embarrassing. Some go so far as to claim that the family was and is the
main obstacle toward women's self-fulfilment (see, for example, the work
of Sheila Rowbotham, *Hidden from History: Rediscovering Women from
the 17th Century to the Present* [1975]; and Evelyn Sullerot, *Woman,
Society and Change* [1974]). For some women, possibly increasingly so,
this may be true, but before one can assess such claims one needs to know
exactly what the history of women in the family is. In other words, even if one
holds that the family has kept women back one must deal with the history of
their family role; indeed only the historical dimension could offer evidence
for an assessment of the critical position, beyond mere assertion. I will try
to show that far from being a major stumbling block, the family has been
the stepping stone toward female emancipation. This is not to suggest that
we can recount a story of past bliss for the heroine-housewife. What follows
is rather a story of struggle, suffering and sacrifice, which did however bring
some results, and which does form a definite history, not a boring
description of the constant Hausfrau.
2. See Part III for a discussion of the legal battle for women's rights.
3. Laslett, *The World We Have Lost;* Olwen Hufton, *The Poor of Eighteenth
Century France 1750-1789* (1974).
4. For a discussion of pre-industrial marital arrangements see J. Michael
Phayer, 'Lower Class Morality: The Case of Bavaria', in the *Journal of
Social History* (1974), pp.79-85; and Edward Shorter, *The Making of the
Modern Family* (1975), pp.54-78.
5. For a discussion of family structures see Peter Laslett, ed. *Household and
Family in the Past Time* (1972).
6. Lutz Berkner, 'The Stem Family and the Development Cycle of the
Peasant Household: An 18th Century Austrian Example', in the *American*

Historical Review, 77 (1972), pp.398-418.

7. For information on the biological determinants of women's physical lot see the work of Rose E. Frisch, 'Weight at Menarche: Similarity for well-nourished and undernourished girls at differing ages, and evidence for historical constancy', in *Pediatrics* 50, (1972), pp.445-50; and 'Critical Weight at Menarche, Initiation of the Adolescent Growth Spurt, and Control of Puberty', in M. Grumback, G. Grave, and F. Mayer (eds.), *Control of the Onset of Puberty* (1974).

8. A solid study of the role of the midwife is certainly needed. For a brief description see Harry Graham, *Eternal Eve: The Mysteries of Birth and the Customs that Surround It* (1960), and Walter Radcliffe, *Milestones in Midwifery* (1967).

9. Bouneceau-Gesmon, *De la Domesticité* (1875), p.37.

10. Dr V. Raymond, *Etudes Hygieniques sur la Santé, la Beauté, et le bonheur des femmes* (1841), pp.50-51.

11. John Knodel and Etienne van de Walle, 'Breast Feeding, Fertility and Infant Mortality: An Analysis of Some Early Germany Data', *Population Studies,* 21 (1967), pp.109-31.

12. David Hunt, *Parents and Children in History: The Psychology of Family Life in Early Modern France* (1970), offers a good insight into the attitudes and treatment of children in early modern France.

13. The age of puberty has been falling on an average of three to four months per decade for the last 125 years. There is evidence that the onset of puberty is class-specific. In a study of women in Manchester in 1820 it was found that the age of menarche among working women was 15.7 compared to 14.6 for girls of the middle class; see J.M. Tanner, 'The Trend Toward Earlier Physical Maturation' in J.E. Meade and A.S. Parkes (eds.), *Biological Aspects of Social Problems* (1965), p.51. The nutritional factor seems to be most important in accounting for such differences. Recent medical research suggests that the onset of puberty is related to a girl's critical weight as we noted earlier. The age at which this weight is attained is probably related to food consumption and social class. See R.E.F. Frisch, 'Critical Weight and Menarche', in Melvin Grumback (ed.), *Control of the Onset of Puberty* (1974), pp.403-23.

14. Dr Allbutt in his popular manual *The Wife's Handbook* (1886), noted the anxiety that mothers felt in approaching this subject to their daughters, p.50.

15. For an historical discussion of the rise of illegitimacy see Edward Shorter, 'Illegitimacy, Sexual Revolution and Social Change in Modern Europe', in *Journal of Interdisciplinary History*, 2 (1971), pp.237-72; also *The Making of the Modern Family*, pp.80-98.

16. Edward Shorter, 'Female Emancipation, Birth Control and Fertility in European History', in *American Historical Review*, 78, (1973), developed this concept. While there are major problems with the Shorter thesis (most specifically, as regards our discussion, his timing of the sexual revolution and the role of the middle class therein), it is still useful. Critics of Shorter have raised important questions; for example, how sexually liberated was a woman who had to endure repeated pregnancies? Some believe that the rise in illegitimacy rates (which is Shorter's main source of justifying a sexual revolution) was a result of heightened male aggression and that there was no change in women's sexual attitudes. Obviously it is

extremely difficult to ascertain the exact nature of the relationship between men and women at this time. However, the implication of those who argue that there was no change in women's sexual instincts is that there was some type of rape epidemic. It is difficult to believe that this would have occurred without comment. Indeed what contemporary comment there was noted altered behaviour on the part of both sexes. However, the nature of change at this time was far more subtle than Shorter has described. Increased fertility accounted in part for the increase in births both legitimate and illegitimate, as we will discuss in this chapter. In addition, there was a change in behaviour patterns. One cannot possibly argue that a woman who found herself pregnant and abandoned, even once, would consider herself sexually liberated (although she might derive some comfort in the fact that the act was with a man of her own choosing). It is more useful to consider the period 1750-1850 as one of an important transition rather than of an acommplished sexual revolution. The increase in illegitimacy rates was a sign of new behaviour but it also indicated that tradition wrought many grave problems for women. Tradition provided little control for women over their biological processes; sex meant more babies, which limited sexual freedom to a few years of youth for many women. Before women could freely enjoy new intimacies with mates of their own choosing they would need to develop a new attitude towards birth control for one thing. It would take time to solve the problems brought about by the conflict between tradition and innovation. The history of these developments that eventually enabled women to perceive the dawning of a sexual revolution are discussed in the text and will have a focus different to that which has been presented by Shorter.

Another indicator of new behaviour was the rise in marriage rates (which Shorter does not emphasise enough). Again some have argued that this also was a sign not of new values but of the further subjection of women. The argument here is that as economic pursuits diminished (most specifically in agriculture and domestic manufacture) women were forced more than ever before to find economic sustenance, i.e. a man. There are several problems with this line of thinking. First, it is not at all clear that women faced an economic crunch, as we discussed earlier. Granted that we have a very limited comparative base, the trend in terms of the number of women formally employed did show an increase into the nineteenth century. The point is that the increase in the number of women workers was in line with an increase in women marrying. Second, if economic times were depressed why did births increase particularly within marriage? One could argue that women found their jobs so awful that they chose what seemed to be the lesser of two evils. This type of sentiment was not articulated however. Quite the contrary, the festivities of marriage took on growing importance from the late eighteenth century onwards as bridal dresses and parties became more elaborate.

A more substantial argument is the cultural conditioning debate. Current interest in psychological implications of societal behaviour has led some to conclude that women married and continue to marry because of the forces set by society. There is no denying the fact that women were conditioned to behave according to norms; a crucial standard held that to be successful was to be married. However, role playing goes on at all ages and for both sexes. The question that needs to be asked is whether women marrying in the nineteenth century or even today were reacting merely to a long established traditional role which was becoming less necessary given the changes in women's employment patterns or did marriage change, providing women with new goals, notably emotional sustenance? The implications of this question will be discussed in the text.

17. Aristotle (pseud.), *Aristotle's Complete Master-Piece in three parts, Displaying the Secrets in the Generation of Man* (1795).
18. Alex Comfort, *The Joy of Sex*, (1974), and Dr David Reuben, *Everything You Wanted to Know About Sex* (1974).
19. This is the concept implicit in the analysis of women and modernisation in Sheila Rowbotham, *Hidden from History: Rediscovering Women in History from the 17th Century to the Present* (1975); and Ester Boserup, *Women and Economic Modernization* (1970).
20. See Phayer, 'Lower-Class Morality', pp.79-85.
21. Ibid., p.89.
22. See note 13.
23. The *British Mothers Magazine* (Oct. 1849), p.240.
24. W. Giles, *A Guide to Domestic Happiness* (1836), p.5.
25. The *Ladies' Pocket Magazine* (1829), p.55.
26. The *British Mothers Magazine* (Oct. 1849), p.240.
27. Dr Henry A. Allbutt, *The Wife's Handbook*, p.58.
28. Dr. P. Bouardel, *Le Secret médical* (1887), p.87.
29. Dr Louis Seraine, *De la sante des gens mariés* (1865), pp.112-16.
30. *Le Petit Journal* (1906), p.3.
31. For a good discussion of the subject see Phayer, 'Lower Class Morality'.
32. P. Bureau, *'Indicipline des moeurs'*, (1927), p.60.
33. Albert André, *Traité Practique Formulaire des contrats de mariage,* 3rd ed. (1905), pp.6-7; Raoul Grasserie, *Du Contrat de Mariage des Commerçants* (1896).
34. *L'Alliance des Familles* (1876) is typical of the journals that carried such advertisements.
35. Dr Louis Fiaus, *La femme, le mariage et le divorce. Etude de physiologie et de sociologie* (1880), pp.27-8.
36. The *Family Economist,* I (1848), p.44.
37. The *Ladies Journal* (1847), p.3.
38. The *British Mothers Magazine* (1850), p.129.
39. Pariset, *Manuel*, p.6.
40. Richard Carlile, *Every Woman's Book; Or What is Love* (1828), p.8.
41. Michael Ryan, *The Philosophy of Marriage,* pp.114-15.
42. Gustave Droz, *Monsieur, madame et bébé* (1866), p.112.
43. Pariset, *Manuel*, p.9.
44. J.A. Banks, *Prosperity and Parenthood* (1954), pp.32-47.
45. M. Jeanne Peterson, 'The Victorian Governess: Status Incongruence in Family and Society', in Martha Vicinus (ed.), *Suffer and Be Still: Women in the Victorian Age* (1972), pp.3-19.
46. See the work of Charles Harris, *Islington* (1974); F.M.L. Thompson, *Hampstead: Building a Borough 1650-1964;* and Alan Armstrong, *Stability and Change in an English Country Town: A Social Study of York 1801-1851* (1974).
47. Pariset, *Manuel*, p.10.
48. Isabella Beeton, *The Book of Household Management* (1861).
49. One French domestic manual written by the household sage Mme Pariset (*Manuel*, p.14) stated that it was necessary that a husband and wife have two bedrooms with a sitting room in between, so that in case one was ill the other would not be bothered. In fact this was rarely possible in the cramped housing of the French middle class but it correctly shows the drive for personal privacy within a nuclear family context.

50. See the work of J.F.C. Harrison, *The Early Victorians 1832-51* (1971)
51. Emily James, *Englishwoman's Year Book and Directory, 1899-1900*, p.91.
52. Marcel Cusenir, *Les domestiques en France* (1912), pp.172-4; Marie Delorme, 'Les domestiques', *L'Enseignement menager* (1906), p.229; Mme V. Vincent, 'La domesticité féminine', *La Reforme sociale*, p.3.
53. See Patricia Branca, *Silent Sisterhood* (1975), chap.3.
54. Pariset and Celenart, *Nouveau Manuel*, p.28.
55. T. Webster, *An Encyclopaedia of Domestic Economy. . .* (1845), p.347.
56. For a discussion of the demand for increased privacy for the family as a whole see Shorter's *The Making of the Modern Family*.
57. This new science was found in a variety of reading materials; in household manuals, for example, see John Walsh, *A Manual of Domestic Economy: Suited to Families Spending 100 pounds to 1000 pounds a Year* (1853); women's periodicals, such as *Journal des Demoiselles* (June 4 1870).
58. Ris-Paquot, *Le Livre de la femme d'Interieur* (Paris, 1891), p.57.
59. Pariset and Celenart, *Nouveau Manuel*, p.57; *Economy for the Single and Married. . .*(1845), pp.35-6.
60. Pariset and Celenart, *Nouveau Manuel*, p.52; Beeton, *Household Management*, p.2.
61. Eliza Warren, *How I Managed my House on Two Hundred Pounds a Year* (1865), preface.
62. Pariset, *Manuel de la Maîtresse*, p.6.
63. Mme L.D. Alq, *Le Maître et la Maîtresse de Maison* (1880), p.133.
64. Advertisements and articles on the various makes and marvels of sewing machines appeared in the *English Woman's Domestic Magazine* (1867), pp.333, 403, 485, 541, 587, 626; similar writings were found later in France, for example, *La Femme au Foyer* (1910), p.21.
65. J.A. Banks, *Prosperity and Parenthood* (1854), p.58.
66. The *Mothers' Companion* (1888), p.103.
67. The *Housekeeper's Magazine and Family Economist* (1826), p.2.
68. V. Maquel, *Le Bonheur dans la Famille ou L'Art d'être heureux.* (1853), p.149.
69. M.G. Beleze, *Le Livre de Menages*, p.112.
70. *La Femme au Foyer* (5 June 1910).
71. R.H. Graveson and F.R. Crane (eds.), *A Century of Family Law 1857-1957* (1957).
72. Neil J. Smelser, *Social Change in the Industrial Revolution: An Application of Theory to the Lancashire Cotton Industry, 1770-1840* (1960).
73. Some of the more popular works were: Dr Bull's *Hints to Mothers* (1833); Dr Conquest's *Letters to a Mother* (1842); Dr Allbutt's *The Wife's Handbook* (1886) and *Every Mother's Handbook* (1897); the *British Mother's Magazine* and *The Mother's Friend*.
74. For a discussion of the woman patient as victim of male medical conspiracy see Ann Douglas Wood, 'The Fashionable Diseases: Women's Complaints and their Treatment in Nineteenth Century America', in *Journal of Interdisciplinary History*, III (1973).
75. Dr Desbruêres, *Hygiene des Femmes* (1845), p.xxii; Dr Michael Ryan, *The Philosophy of Marriage. . .*(1837), p.202.
76. Dr Bergonier, *Le Guide Maternal ou Médicine Pratique de la Mère de Famille* (1842), p.79.
77. Dr Fraissines, *Hygiene de la Femme Pendant la Grossesse* (1857), pp.12-13. The doctor recommended that the woman who wished to be certain of her state should take her urine to her doctor so that he might examine it for *Kyesteine* which Fraissines believed to be the surest sign of pregnancy.

78. Dr Desbruères, *Hygiene,* pp.80-82.
79. Dr V. Maquel, *Etudes Hygièniques sur la santé, la beauté et le bonheur des femmes* (1858), p.18.
80. Bergonier, *Le Guide,* p.184.
81. For a contemporary discussion of the decline of wet nursing in France see Fraissine, *Hygiene,* p.60; Ris-Paquot, *Le Livre,* p.913; secondary literature on the topic can be found in Shorter, *The Making of the Modern Family,* and a good statistical analysis by George D. Sussman, 'The Wet-nursing Business in Nineteenth Century France' in *French Historical Studies,* IX (1975), pp.304-28.
82. For a discussion of the problems of wet nursing in England see Dr Edward Tilt, *The Elements of Health and Principles of Female Hygiene* (1852), p.47; *The Mothers Medical* (1843), p.8; in France, Fraissines, *Hygiene,* pp.62-3; Ris-Paquot, *Le Livre,* p.413.
83. Pariset and Celenart, *Nouveau Manuel,* p.466; see also Shorter, *Modern Family,* chap.5.
84. Ris-Paquot, *Le Livre,* p.414.
85. Conquest, *Letters,* pp.92-3.
86. Literature lamenting the declining willingness of women to nurse their children appeared as early as 1802: Dr J.M.R. Pontainier, *Dissertation sur les Advantages de l'allaitement maternal,* p.9.
87. Bull, *Hints* (1877 ed.), p.40.
88. Desbruères, *Hygiène,* pp.182-3.
89. V. Raymond, *Etudes Hygièniques,* p.512.
90. A series of articles written by Dr R. Bakewell entitled 'Infant Mortality and its Causes', printed in the popular *British Mothers' Journal* (June-December 1857) poignantly depict the seriousness of the problem of misuse of medicines by mothers.
91. Doctors in general had little to offer mothers who came to them with sick infants. Medical ignorance was as gross as that of the mothers. The following story reflects the situation: ' "Ah! poor thing, it's gone at last", said a fond father to a friend, alluding to the death of a baby two months old, "but we did all we could for it, and there's no use repining. It was only ill a week, and during that time we had four doctors, who gave it eight calomel powders, applied one leech to the chest, one blister to the chest, six mustard plasters and gave it antimony wine and other medicines in abundance. Yet the poor thing died!" ' from 'Physics and Infancy', in *The Family Economist,* I (1848), p.96.
92. See 'Women in Domestic Life', in the *Magazine of Domestic Economy* I (1935-56), p.67 for one of the earlier discussions on the importance of the mother's role in child rearing.
93. The anxiety over the problem of adolescence can be seen in a long series of letters that appeared in *The Englishwoman's Domestic Magazine* (1869-1870), on the question of disciplining teenage daughters.
94. Allbutt, *The Wife's Handbook,* p.53.
95. For a fuller discussion of the history of birth control see Patrician Branca, *Silent Sisterhood* (pp.114-43); Norman Himes, *Medical History of Contraception* (1936); for an American discussion of the same phenomenon see James Reed, 'Birth Control and the Americans' (unpublished PhD thesis, Harvard, 1974)
96. Allbutt, *The Wife's Handbook,* advertisement.
97. J.A. and Olive Banks, *Feminism and Family Planning* (1964), *passim.*
98. Rene Villerme, *Tableau de l'état moral et physique des ouvriers employés dans les manufactures, de laine, et de soie* (1840).
99. Fritz Schuman, *Auslese und Anpassung der Arbeiterschaft in der*

Automobil industrie (1911).

100. Robert Tressell, *The Ragged Trousered Philanthropists* (1914), p.49. This novel presents an unusual insight into working-class life in England in the late nineteenth century.

101. For a discussion of birth control and the working classes see Shorter, *Modern Family;* and Daniel Scott Smith, 'Family Limitation, Sexual Control, and Domestic Feminism in Victorian America', in Mary Hartman and Lois Banner, *Clio's Consciousness Raised* (1974), pp.119-36.

102. This information was found in Edward Shorter's, 'Female Emancipation, Birth Control, and Fertility in European History', in the *American Historical Review* 78 (1973).

103. F. Zweig, *The Worker in an Affluent Society* (1961) discusses the parent-child relationship at some length.

104. Edward Shorter and Charles Tilly, *Strikes in France* (1974).

105. For an historical discussion of the lot of working-class wives see the work of Peter N. Stearns, 'Working-Class Women in Britain 1890-1914', in Vicinus, *Suffer and Be Still,* pp.100-20; and Laura Oren, 'The Welfare of Women in Labouring Families: England 1860-1954', in Hartman and Banner, *Clio's Consciousness Raised,* pp.226-44.

106. Maurice Halbwachs, *L'Evolution des besoins dans les classes ouvrières.* (1933).

107. Tressell, *The Ragged Trousered Philanthropists,* p.58.

108. Stearns, 'Working-Class Woman', p.104.

109. Ibid., p.105.

110. Shorter, *Modern Family:* Alfred C. Kinsey, *Sexual Behaviour in the Human Female* (1965).

111. Michael Anderson, *Family Structure in Nineteenth Century Lancashire* (1971).

112. See Richard Sennett, *Families Against the City: Middle-Class Homes of Industrial Chicago, 1872-1890* (1970) for a debatable discussion of the advantages of the extended family in America.

113. Ernst Duckerstoff, *How an English Woman Lives* (1899), p.40.

4 FROM BEHIND CLOSED DOORS: WOMEN IN SOCIETY

No account of the modern woman's growing pains would be complete without a look at the drama of what has become known as the *woman's movement*. The many vicissitudes the modern woman has seen as she pursued her personal development are reflected in the woman's movement of the nineteenth and twentieth centuries. An important stage of women's history began when pioneering women dared to come out from behind closed doors to tell of their plight and their visions for a world without sexual bias. They were the first feminists. Many will feel that the history of feminism is familiar enough and that the sins of
• society against women have been amply chronicled. While it is true that the rise of feminism has received a disproportionate amount of attention, it is far from being understood. More important, the story of the relationship between the rise of feminism and the personal struggles of the common woman has not been explored. We leave the first task for the astute student of women's history and attempt the latter in the following pages.

We begin with a series of questions regarding definition. Question one simply involves putting feminism into its historical frame. What were its origins? Tracts defending the rights of women were issued from the early 1790s onward — the two most relevant precedents are those of Mary Wollstonecraft, *A Vindication of the Rights of Women* (1792) and Olympe de Georges, *Declaration of the Rights of Women* (1791). Clearly the roots of feminism are deeply entangled with the general revolutionary ferment of the late eighteenth century. The ideologies underlying the French Revolution stirred many women and men to scorn the degradation to which women were subjected. Earlier the belief in the dignity of *man* popularised by the *philosophes* of the Enlightenment raised the consciousness of women as well as men. While theoretically the new philosophy of liberty and equality was proclaimed for all, it was slowly realised that man did not include woman; witness the new language *citoyenne* and *citoyen*. From then on sporadic pamphlets appeared urging greater legal equality for women in home, school or society. Feminist philosophy owes much to men like the Utopian Socialists; Charles Fourier, for example, believed that women's advance to equality with his own sex would be the true measure of general social progress.

By mid-nineteenth century a woman's movement was definitely discernible as it gained focus and numbers. Women played a role in the revolutions of 1848. In countries like Italy and Hungary, this was mainly supportive, as noblewomen organised nursing brigades and cheered the troops on. But in Berlin and even more in Paris women organised on their own – one French group even forbade male attendance at the meetings – and studied problems ranging from the difficulties of domestic service to the need for direct political expression through extension of the vote to women. A desire to extend the justice advocated for men was definitely in the air.

Yet even after this, feminism seems more often to be a list of names than a definable movement. Feminist groups were small. Exceptions, such as the massive petitions for suffrage produced in England shortly before World War I, proved episodic and indeed incomplete, for formal organisations boasted at most a few thousand members. In the absence of numbers, we are forced to seek the feminist crusader and come up with names such as George Eliot, Florence Nightingale, Rosa Luxemburg, and Emmeline Pankhurst. The temptation to create a feminist hall of fame is great. But what did these pioneers have in common? They were women. They in some way envisaged a better world for women. But so did people like Mrs Beeton, who tried to improve the housewife's lot; and so did a host of men. Pioneering women might easily ignore each other or even, actively or potentially, disapprove of each other. Emily Davies, an advocate of jobs and education for women, did not want women to strive for the vote. Isadora Duncan's search for self-expression in the world of the creative arts took her in quite a different direction from, say, the suffragettes.

Problem two, when we compare individual advocates of women's rights or, particularly, organisations, we find constant disagreement and quite serious differences. Working-class organisations and ideologies differed immensely from one country to the next, but everywhere they developed with some energy and within a broadly comparable framework. Not so feminism. What we know of feminism is based almost entirely on an Anglo-American model and while feminism can be appropriately identified elsewhere it is a distinctly different phenomenon. This is not, we must stress, simply a question of social-industrial lag. Feminists did concern themselves primarily with the problems and presumed aspirations of urban women, so it is understandable that French feminism displays a weaker and less consistent historical strand than, say, English feminism around 1900. But the French never imitated the English model, even as their society became comparably urbanised. Witness the relative lack of concern over the vote, despite the fact that English women provided not only a model of suffrage agitation but actual achievement of the vote almost thirty years before their French sisters won suffrage, without any particular movement at its base even then.

French and indeed continental feminism generally was not as radical as the English and never succeeded even briefly in arousing massive support. French leaders faced not only a less urban society but also the strong force of the Catholic church. Still more important, and here not only in France, was the absorption, at least in theory, of many feminist demands by socialist parties of various stripes. The process began early. Fourier envisaged full educational equality and radical reforms in marriage. The Saint Simonians also preached equality of the sexes. In 1848, the Fourierist, Victor Considérant demanded that women be given the vote. Here was the inception of the envelopment of the feminist cause by a minority political movement acting on theoretical and disinterested grounds. French socialists tried to couple the liberation of the proletariat with that of women; and it proved almost impossible even for upper-class women not to yield to the lure of socialist support and merge their cause with that of the workers. The theory was splendid, for in remaking society all oppressed groups might gain; but the practice gave women a less distinctive voice than that of Anglo-American feminists who had no serious socialist movement to rely upon and who worked up their own set of demands. While women participated ardently within French and German socialism, socialist leaders paid lip service to the female cause, for their main concern and main constituency rested with male labourers. It was not until 1935, for example, that the French socialist party fully accepted its long-proclaimed ideology of equality between the sexes.[1] The daily tension between men and women workers inevitably limited concern with the female cause. Yet French feminists continued to rely on the will of men even to obtain a hearing for their own proposals. They constantly stressed their desire to stand by men, not to overcome them. Never did they imply superiority of the female; as a feminist journal stated, 'We advocate nothing of the kind. Feminism is purely and simply the doctrine of the natural equality and balance between the sexes.[2] The desire was liberty for all.

In England feminists ultimately had to create their own cause, absorbed by no one political party. This approach involved immense strain, but it seems to have worked better as ultimately all major parties responded in varying degrees to feminist demands. After all, as already noted, English women won the vote first. Yet German women, working through socialism, gained the same — right after World War I — but without the public display of their British counterparts. Despite a lag in suffrage French women gained in other areas of law at approximately the same pace as the British. European feminism involved distinctly different sets of movements, depending on each national political context; but it cannot really be said that its aspirations or its achievements were radically different. One might ask, given the major differences in feminist organisations and tactics, whether the changes which did come about occurred because of or in spite of feminist agitations.

This leads us to the central question: whom did the militant feminists represent? If they prove unrepresentative, which segment constitutes the more genuine process of growing-up, the articulate advocates of reform or the silent women who bought sewing machines and learned how to be good wives and mothers?

Let us look at the general problem first. From relatively early days, when given a chance, many women have expressed hostility both to feminist causes and to the die-hards of the old school. But the majority remained apathetic. Expressed hostility to early feminist causes was limited but real; there was as a letter to an English woman's magazine in 1870 on the question of suffrage witnesses

> The women who do have such a wish [for the vote] form but a very small proportion of those whose opinions they say they represent. I think most sensible women will say that they prefer their own sphere to that offered them in the terms and inference of the Bill. The opinion of most women on the subject of this Bill will be that they prefer their domestic husbandry and its consequent joys and cares, to the great privileges of having a vote at each election . . .[3]

As late as 1914 a poll taken by a French women's magazine indicated that the majority of women were uninterested in the vote. The poll revealed that 143,983 women said 'No' to the question 'Do women wish the vote?' while only 96,924 said 'Yes'.[4]

Advocacy of new work roles for women struck an even less responsive chord by the majority who commented. In 1872, another English reader expressed the following statement:

> There is plenty of unpaid work for women to do in the world if they

like to do it. When it comes to paid work, remember that most men who can afford it marry and each provides for a woman. Would the lady lawyers, etc., as a rule, each marry and provide for a man? It seems only right that what produces the greatest food for the greatest number should continue.[5]

Here, clearly, the role that most married women had painfully carved out for themselves seemed pitted against feminist pleas. Small wonder that an outspoken attack on feminism called *The Girl of the Period*[6] — by a woman, Eliza Lynn Linton — sold hundreds of thousands of copies. And of course the dilemma continues. Many feminist causes draw strong objections from other women. A German poll of the early 1950s showed that the majority of women believed that no mother should work until her children were at least ten years of age. They thus opposed feminist demands for day care centres and protection of job opportunities. The irony of the situation is made even more apparent when one realises that many of these opponents were themselves working mothers.[7]

The question of the representativeness of various feminist demands must plague any assessment of the modern women's history. Sometimes, as perhaps with the German poll, women mouth conventional beliefs to enquirers — mothers should care for children — while in their actual behaviour show openness to the more varied lifestyle the feminists suggest. Is the problem here one merely of a time lag? Indeed many feminists, from the nineteenth century onward, were years ahead of their time. The struggle for advanced educational degrees for women is an example. Most women in the nineteenth century could not afford higher education (most men could not either) so the feminist strivings for university places in France and England meant little even to the middle classes. But in the twentieth century, with universities more open, increasing numbers of women desire better education and profit from the vision of the pioneers.

The issue of representativeness can be refined further. Most feminists were from the upper class and the upper middle class. This is logical, both because such women had time and resources for new activities and were steadily evolving a new life style involving new forms of self-expression, especially the middle class woman. By this very token however feminists, despite their best efforts, found it difficult to communicate with working-class women. Advocacy of protection of married women's property, an important legal issue in England in the 1870s and 1880s, drew middle-class support but meant little to most working-class woman who brought no dowry and little property into marriage. Legislation such as divorce laws which gave women a right to maintenance might prove of immense benefit to working-class women, but as a cause they drew no active support below the middle class.

This is not to say that feminists were not interested in specifically working-class causes. In 1888 Annie Besant, who had made important breakthroughs in the free dissemination of birth control information, over a decade before, organised a strike by female match workers in a London factory. The strike, one of the first by low-skilled women operatives, won many of its goals; even if no enduring women's labour movement resulted. Two decades later individual advocates such as Barbara Drake in England addressed themselves to the joint problems of inferior working conditions and lack of unionisation among women. Again some results could be cited, as a few unions were organised and strikes for better conditions conducted even among domestic workers in rural areas. Nevertheless the main dynamic of women's unionisation, except in white collar ranks, remained outside the feminist orbit. The view of work taken by most women precluded extensive interest in unionisation; work was a temporary or at most supplementary concern, and a definite job commitment was essential for organisation. Women did unionise, but at a rate far below that of their male counterparts. Their strike rate may have been a bit higher, again compared to men, but it still lagged; strikes had a spontaneous element and could rouse workers of either sex.[8] With few exceptions, where women struck or joined unions they acted with men, on group or class grievances, not as women specifically.

Part of the problem was obviously discrimination. There is no question that even in countries where socialism was strong, with its theoretical commitment to equality, women encountered discrimination by male labour organisers. In Britain, where trade unionism had a less doctrinal base, women on occasion specifically resisted organising efforts because the unions had ignored them before; in machine work, for example, despite the promptings of union leadership, men voted overwhelmingly and repeatedly to keep women out until shortly before World War I — by which time many women had lost what interest they might have had in participation. Nevertheless a respectable percentage of women textile workers and white-collar workers were unionised around 1900 — perhaps 10 per cent of the total. Almost invariably, however, they belonged to unions with predominant male membership and male leadership; in textile unions, for example, men granted women second-level representation on governing councils, but never top positions. Thus despite blatant sexual discrimination feminists did not perceive unionisation as a central issue. The point is best made by drawing the comparison. In the newer areas of women's work, white-collar employment, one does find strong feminist stirrings. The more middle-class the occupation the more the feminist overtones to be found in the demands put forward. The efforts of women teachers, particularly at the secondary level, to unionise is a case in point. Specifically female issues were always at the top of the list of union demands. Among the goals cited were the right to equal pay for equal work and the right to work after marriage. This is only one example of the strong connection between feminism and middle- class and upper-middle-class women's striving for a new life style. However, it should be noted also that the efforts to unionise women workers at all levels were generally sporadic and failed to have enduring impact.

Unionisation aside, feminists had further difficulties dealing with the issues that confronted working-class women most directly. The cloudy realm of legislation applied to women's work troubled feminists as well, whereas women actually on the job showed less concern. Beginning in the 1840s (as with the 1847 law limiting the hours of work for women in British factories to ten per day) middle-class reformers, mainly male, sought to alleviate the burdens of employment for women. In France a law of 1899 similarly restricted hours of work in all factories in which women were employed. Laws also made special provision for sanitary facilities, limitation of night work and the like. This protective legislation clearly stemmed from a belief that women and men were not equal on the job, that women needed special state intervention.

Thus, a definite theoretical problem was raised, one with which feminists are still grappling i.e. that the laws in principle deliberately separated men from women. In practice their impact was often less discriminatory than the impulse behind them. The French law of 1899, for example, applied to men in factories where women were employed, even though it was the special frailties and home duties of women with which the law concerned itself. This is one reason why workers did not normally object to 'special' legislation. Furthermore, as we have seen, general working-class culture was reflected in women's job culture; both were compatible with a differentiation between men's work and women's, for women did have extra roles, as home managers and mothers, which special legal protection could facilitate. For the feminist, the issue of inequality in law was seen as outright discrimination. One of the most vigorous battles waged by French feminists was against the 1892 law which prohibited women from working at night. Journals such as *La Fronde*, under the guidance of Mme Durand De Valfère, and *La Femme Affranchie*, bemoaned the inability of women to pursue occupations such as bread carriers or dairy workers for whom night work was an essential.[9] From this point of view special legislation was just another way to subject women. In theory there was a real issue here. In practice the situation looked different. Few women strove to be bread carriers; few working-class women sought night work of any sort. Exclusion there was, but it was not necessarily felt or realised by its objects.

At an extreme, therefore, the ratiocinations of middle-class women, who on record never applied for bread carrying work, were highly important as a matter of principle but irrelevant to the lives of women working at manual or clerical jobs, for whom any alleviation might be welcomed. The feminists were not wrong. Laws applying to women alone could and did limit opportunities. But in the actual circumstance, this kind of debate was not even a dialogue of the deaf — it was not a dialogue at all, for few women workers would even be aware of the issues. And concerns of even greater abstraction, such as suffrage, were remoter still. The few massive petitions for women's suffrage included no significant working-class component. Some identifying with class more than sisterhood, might see these issues as distractions from the main issue of improving conditions for workers regardless of gender. Even white-collar workers found little relevance in the most publicised feminist efforts. Here, obviously, is one source of the comparative distinctions within feminism. It was not unrealistic to merge women's causes with broader reform or evolutionary movements such as socialism, which was by and large the pattern on the continent; yet we have already mentioned the risks involved here, of which the leading one was subjection to a male-led movement dominated by male issues. Yet where feminism struck out alone, as in Britain, there could be little pretence of realistic contact with women workers.

This limits the issue of representativeness to the middle-class, particularly that majority of the middle-class female population that was not formally employed. But one must be careful not to overgeneralise. Most middle-class women were not active feminists. Most benefited from feminist advocacy without participating in it. Some were sympathetic but too busy for active involvement.

The radical feminists can be judged correct in their goals of complete and rapid equalisation of rights between the sexes and their related attack on the traditional functions of women in society. Their methods may be deemed appropriate. But no dispassionate judgement can equate them with a wide segment of middle-class opinion.

Having indicated all the problems of representativeness, it is more interesting to note that feminism won its widest gains when it expressed the new position that women were winning in more central aspects of their social life. In education and in the eyes of the law, reform was essential, both areas of change expressed the new self-awareness of hosts of ordinary middle-class women. In family law, feminists made great strides in conveying into law what was already a *fait accompli* in ordinary family life. Married women gained new rights over personal property thus expressing more fully the new developing concomitant relationship with their husbands. Likewise the emotional investment made by modern mothers to their children demanded legal recognition. When Caroline Norton separated from her husband in the mid-1830s, the latter took the children away and for two years forbade her even to see them, as was his right in law. Caroline Norton wrote to every member of the British parliament and penned pamphlet after pamphlet demanding recognition of her right to motherhood. The result was a new child custody act passed in 1839 giving women control over their children, in cases of divorce or separation, until the age of seven (during the children's tender years), after which fathers had right to custody but with maternal visitation rights guaranteed [10] — in sum, a first step toward the modern system of custody arrangements. While recognising Norton's diligence, what is more important to grasp is that what happened here was in essence a recognition of the new culture of motherhood — else an all-male parliament would have had no reason to pass a new law. And so it was with most of the new domestic legislation in which individual advocates (sometimes men as well as women) and early feminist movements participated.

Thus, the feminist movement is best viewed in the context of the social history of modern women. Its divisions, its lack of complete representativeness even of the modernised middle-class, its periodic tendency to go to extremes, are best noted within the mainstream of women's history. It did elicit significant support for many causes. It did effect change which, if initially of interest only to a few, could later alter the behaviour of many, as in the case of opening the higher professions or gaining new rights in divorce.

French feminism, rather episodic and often focused on peculiar disabilities forced on married women by the Napoleonic code, was far less effective than its English counterpart. This is a major factor in the belated liberalisation of dissemination of birth control information, attainment of the vote, and more recently even legalisation of abortion. Here the situation was complex, for French women in fact practised birth control and probably had far more abortions than their English neighbours, despite legal differences; how much the delayed achievement of suffrage mattered is open to debate. Nevertheless feminism did have an impact. On the whole it moved in the same direction that women were moving in their other spheres of activity. It is not unfair to see key feminist demands as a vanguard movement, though it would be wrong to see the history of modern women purely in feminist terms. We must be careful not to give the credit to the articulate feminist for those changes which were brought about silently and privately by the ordinary woman.

Our discussion of women in society falls most easily into three major segments, as already suggested: first, legal change, particularly for married women, in which feminist advocates played a key role reflecting fundamental societal change; second, the opening of education and the professions, where feminism initially articulated rather limited interests but combined with other social forces for expansion of opportunities regardless of sex; and third, feminism as a political force. In all three aspects, feminism was fundamental to the female's growing-up process, but we should avoid equating it with protest in the conventional sense. Women might protest outside feminist circles, as in the case of working-class women who joined men on strike. Or, within feminism, they might see legal change as a logical ratification of something already fundamentally achieved. A current of protest arose among certain women as women, but feminism as a whole is best seen as part, a vital part, of the all-encompassing change in women's roles in modern society.

The Double Standard

Changes in family law, to the woman's benefit, varied in their pace and precise nature from one country to the next, but their basic direction was similar. From a situation around 1800 in which married women were virtual nonentities before the law, whether under English common law or the new Napoleonic code, a wave of legislation expanded women's rights in areas ranging from property rights to divorce.

In the nineteenth century under English common law a married woman could not sue or be sued or be called as a witness. She had no legal rights of property ownership, for anything she owned, earned or inherited belonged to her husbad. The doctrine was aptly summed up as 'my wife and I are one and I am he'. By the same token only the father could determine where children of the marriage would live and how they would be educated. In France, married women could protect certain kinds of property by marriage contracts (so could English wives but the scope was more limited). Nevertheless earnings or other acquisitions subsequent to the marriage placed her under the same types of disabilities as existed in England. The Napoleonic Code required a wife to obey her husband in return for the latter's 'protection'. Hence a wife had to reside wherever the husband determined, could not buy or sell goods or enter into any contract without his permission. Again the husband had full control of the children. Even a widow seeking to remarry had to submit the question of child custody to a family council composed of her dead husband's relatives.

In both France and England women found divorce opportunities virtually nil. French law made divorce illegal for both marriage partners. A woman found guilty of adultery could be sentenced to two years' imprisonment, while a husband was held liable only if he actively maintained a concubine in the conjugal home. Even in this case the husband was only fined. In England men could divorce their wives on grounds of adultery alone, but the reverse was not possible. Needless to say laws enforced the traditional religious view of marriage as designed for procreation, by prohibiting dissemination of birth control information and devices.

There was much then, for women newly conscious of themselves as individuals, to attack. The new type of marriage based on emotional ties made laws protecting the family as an economic entity under male control obsolete and a barrier to smooth personal contacts within marriage. Divorce followed from a desire to escape a marriage in which emotional fulfilment was not found. And obviously the rights of mothers had to be strengthened; this was in fact the first area in which a highly traditional legal structure was dented.

Caroline Norton's battle for custody of her children, after a separation from her husband in the 1830s, has already been cited. But the limited gains embodied in the act of 1839 provoked continuing controversy, for paternal control was only modified by the 'tender years' doctrine, not overturned. Articles by both men and women returned to the theme during subsequent decades. A paper in 1884 showed how slowly the culture changes even after the limited reform:

Although the law now recognizes rights of property in married women, it does not recognize in them any right over their children. The children belong to the father. He may take them away from their mother, educate them where and how he pleases, bring them up in any religion, or if so minded, first in one religion and then in another. If he is poor, and the mother rich, he may compel the mother to maintain the children, although he chooses to take them away from her care. He may leave the guardianship of them after his death to a stranger, or even to his mistress, and the mother has no redress; and if, at his death, the father appoints no guardian, and the children are left with the mother, the law recognizes in her no right, in case of her own subsequent death during their minority, to appoint a guardian in her stead.[11]

Under incessant pressure the law was further changed. In 1886 the Guardianship of Infants Act provided that on a father's death the mother should be her children's guardian. By 1925 the traditional situation had been almost totally reversed in England, as the mother gained virtually exclusive control of children, with fathers' rights nominal. In a famous section of the Guardianship of Infants Act of 1925 the welfare of the child was stated as the first and paramount consideration in all matters of custody. Given the modern culture of motherhood and the new functions mothers undertook with regard to their children, this provision was and is normally interpreted in the courts that in cases of separation or divorce, mothers maintain control. Now that emotion, not economics, is the family base, mother, not father, knows best. Here is one legal area where women overcame centuries old traditions of inequality.

Feminist groups in England (and in the United States, where the same evolution occurred) supported the legal changes in the position of mothers. The legal success reflected basic changes in culture, not just specific agitation. In countries such as France and Italy, however, the law changed less than did women's actual functions as mothers despite strong feminist agitation. Fathers maintained predominant legal rights over their children (although they may not have chosen to exercise them). Feminist demands were not ignored completely. The principal legal change on the continent involved the right of mothers to acquire custody in case of the father's death. Feminist groups in France and Italy were concerned primarily with the rights of motherhood. A free woman, said one definition, will be 'honoured in the family as equal to the husband, having the power and capacity to direct with him the education of the children...'[12] Again, specific demands for legal change were rare. An English observer attributed this to the unofficial power of French women in their families: 'Though legally women occupy a much inferior status to men in practice they constitute the superior sex. They are the power behind the Throne.'[13] It was also true that divorce in France, even when legalised, remained less common than in England, making child custody questions of diminished importance.

French feminism was more concerned with a different kind of attack on the legal double standard; again, the same applies to Italy as well. Feminists here were much more distressed with the legal situation of illegitimate children. The cause was in essence the same as in England and the United States: to gain legal protection in family matters. But the issue, frankly, was less pertinent. Perhaps it derived from a belief among upper-class women, the strength of the feminist movement, that their husbands frequently strayed and that there was a clear way to prevent this. Whether they were correct, whether their husbands did have an unusual tendency toward extramarital relations, is really not at all certain; the French reputation in such matters may be more a matter of male boasting (or, in Anglo-American countries, of male silence than real behavioural differences). French feminists had a clear target here: Article 340 of the Napoleonic Code. During the French Revolution egalitarian legislation, seeking to make all children equal whether legitimate or not,[14] set up an elaborate procedure to establish the paternity of an illegitimate child, thereby making the father responsible for economic maintenance and protecting mothers. Here, in the eyes of later feminists, was simple justice, a real means of preventing the sexual exploitation of women. But the passing of Article 340 of the Napoleonic Code forbade the search for paternity. And the indignity toward women was further carried by Article 341 which insisted upon the search for maternity. The state, not wanting responsibility for upkeep of bastards, left the entire burden to the women — who were, as a practical matter, easier to find and, given their political disabilities, of little consequence. This was a glaring example of the double standard, for women were held to domestic responsibilities while men were theoretically free to pursue their pleasures as they chose.[15] Whether the issue deserved the attention it received may be questioned, but one must keep in mind the rising number of illegitimate births in the first half of the nineteenth century. Serious demonstrations were staged over the inequities of the Code and specific organisations formed to fight for change. The host of arguments presented all revolved around the need to remove this glaring example of the double standard. If men were made economically responsible for their actions they would be less likely to take advantage of women. Reform would also bring greater harmony into marriage, by encouraging fidelity. And the whole society would be moralised if needless sexual exploitation was discouraged. This was a vibrant issue, and not only among French feminists. In Norway feminist advocates such as Katti Ankin Moller and Johan Castborg demanded legal recognition of the equality of illegitimate children, and in this case they won through a law of 1915 which gave illegitimate offspring the same rights as legitimate children, meaning that the father was to be economically responsible in all cases.[16] In France the campaign waned without result, as feminists turned in 1914 to support of pacifist efforts against the War. Given the very high rate of abortion in the latter half of the nineteenth century it would appear that women were forced to take the law into their own hands.

Battles over the double standard were most poignant in their concern for the plight of the prostitute. There was no question that prostitutes faced serious legal disabilities. In France and in port cities of England they were subjected to compulsory internal examinations to detect venereal diseases and liable to detention in lock hospitals. In France, this procedure was inaugurated early in the nineteenth century by Napolean, concerned particularly with protecting the health of his troops, who established the 'police des moeurs'; it was then copied for English naval centres by a law of 1864. Abusive treatment of prostitutes did not go unnoticed. Individual crusaders such as Josephine Butler[17] in England and Avril St Croix[18] in France championed the civil rights of prostitutes, who suffered both mental and physical cruelties from arbitrary detention. In England, the Contagious Disease Act was repealed finally in the 1890s. Here the motivating force came not only from women but also from male reformers, particularly doctors, who judged the whole procedure counterproductive in driving diseased prostitutes into hiding. French doctors also noted that police harassment made prostitutes fear hospitals, though here no reform was forthcoming. Ironically, feminist support was divided over this issue. In England leaders such as Emily Davies and Maurice Dennison refused to back Josephine Butler's efforts, largely to avoid antagonising public opinion by associating the woman's cause with a tainted subject. French feminist movements made no effort to repeal the requirement for medical examination of prostitutes. For the prostitute was a fallen woman. Feminist visionaries saw her elimination only as the result of a total revamping of society, for with suitable jobs available women would not have to sell their bodies to live. With few exceptions, attention to the real problems of existing prostitutes was taboo, and so their legal situation remained unchanged in most cases.

A similar hesitancy or moral conservatism extended to feminist association with efforts to legalise contraception. Here, the behaviour of ordinary women definitely preceded formal public championship, although the legal limitations on the sale of birth control literature and devices severely hampered individuals who sought new control over their own bodies. Throughout Europe appeals were issued to alleviate the perils of repeated pregnancies for married women. But feminists were divided on the method of attack and indeed the importance or suitability of the whole issue. Many believed in family limitations but were reluctant to push the cause lest it detract from what they deemed more important issues, such as the vote. Others, vocal on the issue, saw the solution in celibacy — which was perfectly legal. Mona Caird, an English journalist, advocated separate bedrooms as the best reform possible in married life. Edith Ellis went further, recommending separate residences. Some feminists opposed contraceptives on the grounds that these were just another male device to exploit women for their own pleasure. The extreme position was taken in Britain by Christabel Pankhurst whose pamphlet *The Great Scourge*[19] warned women of the horrors of sex with men. This minority position inevitably drew much public attention and antagonism from both men and women. Soon some equated the whole woman's movement with anti-male biases and lesbianism. Obviously this could only detract from the other goals of feminism. It also convinced many women's leaders that the issue of contraception was simply too controversial.

Despite these problems, individuals did make headway with the more obvious solution to the problem of exploitation through sex. In England the efforts of Charles Bradlaugh and Annie Besant to make birth control literature available prompted the first legal confrontation, in the late 1870s. The two were brought to trial in 1877 for selling a revised edition of Dr Charles Knowlton's *Fruits of Philosophy,* first published in the 1840s. The trial, highly publicised, served to educate the public on the archaic nature of anti-contraception laws. Bradlaugh and Besant were acquitted and went on, with others such as Edward Truelove and Dr William Allbutt, to propagandise widely and successfully for adequate knowledge of artificial birth control techniques.[20]

Attempts to provide the same information to French women were less well received, even though many French feminists saw the right of women freely to regulate their fecundity as essential for female emancipation.[21] But overall the attention given to liberalisation of birth control laws was slight, compared to causes such as pacificism, and thus the official prohibition of the sale of birth control devices went unchanged until 1974. In Holland, in contrast, birth control clinics were opened in the early 1880s, without fanfare; the first was that of Dr Alletta Jacob in 1881. The work of Dr J. Rutgers expanded the clinics, which then spread to England, under the sponsorship of Marie C. Stopes, and to America through the efforts of Margaret Sanger. In 1930 the first international birth control clinic conference was held in Zurich, indicating the importance of the movement for women throughout the industrialised world.

The more courageous dealt with the related subject of abortion. Here French doctors took a leading role in attempts to liberalise abortion around the turn of the century. They pleaded, as they still plead, that abortions occurred whether legal or not, but under the worst possible conditions. They held that legalisation was the only moral thing to do, for it would save the lives and protect the health of thousands of women yearly. In many countries therapeutic abortions were permitted, whereby women were granted abortions if their lives were endangered by a pregnancy. But further reform would have to wait until the 1960s. Even now, French women still struggle to enforce the right to abortion granted only in 1975 and American women too continue to fight to maintain their newly won right.

Feminists had no trouble, however, championing the economic rights of married women. In the second half of the nineteenth century the economic disabilities facing married women were gradually altered in both England and France. The effort was launched by a pamphlet written in England, by Barbara Bodichon (née Leigh Smith) in 1855, entitled *A Brief Summary in Plain Language of the Most Important Laws Concerning Women.*[22] A reform group, the Law Amendment Society, received the pamphlet and set out to propose legal changes to give women property rights and the power to make wills — rights single women already had. Bodichon herself organised a committee calling for signatures on a petition to support these reforms; 26,000 signatures were collected, which made an impressive showing when the document was presented to Parliament, especially when by mistake the petition unrolled and covered the whole length of the chamber of the House of Lords. Within two years the Married Women's Property Bill was introduced. Needless to say feminist enthusiasm was rising, only to be quickly deflated as the bill was immediately rejected. Opponents, seizing on the novelty of the issue, claimed that the act would disrupt society by destroying the home and turning women into hateful, self-assertive creatures with whom no man could live. The *Saturday Review,* a vocal and boorish anti-feminist organ, suggested that the proposal would set at defiance the common sense of mankind and would revolutionise society, and that it smacked of selfish independence, which jarred with poetical notions of wedlock. But it was in fact the new idea of equality of marriage, already widely carried out in practice, which won the day. Women's magazines, quite domestic in their format, even hailed the significance of the measure:

> During the last Session of Parliament several measures have been discussed which prove the great advance public opinion has made, and the liberality in which it estimates the necessity of new and effective legislation for women. The measures which have been introduced clearly prove that the idea of general inferiority and secondary position and consideration of women is rapidly passing away to give place to the more general and more enlightened appreciation of their wants and rights.[23]

Subsequent acts in 1882 and 1893 provided women with exclusive rights to all their property and provided generally that a wife should be in the same position with respect to property as the husband. This new legislation, one of the first female advances in the broader society, affected masses of women as it allowed all married women to protect their economic independence, a possibility previously limited to the special arrangements open to upper-class women alone.

Legislation in France was in a sense less necessary, as more French women drew up traditional marriage contracts thereby protecting the real property they brought into marriage. This provided only minimal protection. Dedicated feminists recognising the inequities campaigned vigorously against the formal law. Earlier attempts had been made. Utopian socialists such as the Saint Simonians urged legal reforms in this area. Later in the century Maria Deraisnes formed a society for the improvement of women's lot, and in 1881 the society addressed a petition to parliament demanding the right for women to conduct their own business affairs. The first sign of relief came in 1881, when married women were allowed their own accounts in savings banks. In 1886 employed wives were granted separate pension dues and benefits, though husbands still legally controlled their salaries. In 1890s the socialists proclaimed the wife as a slave, in dramatic speeches to the Chamber of Deputies; economic equality was essential for a wife to develop herself freely. Individuals such as Mme Schnall directed their efforts toward gaining the right for wives to control their wages without their husbands' consent. New laws soon followed. In 1891 women won the right to inherit from their husbands and in 1893 they were allowed to manage their own property completely free of their husband's direction. Complete control of their wages came in 1907.[24] Similar reforms occurred in Germany, the Scandinavian countries, and the United States. Married women gained basic legal recognition in Norway in 1888 and in 1927 were recognised as equal partners in marriage. The Society for Married Women's Rights was formed in Sweden in 1873, and the next year laws granted married women the right to dispose of their own property and any earnings. All vestiges of a husband's legal tutelage over a wife were abolished by a new marriage law of 1921.

In property and basic legal equality, then, feminism, a general spirit of reform, and the changing nature of marriage combined to produce substantial results. The new laws signalled the growing stature of women in the family while making marriage conform to the needs of female self-expression and equality.

Property reforms drew wide support, even from socialists who in principle opposed property. Despite conservative carping, they did not disrupt marriage but rather expressed the new marital relationship developing particularly in the middle class. Few voices were heard in opposition and feminists, while by no means solely responsible for change, presented a united front. Indeed some of the earlier women's rights organisations were formed over this general issue precisely because it coincided with women's interests and women's new situation in marriage.

Ironically, the same reasoning applied to changes in divorce law. Marriage was now based on emotion, not on economics which had made it impossible to break it up. Traditionally, formal divorce had been an upper-class preserve; between 1650 and 1850 the grand total of divorces in England was 250. Non-legal divorces are uncountable, when one party simply walked away from the other and set up a new life in another village or town. In the years after 1815 demand for a cheap, simple, but legal form of divorce grew increasingly loud. Middle-class people, who could not easily walk away and hide and who pioneered the new marriage relationship needed an escape route when the needs were no longer filled. The first reform came, again in England, in 1857.

It was patently inequitable, but it did allow divorce. This Matrimonial Cause Bill allowed a husband to petition for divorce on grounds of his wife's adultery; a wife had to adduce misconduct in addition to adultery on the part of her husband. Further reforms reduced the required separation period before divorce, and the most important legislation, passed in 1884, awarded financial maintenance (as well as child custody) to the successful petitioner. Only with maintenance legislation did divorce become a real possibility for women. Finally, a new Matrimonial Causes Act in 1923 set the same grounds of divorce for both sexes.

On the crest of the revolution divorce on grounds of incompatibility or mutual consent was introduced in 1792 in France. But the Napoleonic Code soon restricted the ground to adultery, cruelty or grave injury; few people actually divorced under these provisions and in 1816 divorce was abolished completely. No serious change occurred until 1884, when divorce on grounds of cruelty or injury was re-established; law courts in practice made increasingly liberal use of these provisions, judging the mere refusal to return home an act of cruelty which allowed the deserted spouse to obtain a divorce. One wife even obtained a divorce when her husband did nothing when she was insulted by their servant.

While one can argue divorce as a logical concomitant of new marriage relationships, its use in the nineteenth century was extremely limited. For many relationships worked, while tradition (including religious prohibitions on divorce) inhibited others from acting when the relationship failed. Even in England the annual number of divorces was only 277 between 1876 and 1880, rising to 335 by 1885 and 500 by the end of the century. The twentieth century situation proved different: divorces mounted to 2,800 per annum in the 1920s rising to 10,000 in the early 1940s, representing a peak of seven per cent of all marriages. After the Second World War divorces rose to 30,000 a year, a level maintained since then.[25] In France similar trends were at work; in 1900 a mere 7,363 divorces were granted, but in the 1920s the number more than tripled, to an average of roughly 20,000 per year.[26] Divorce law, steadily advanced in the nineteenth century context, proved to have a rather different impact in the most recent decades.

Overall, the success rate for women's rights-in-family was good. Many women leaders, such as Annie Besant, got their first taste of battle over issues such as contraception. Some of the most solid, if unspectacular, women's movements developed over glaring inequalities in marriage law. Only on those issues which dealt with sexual behaviour was support divided and advance slow. This proved to be a major qualification to women's gains, but what was achieved was in many ways spectacular. Within roughly eighty years married women were equal to their husbands under the law. The combination of general societal change, which demanded recognition in legislation and specific advocacy of reform could not find a better illustration.

Education: The Woman Has A Mind of Her Own

Education was a slightly different case, though here, too, women advanced steadily. Educational gains reflected women's new importance in home and in certain key jobs; they also prompted further gains. The feminists had a clear target in mind: access to the top levels of education and the professions. But there were many other aspects.

The concept of education for women was first widely discussed in the late eighteenth century, and the debate gained intensity through the following century. Debate it was, for it reflected the conflicts brewing over the changing position of women in society. There was growing agreement that women should have access to a proper education, although at every stage of the expansion of educational opportunity men received pride of place. Men's educational lead over women remains an aspect of modern society, and must not be overlooked. The school debate focused attention on the nature of proper education for women, and this involved a judgement of the female's role and intellectual capacities in comparison to those of men. Several positions were taken. Conservatives and anti-feminists insisted that women were by nature intellectually inferior to men. No education could remedy this basic fact of life, though an appropriately limited education might be highly desirable (for there is nothing neater than a self-fulfilling prophecy by which women, educated less intensively than men, would emerge less knowledgeable). Leading educational reformers espoused this view, including Jean-Jacques Rousseau as well as socialists such as Pierre Proudhon. It was Proudhon who claimed that women's intellectual and moral value amounted to only a third of men's; he could envisage only two possible roles for women, housewife or prostitute. Rousseau, bypassing training for the latter career, recommended that a domestic education was alone suitable for women. In this same camp, but so diverse in basic political philosophy, were self-proclaimed conservatives such as Joseph de Maistre who thought formal knowledge dangerous to women. Pseudo-scientists joined the parade. Phrenologists equated brain size with intellectual capacity, which automatically left women behind. At the extreme were the contentions that any formal education was detrimental to women, even to their physical development. A great controversy developed over this point in America with the appearance of Professor Edward Clark's book, *Sex in Education,* which claimed that higher education in particular drastically affected women's reproductive functions.[27]

A more moderate position accepted intellectual equality between men and women, but laid stress on their different roles: women's education should be first and foremost practical. This was itself a radical challenge to a tradition which for centuries had seen fit only to educate males outside the upper classes. Education was central to the extension of middle-class culture, and while women might be treated as a separate entity they were not left out. By the later nineteenth century the new woman was by definition an educated woman. Jules Ferry, the French Minister of Education in the 1880s, author of the compulsory school requirements that applied to both sexes, showed the rethinking of women's position. He had a highly pragmatic reason for his belief that women must be educated as well as men: for a woman controls the child and secondly because she controls the husband.[28]

Soon from all camps came criticism of the state of female education. Conservatives lamented the lack of training in practical household skills; for most girls exposed to any schooling, reading of the Bible and learning the catechism constituted the sum total of instruction. For the rich, boarding schools or governesses offered lessons in music, dancing, art, needlepoint and a foreign language. Moderates and egalitarians alike in the rising middle class found this a frivolous approach. 'Useful knowledge' became the watchword. Thus reforms at the elementary level found girls sitting beside boys.

Secular day schools were established to provide children of both sexes with a primary education stressing the three *r's* along with rote learning of geographical locations, historical dates and some elementary science. However, beyond the elementary level the 'useful knowledge' approach distinguished between the sexes in training. Educational reformers who did urge more than basic knowledge for women emphasised domestic science: practical mathematics, for the keeping of accounts (there was no need for women to be acquainted with theoretical branches such as algebra or calculus); knowledge of sewing (beyond ornamental needlework); and even training in cooking. Schools specialising in the new domestic economy for girls proliferated in both France and England. They had limited appeal, for working-class girls had scant time for education of any sort and middle-class girls received practical training at home after completing primary instruction in school. Domestic training loomed large in the thinking of educators planning curricula for women, and elements of this thinking persist to the present day.

By the second half of the nineteenth century national governments became more active in the control of education. They were spurred by a general desire to educate the citizenry and were roused by critics of the education most women received. Thus the famous Taunton Commission of 1864 in England specifically surveyed educational facilities for women and was quite explicit in insisting that more schools provide girls with a sound basic education. Ferry's reforms in the 1880s in France capped a steady development of educational outlets for women at the primary level. Even though primary education was made compulsory for girls and boys at the same time, differences persisted; far more girls than boys fulfilled their requirements at religious schools, until after 1900, and of course far more stopped when their primary school requirements were completed. Nevertheless a revolutionary change was underway. By 1900 almost as many women as men were literate in countries like France and England. Even if they were still less likely to be avid readers, an end had been put to male predominance in a basic skill. The spirit of reform touched all industrialising countries. The first girl's school in Gothenburg, Sweden, was opened in 1815. Hasta Hamsteem crusaded for women's education in Norway, where secondary opportunities were improved with the opening of specialised training schools in 1876 and the admission of women into the classical *gymnasium* in 1882.

Reform could not end with primary education. Feminists entered the scene with increasing force toward the end of the nineteenth century, concentrating on changes at the higher levels of education. Primary education was extended to women largely as part of a general reform effort and solid middle-class interest. The crusade for access to the educational summit was more remote, and this is where special advocates were essential – and where feminists, largely upper-class and highly educated themselves (even if partly self-taught), had a distinct interest. French pioneers in the fight against sexual discrimination at secondary and university levels included Maria Deraisnes, Léon Richter and Adolfe Guercoult. The feminist journal *La Femme Affranchie* clearly expressed the sentiments behind the campaign: 'the real woman will be the woman emancipated by a rational education which, without distinction of sex and without distinction by class, will give freely to all intellects the culture that is demanded and the knowledge that each mind can assimilate'.[29] As early as the 1860s, under the reforming educational minister Victor Drury, a number of secondary schools (*lycees*) were opened for girls. Yet the programmes remained more superficial than secondary training for boys in this highest level of French secondary education. Organisations such as the *Société d'Etudes,* under the leadership of Mme Jeanne Odo, fought the disabilities created by the continuing discrmination against girls in education. The result of such campaigns was not only some improvement in secondary curricula but, in the 1880s, the opening of the Sorbonne to women – though only certificates, not degrees, were initially granted.

Feminists eagerly embraced the educational cause in England. Secondary education for girls owed its beginning to the pioneering efforts of Miss Buss, who founded the North London Collegiate School for Ladies, and Miss Beale's school at Cheltenham, both established in the 1850s. In 1872 the Women's Education Union was organised with the purpose of coordinating the efforts of those interested in promoting schools for girls. The Girls' Public Day School Company opened its first school in Chelsea and by the mid-1880s there were twenty-two more schools. These provided as thorough and sound an education for girls as the grammar schools offered boys.

Breakthroughs in higher education naturally followed. By the 1870s Swedish women were allowed to take matriculation examinations for university entrance; by 1873, in fact, they could sit for all academic examinations except theological and the higher law degrees. Ten years later Ellen Fries was Sweden's first woman PhD. In 1884 women in Norway gained admittance to study in faculties and colleges. Progress in England followed a similar path. University College in London opened its doors to women as early as the 1830s. The opening of Queen's College in 1848 and Women's College at Bedford Square in 1849 contributed to the cause of better education. By 1878 a new charter for London University empowered it to extend all its degrees and prizes to women. The most prominent figure in the attempt to equalise opportunities in English high education was Emily Davies. Davies succeeded first in opening the local examinations in Oxford and Cambridge to girls. She then turned her attention to the universities themselves. But Oxbridge remained unmoved, so Davies founded her own college, in Hitchin, in Hertfordshire; this ultimately became part of Cambridge University as Girton College. In 1871 Cambridge began to admit women, and Oxford followed suit in 1879. Women were still not granted degrees, however, and this restraint was not removed until after World War I.

Despite a sometimes halting advance, women's education had become a reality within less than a century. Most feminist demands were realised by 1914, with expansion of facilities and upgrading of curricula at all levels. Although co-education at university level, as the only practical means of training girls was a concept ahead of its time, feminists pushed this cause as early as the 1890s.[30] Special efforts were made to improve physical education and sex education for women. Here too most early attempts failed, although in Sweden, through the efforts of Mrs Elise Ottesen-Jensen, founder of the National Union of Sex Education, courses on sex were made compulsory by 1933. The debate about quality and equality in physical training and sex education continues.

The classic gains of the feminists must be interpreted with care. While the spread and improvement of general education proved an essential aspect of women's modernisation, reforms at university level were more relevant to later generations than to women at the turn of the century. Even today attendance is restricted by economic and cultural factors. Education beyond the secondary level is still very much an elitist venture in Europe, even for the middle class; and while this is true for both sexes, women rarely make up more than a third of the university population. Yet continuing, and recurrent handicaps should not obscure the tremendous advance. By the end of the nineteenth century education had become a fact of life for most girls and their intellectual horizons were expanded.

But expanded in what direction. Few feminists urged better education as an alternative to marriage and domestic duties.[31] Even *La Femme Affranchie* claimed that its efforts to improve female education were designed to bring greater harmony into marriage.[32] Schools undeniably provided new social as well as cultural stimuli for women. Despite the prevalence of all-girl and all-boy schools, greater contact with the opposite sex was available as informal meetings after school and organised activities set up preliminaries to courtship among young couples. Here the change was most striking for the middle class who were taken out of the purely domestic sphere at an early age. Education could provide women with intellectual interests similar to those of their husbands after marriage, permitting the modern couple to share cultural and social activities more fully. For most women education did not change basic goals. It enhanced marriage prospects by making the woman more interesting and useful and also by expanding her social contacts. Whether this led directly to marriage or not, education served to increase a sense of independence, of individual resources, which was a vital aspect of women's new self-image.

The Right to Work?

Eventually education was related to better jobs for women. Hundreds of thousands of women were ready to pursue new economic interests by the later nineteenth century. We have seen that new work opportunities kept pace with supply for many women. Working-class girls particularly, now better educated, found jobs as sales or office clerks. Their primary education was fundamental to their ability to shift from domestic service and other traditional work.

Education had a more pronounced impact on middle-class women. For the first time in women's history respectable work outside the home was available for middle-class women from families of a certain economic and social standing. Expansion of the education sector opened up new jobs which in turn demanded new training as part of this process. Modern compulsory education dramatically heightened the demand for teachers. Women's role as nurturer of children, and their availability at low salaries, made them prime candidates to fill the new needs, and by the end of the nineteenth century women dominated the teaching field, which had never before been open to them save in limited instances as members of religious orders. By the 1860s in America, one out of every five women would spend some part of her life as a teacher.[33] Here was a way for middle-class women to find not only a better education but also economic independence, beyond the family unit, thereby enhancing their sense of individuality.

The advent of the woman teacher inevitably changed the process of education as well, for women extended to the schools the concepts of child care they had developed in the home. Teaching methods were dramatically altered under women's influence. Women gradually eroded the tradition of strict rote learning dosed with heavy corporal punishment to ensure discipline. With women at the front of the class a new philosophy of education was developed. The child as student was to develop his or her own personality through a system that stressed positive learning rather than negative reinforcement. It is true that educational theorists, mainly men, wrote up and supported this development, but it was female primary school teachers who carried it through, often initiating the change without significant contact with theory but simply through a natural adaptation of middle-class child-rearing concepts. The full implications of the unprecedented power women gained as teachers, as they largely monopolised the training of children into their adolescent years, is yet to be fully recognised.

Although key supervisory positions remained in the hands of men, women found their way into posts of educational inspectors and health supervisors — in France the nomination of a woman to the *Conseil Superieur de l'Instruction publique* was unprecedented — thereby making their presence and power all the more pervasive. And in teaching there was from the beginning a greater approximation of equality between the sexes with regard to such matters as conditions of work and benefits for a given job than in any other profession. Relatedly, organisation, traditionally very difficult for women, was more successful in the teaching corps than in virtually any other job category. As early as 1883, for example, women teachers began to organise themselves in Norway.

Nineteenth century society and government encouraged these new ventures by women in the public sector. By the 1880s in France every department was required to establish a training college to prepare women teachers. In Sweden the first women's teachers' college was established in 1860, while Norwegian women were admitted to teachers' colleges thirty years later.

Other 'respectable' jobs followed from the new education available to the middle class. Nursing was upgraded by professional training, and here again women as providers of family health care logically entered and quickly dominated the occupation.

While the gains were significant so was the battle. The changing nature of women's work aroused discussion as agitated as that over education itself, and the feminists found ample grist for their mills. Few people by the end of the nineteenth century contested the idea that even 'respectable' women should have the right to work, and this was a clear sign of women's new social influence. But work at what? Teaching, nursing, librarianship were all very well, but feminists uniformly supported the position that women had the right to pursue any economic endeavour they might choose. Emily Faithful[34] in England and Maria Martin in France campaigned vigorously to open up avenues of work traditionally reserved for males, ranging from printing for working-class girls — Faithful established her own publishing operation — to the liberal professions for the better educated. For some the right to work issue was the most important problem facing women, for inequalities were glaring. The *Journal des Femmes* urged this position: 'It is time for our feminist groups to concern themselves very actively with this practical side of feminist demands. It is not for a tiny elite but for all women that we demand the right to earn one's living by manual or intellectual work, with no limits to women's liberty and no legal inferiority *vis-à-vis* man.'[35] According to this view, other feminist causes such as the suffrage or overall equality before the law were judged useless if economic emancipation did not come first.[36] However, failure to come to an agreement on the priority of issues or the tactics to be used, diluted the feminist effort in many fields and provoked outright internal battles among various factions.

Nevertheless, a steady current of pressure for economic emancipation existed from the later nineteenth century onward. The most difficult battle was the struggle to open up the liberal professions, in both England and France.[37] Without degrees from the most prestigious universities such as the Sorbonne or Oxford it was extremely difficult for women to gain professional status. In any school, admittance had first to be won to the courses required for a professional degree. Women were discouraged, for example, from attending the biology and anatomy courses required for a medical degree. Through the efforts of pioneering individuals such as Elizabeth Blackwell, Elizabeth Garrett Anderson and Sophia Jex-Blake, the English medical profession was opened to women by the late nineteenth century.[38] Karolina Widerstrooms in 1889 became the first female doctor in Sweden. The legal profession proved a hard nut to crack, as we have seen. The Norwegian Association for Women's Rights, led by Hasbart E. Berner, worked to open up all professions for women, and in 1904 Norwegian women gained the right to practise law. Jeanne Chauvin campaigned successfully for the same right in France. As in education, by 1914 the basic legal rights were won in gaining admittance to the professions. Women could acquire education and admission to all professions (except the clergy in most major churches).

Freedom and ability for the professional women remained somewhat separate. Few women actually became doctors and lawyers. Their own cultural conditioning, which taught them to seek other goals, and discrimination from potential colleagues discouraged all but the very bold. Semi-professions, often regarded as providing temporary work experience until marriage, remained the most pervasive result of education and legal change. This was and still continues to be an obvious cause for feminists, but once formal legal barriers were removed the target proved somewhat elusive. Statutes are easier to attack than attitudes.

Women At the Front: Poltical Protesters

While feminists fought for educational, professional and legal rights they were increasingly attracted to the most striking public handicap for women, disfranchisement. The challenge here was obvious, although we have already noted that committed feminists as well as women in general were seriously divided over its importance. The French Revolution launched a long series of political struggles to extend suffrage — to men. For articulate women, and their male supporters, to take up the same cause was a logical result of a philosphy that held both sexes to be equal.

The principle of sexual equality, applied to voting rights, attracted a few high-spirited women during the French Revolution itself, even as most revolutionaries hesitated about granting the vote to the bulk of the male population. Mme Roland, Mme de Staël and Olympe de Georges petitioned both the Constituent Assembly and the Convention specifically on women's rights. Roland and de Georges found the guillotine the reward for their radicalism, while de Staël had to flee France during Napoleon's repressive regime. The women's cause gained momentum with each new French upheaval. Madam Herbinot de Mauchamps took up the cause in the 1830s, founding the journal *La Gazette des Femmes* (run exclusively by women) which demanded female suffrage.

The revolution of 1848 stirred up strong interest in women's rights, again primarily in France. We have already noted that socialists such as Victor Considérant took up the cause, demanding a vote for all adults of both sexes. Feminist clubs and newspapers were formed. Posters dramatically printed on yellow paper appealed for women's rights to vote and were widely distributed. Jeanne Deroin founded a suffragette paper, *La Politique des Femmes,* and on 23 March 1848 went to the *Hôtel de Ville* to ask for the vote. In 1849 she stood for election to parliament and won 14 votes. The strength the feminist cause gathered in 1848 can be seen in the repressive measures taken to quell it. In the late summer of '48 women's organisations were banned and women were prohibited from other political meetings.

Ironically women participated massively in the radical phases of the 1848 revolutions, and not only in France. They set up barricades in the Parisian June Days, they formed unions to petition or strike for better conditions in laundries or textile factories. Women teachers, although a small minority, were active in various revolutionary causes. The suffrage issue remained in the hands of those convinced of the philosophy of equality between the sexes and the primacy of political expression — and these were as often men as women. In 1851 Pierre Leroux introduced the first parliamentary bill to grant women voting rights in municipal elections, but without success. French feminists concerned with the continued ill fate of their cause turned increasingly to the small socialist movement for support. It was not until the establishment of the Third Republic in the 1870s that the issue of women's rights was again to come before the public. Mme Barbarousse claimed the right to vote on grounds that the basic laws of the Republic enfranchised all citizens; but in 1885 the courts decided that as far as the vote was concerned 'Frenchmen' was to be literally defined. All adult men could vote, but no women.

Here was inequity too great to be ignored. Hubertine Auclert, France's leading suffragette, organised the society *Suffrage des Femmes* and attained much notoriety through her quarrels with public officials and refusal to pay taxes. She failed to have a large following. Even devoted feminists regarded her tactics as too extreme. Her efforts mark the only time that French feminists resorted to direct action to attain the vote. A bill to grant women the vote was introduced in 1901 by the reformist socialist Viviani. The Chamber of Deputies accepted a similar measure – but in 1919, by a vote of 344 to 97, the conservative Senate blocked the proposal. In light of this resistance plus the achievement of female suffrage elsewhere, French feminist agitation between the wars was exceptionally orderly, though interest remained high. *La Femme Affranchie* continued to proclaim suffrage as essential for the liberated woman: 'The true woman will be she who can defend her interests and rights with the ballot, who having become a citizen will cease to be indifferent to social progress and instead will make herself the active creator of it'.[39] Groups such as the *Solidarité des Femmes* led by Dr Madaline Politier petitioned the socialist party directors, urging greater support for female suffrage on the grounds that the vote would educate and enlighten women who would then vote socialist. If World War I disrupted agitation, it was resumed immediately thereafter by groups such as the National Union for the Women's Vote, led by Mme de Witt-Schlumberger and Cécile Brunschwieg; the National Union for Woman's Suffrage, founded by Mme Le Vert-Chotard in 1920; and the French Union for Women's Suffrage which claimed to have 100,000 members by 1929.

Even at this late date, however, even with respectable leadership and tactics, the crusade for the vote went unheeded. Female suffrage was obtained only in 1944, and then only by a decree issued by General de Gaulle as leader of the post-war regime. Was the tardiness of the achievement of suffrage a sign that French women were unusually backward or oblivious to oppression or was it a symptom of an unusually weak feminist movement. It is clear that, by the turn of the century, the vote was not the prime cause of organised feminism in France. We have seen that the dominant issues were the attack on key provisions of the Napoleonic Code and on economic injustice; gains in these areas modify any impression of an impotent feminist movement and may have confirmed the view that the vote was not an essential priority. The desire to co-operate with the socialist party, which put a host of other issues first, and the related and very conscious reluctance to engage in the disruptive tactics of English feminists — for fear of antagonising male support — played an obvious role in French developments. Yet it is also clear that few people were prodding feminists or any other group to work for women's rights. We remain with the irony that the most revolutionary of countries, where political feminism was born, was virtually the last to grant women the vote. The informal power that women wielded within families, the persistence of a large, traditionalist agricultural sector which retarded modernisation in so many respects, and probably a less tolerant atmosphere among men, trained to view public affairs as their province, account for the delay in the achievement.[40]

Despite French origins the political struggle was taken up much more vigorously, and ultimately more successfully, in England. The first fully fledged statement of the case for female suffrage was penned in 1825 by William Thompson, in his *Appeal of One Half of the Human Race against the Pretensions of the Other Half.* During the political turmoil prior to the 1832 Reform Bill, concerned women, like many workers, believed that they would be included in suffrage extension. Like their French counterparts, they quickly learned that the battle would be long and bitter and that man did not include woman, for the great 'Reform Bill' specifically and exclusively enfranchised 'male persons'. This was actually the first statutory bar to women's vote in England and provided the focus of attack and source of resentment from which the suffrage movement grew. Even in August, 1832, Henry Hunt petitioned parliament for the right of unmarried women, who met appropriate property qualifications, to vote (married women were long held to be different because their vote would be under the husband's control); the petition was withdrawn, and the long struggle began.

The English situation was particularly ironic in that a woman ruled the country while women lacked the vote. The first Chartist efforts, in 1838, included a proposal for female suffrage but this was dropped in favour of males alone. In 1843 Mrs Hugo Reid, making her plea for equity in suffrage, wrote that

Of course, we do not mean that all women should possess a privilege which has as yet only been conferred on particular classes of men; we only mean to insist that the right is the same in both sexes. If there be any particular reason for the exclusion from the privilege of a certain class among men, we would allow it to have weight for excluding the corresponding class of women, but for these alone. We would insist that, with whatever speciousness certain classes among men have been excluded from this right, it does not follow as a matter of course — as often assumed — that ALL women ought to be excluded.

* The |Quakeress| Anne Knight drew up a petition for the political rights of women in 1847. The Seventh Earl of Carlisle petitioned the House of Lords in 1851, and shortly thereafter another pamphlet, written by 'Justitia' (Mrs Henry Davis Pochin) and entitled 'The Right of Women to Exercise the Elective Franchise' kept a modest fire burning.

A significant general statement in defence of women's political rights was put forward by John Stuart Mill in 1865 as part of his campaign platform for election to the House of Commons. From this point onward numerous articles and pamphlets appeared, while organisations were now formed to support the right of women to vote. In 1865 Mill and Henry Fawcett presented a petition signed by 1,498 women asking that suffrage be extended without distinction of sex. Lydia Becker, editor of *Women's Suffrage Journal,* one of the most ardent advocates of the vote for women, lobbied parliament until her death in 1890. A few gains were made, enough to keep the hope alive in the hearts of reformers like Becker but they were far from anything like equality. In 1869 women rate payers were given municipal franchises. A year later Jacob Bright introduced the first women's suffrage bill to get a second reading in parliament. This failed, but hopes were high that success was in sight. Even general women's magazines, rarely roused politically, were confident that the bill would be passed the next time it was brought to the House of Commons.[41] Yet bills introduced almost annually throughout the 1870s never got past the first reading. Many women began to attempt to work through established political parties for their cause; the Primrose League and the Women's Liberal Federation were formed by the early 1890s representing conservative and liberal women respectively.

Then in 1897 a women's suffrage bill again obtained a second reading, and again massive hopes were raised. A huge petition was organised and feminists centralised their efforts in the National Union of Women's Suffrage Societies, with Millicent Fawcett as president. The bill failed. Angry and disillusioned women sought drastic action as the only solution; parliament had to be shaken into realising that they were serious. The leader of this radical wing was Emmeline Pankhurst. Unable to work through the NUWSS which continued to believe in the course of peaceful political reform, Emmeline Pankhurst organised her own group, the Women's Social and Political Union, in 1903. The sole concern of this organisation was obtaining the vote, and the tactics deliberately departed from the plodding efforts of conventional feminists. Pankhurst believed that anything that roused the public's recognition of the woman's suffrage cause was to be employed. Hatred was better than indifference. Her first tactic was to show strength through numbers. Thus mass meetings at the doors of the Houses of Parliament and parades through London were organised. Men continued to be amused and unconvinced. Pressure tactics were then applied. Disruption was undertaken. Male political meetings were broken up. An escalation of violence occurred, as a nervous government arrested WSPU agitators. First to be tried were Emmeline Pankhurst's daughter Christabel and Annie Kenney. Both women refused to pay their fines and were imprisoned. The movement was now newsworthy. Frederick Pethick-Lawrence, the great financial patron of the WSPU, justified the attention-getting tactics, which ultimately involved burning mailboxes, planting bombs in public buildings and the famous blocking of tramlines; the demands justified any means, given the lack of adequate legal outlets, and earlier male campaigns for the vote, as in 1832, had been fought in similar fashion.

But for many, male and female alike, this was behaviour unbecoming to a woman. Feminists themselves diverted their energies into battles over tactics. The supporters of Fawcett's NUWSS were known as suffragists, while the smaller, radical group merited a neologism, 'suffragettes'. Even the WSPU split, only making the radicals more unrestrained. Women chained themselves to buildings; attacked government figures, such as Winston Churchill, personally, burned railway stations – in the first seven months of 1914 a total of 107 buildings were set afire – destroyed museum treasures, set bombs and threw acid on public roads. Each new outburst was met with harsher and harsher treatment by the government, which alone kept this unusual current alive. Feminist meetings and newspapers were repressed, longer jail sentences given out. When, in a notorious and widely-publicised incident, imprisoned feminists went on a hunger strike, they were force fed by means of a tube through the mouth or nostrils. Treatment of this sort horrified public opinion. The government followed, however, by passing the infamous Prisoners' Bill, known as the Cat and Mouse Act, whereby hunger strikers were released when their health was endangered and then rearrested when well.

The militant suffragettes made themselves repulsive to the majority of women's advocates. Anti-suffrage leagues were formed, with significant female participation. Mrs Humphrey Ward was an outspoken leader of women who believed that the crusade for the vote did women more harm than good. Yet the WSPU did serve to bring the 'woman question' to a position of top political priority, particularly between 1905 and 1912. After this the extremism of the radicals clearly outweighed their positive impact, as a public beleaguered by labour agitation, Irish unrest, and fear of war, sought calm. After World War I the women's cause was taken up in quieter fashion, and in 1919 the vote was won. For many feminists, this seemed to cap the whole struggle for equal participation in the broader society.

The unusual calm of French feminism in the matter of suffrage may well have delayed victory, but it is not clear why England alone developed such a militant minority. For suffrage was won elsewhere by women, often earlier than in England, and without great incident. The first country to grant women full political equality was Finland, in 1907. The Norwegian Association for Women's Rights, founded in the 1880s, urged the vote, winning widespread support only in the 1890s; in 1902 Norwegian women achieved the right to vote in municipal elections and in 1913 they received full suffrage. In Sweden societies promoting female suffrage were organised by 1903, under leaders such as Emila Bromee and Ann Margaret Holmgreen; suffrage was granted in 1919. German women won the vote in the constitution of the new Weimar republic, again in 1919, backed by the powerful socialist party. American women conducted a slightly more dramatic campaign than their Teutonic sisters but won the vote nationally in 1917 without resorting to extremism of the English sort. Historians continue to debate the causes of the peculiar English pattern. Were English women more determined than others? Was male resistance more unreasonable?[42] Perhaps radical feminism, in the absence of much revolutionary socialist rhetoric, served as an outlet for the tensions quite general in industrial societies, for men as well as women backed the cause. And obviously the reactions of a nervous government helped fuel the fire.

It is important to keep in mind that in England the militant suffragettes constituted a departure from mainstream feminism, itself directly representing only a minority of women. They operated almost exclusively in London. More important, despite the attention focused on the English case, suffrage was not the primary issue in the feminist movement overall, even in England. Other issues were seen as more crucial. In England, Emily Davies continued to insist that education was the key to the kingdom. In France many feminists focused on revisions in the Napoleonic Code. In both cases gains were made bfore the vote was won. Educational reforms in England were legally complete prior to 1919. Major revisions in the Napoleonic Code occurred in the 1930s in France.

When one places the suffrage campaign in proper perspective one can interpret the full impact of feminism itself much better. Some historians have delighted in pointing out that the world has revolved in pretty much the same direction since women got the vote, implying at least that feminist hopes were dashed. Women did not alter political patterns significantly, despite the hopes of some ardent feminists that they might restructure government in the direction of greater pacificism and social justice. In many countries they voted disproportionately for conservative parties. Under the stress of depression and political turmoil in Germany, more women than men voted for the Nazi party in the early 1930s. French women, after 1944, backed the usual spectrum of French political parties though with a slight preference for the new Christian Democratic Party (the MRP). And if women did not overturn conventional politics as voters they certainly did not, or were not allowed to, enter the political arena directly in any substantial number. There were and are few women politicians. Yet with women as constituents even male politicians had to keep some new concerns in mind. The coincidents of the development of new measures in health, education and welfare with the advent of female suffrage merits attention. Family welfare legislation, including grants to help support large families, had numerous sources, but among them the desire to appeal to women constituents. And, as with male workers earlier, it is clear that one has to allow some decades between winning the vote and clear expression of interests. By the 1960s the introduction of new political issues, such as liberalisation of abortion, suggests that dismissal of the significance of female suffrage has been premature, perhaps even naive.

Indeed many feminist gains must be interpreted in the light of what was ultimately made available or is still being opened up to women. Feminists were not typical women articulating some general female will on the public stage. They were often unrepresentative, they often dealt with issues, such as access to higher education, of extremely narrow concern. But their interests were in line with the more fundamental growing-up process of women in homes and on the job. We have seen that women gained recognition most easily when spokesmen, both male and female, translated into legislation continuing changes in women's position in society. Where the feminists forged ahead, as in aspects of their educational or suffrage campaign, they created opportunities for self-expression that were compatible with the self-image many ordinary women were developing silently. The impact of feminism leads us into consideration of the most recent decades of women's history. Here, gains previously won began to be acted upon by growing numbers of women. The concerns of ordinary women, particularly in the area of contraception and abortion, downplayed by the initial feminist wave, finally gained public attention. And feminism itself, rather a let down in the confusion of the two decades between the World Wars, when other issues held centre stage and when so many classic legal gains had been won, has proved to be a continuing process. The correspondence between women's overall growing-up in modern society and the articulate movements identified as feminist is not complete, but feminism broadly represents the tensions generated by women's changing roles.

Having said all this it is useful to raise the question which is a thorn in the side of ardent feminists: Why was there continual resentment or apathy on the part of the majority of women to the 'woman question?' On the surface there appeared to be a strong reluctance on the part of most women to identify themselves as feminists, even to give moral support to the feminist movement. It has been quickly and very naively asserted by some that this was a clear indication that most women were in fact quite content with their roles in society and did not want change. Some go further and conclude that feminism was the articulated frustration of a handful of women who could not find a man, i.e. feminists were either men haters or lesbians.

If one accepts the position that feminism is best understood as a cultural expression of a society in upheaval there are other factors to consider in explaining the apparent lack of visible support — the apparent lack of a feeling of sisterhood.

One explanation worthy of consideration is that not many women were going to adopt the label of feminism or even be identified with it remotely, given its bad press. The notoriety aroused by the *Saturday Review* is just one example. The hysteria produced by the foul treatment from all sides in the suffragette battle of the early years of the twentieth century in England also added to the tainting of feminism.

However this lack of support from the silent majority does not automatically mean that they were either anti-feminists or even content with their roles in society. As we have seen there were many individual issues that were supported; for example, a mother's right to her own children.

In any assessment of this phenomenon which is not uncommon to other radical movements (the same result was true of the early attempts to organise workers) it is vital to attempt to look at the situation through the woman's eyes. The details of the preceding discussions show that most women did not have the time or energy to devote to abstract arguments about their function in society. In the eyes of a middle-class woman, the problems of managing an efficient household, dealing with domestic servant problems, and managing the new role of mother were omnipresent. Likewise, for the working-class woman, concern for food and clothing to maintain an ever increasing family was all consuming. Thus what would appear to be apathy could simply be the lack of resources on the part of most women to become involved in anything beyond coping from day to day with domestic chores. As we will see by mid-twentieth century women will become more successful in dealing with the domestic problems that plagued their great grand-mothers. The innovations in household management and family planning, however, will raise new problems which we will also discuss shortly and will be closely related to the rebirth of feminism since World War II in Europe and America.

While this might go some way in explaining apathy on the part of the silent sisterhood it does not account for the overt gestures of hostility to feminists by women. It is not at all surprising to find hostility from working-class women. As we have seen, most proclaimed feminists were women from the upper and upper-middle classes. A working-class woman could legitimately suspect what a woman in a grand house with a retinue of servants knew about her problems. No doubt many questioned the importance of the vote in their everyday existence. Would it bring food on her table or stop her husband from abandoning her? The point is that sisterhood is limited greatly by class boundaries especially in the nineteenth century. In addition, as we have seen, the working class woman relied heavily upon tradition to adapt to the new forces found in the industrial urban centres. Maintaining traditions created a sense of security — to abandon or even to question these links with the familiar could leave the woman with nothing and be quite frightening.

For the middle-class woman the situation is not totally dissimilar. There was a growing problem in defining the role of the woman in society with the changing nature of the economic structure and the nature of the family unit, and it is highly probable that many women were encountering an approach/avoidance syndrome. Admittedly over-simplifying a complex psychological perception of mental stress, the problem is that many women might have found themselves confused. There are two ways to deal with a stressful situation — confront it or avoid it. Rejecting the label feminism was one way perhaps of saying there were no problems. In the nineteenth century perhaps most women chose to avoid a direct confrontation with the challenges of the feminists to their life style and decided instead silently (unconsciously) to restructure their role *vis-à-vis* work or the family. The fact remains, however, that every woman who adopted birth control measures was indeed accepting a new role for women in society whether she was consciously aware of it or not.

The conclusion here is more than the sum of the parts. Feminism is more than an aspect of nineteenth or twentieth century reformism. It is more than the female adjunct to the French Revolution. Feminism is the expression of the changing role of women in society. It is the guiding hand for the young girl child who is learning to walk in a world that is much larger than she and very strange, at times even hostile. Feminism is the attempt to give meaning to the X Factor in history. It attempts in all its aspects to deal with the perplexing question: 'What is a woman in modern society?' and in so doing questions the role of everyone, men and women, the young and the old.

Seeing feminism in this light, one realises that its success is not measured by a review of statutes, a survey of female employment statistics or education roll books. Its success lies in its ability to help women (and society as a whole) to deal with the culture shock that urbanisation and industrialisation have produced in the last two hundred years of Western development. As tradition gives way, the link between feminism and women's life cycle becomes most direct as we shall see in the next section.

Notes

1. For a discussion of the role of socialism and feminism for France see
   Theodore Zeldin, *France 1848-1945* (Oxford, 1973); for Germany see Ulrike
   Bussemer, *Die bürgerliche Frauenbewegung und das Vereinsrecht in*

Deutschland von der Mitte des 19. Jahrhunderts bis 1908 (unpublished thesis, University of Berlin, April 1974); Jutta Menschik, *Gleichberechtigung oder Emanzipation?* (Frankfurt am Main, 1971), pp.57-80.

2. *La Femme Affranchie, Organe du Féminisme Ouvrier Socialiste et Libre,* No.2, Sept. 1904; similar sentiments were found in the writings of the French Feminists. Lydia Martial, *La Femme et La Liberté* (Paris,1902), p.29.

3. *English Woman's Domestic Magazine,* vol. VIII (June 1870), p.377.

4. *La Femme au Foyer à la Ville et la Campagne,* no.91 (June 1914), p.183.

5. *English Woman's Domestic Magazine,* vol. XII (June 1872), p.371.

6. E. Lynn Linton, *The Girl of the Period, and other Social Essays,* vols. 1 and 2 (London, 1883).

7. See Helge Prosse's survey of modern women in West Germany in R. Patai, ed., *Women in the Modern World* (New York, 1967); for a similar statement but later see Dr Ingrid Sonnerhorn, *Women's Careers: Experience from East and West Germany* (London, 1970).

8. Michelle Perrot, *Les Ouvriers en Grève en France 1871-1890,* vol.II (Mouton 1974), pp.318-29.

9. *La Femme Affranchie,* no.1 (1904).

10. Caroline Norton, *A Plain Letter to the Lord Chancellor on the Infant Custody Bill* (1839): *English Laws for Women in the Nineteenth Century* (1854); *A Letter to the Queen on Lord Chancellor Cranworth's Marriage and Divorce Bill* (1855). See also R.H. Graveson, and F.R. Crane, eds., *A Century of Family Law, 1857-1957* (1957).

11. Frances E. Hogian, *The Position of the Mother in the Family in its Legal and Scientific Aspects* (Manchester, 1884).

12. *La Femme Affranchie,* no.1 (August 1904).

13. Violet Stuart Wortley, 'Feminism in England and France', in *The National Review,* no.51 (Mar-Aug. 1905), pp.793-4.

14. Crane Brinton, *French Revolutionary Legislation on Illegitimacy 1789-1804* (1936).

15. *La Femme Affranchie,* no.1 (Aug. 1904).

16. Betty Shield, *Women in Norway, Their Position in Family Life, Employment and Society* (Oslo, 1970), p.14.

17. J.E. Butler, *Personal Reminiscences of a Great Crusader* (London, 1896); the writings of Josephine Butler can be found in the Josephine Butler Collection, Fawcett Library, London.

18. Avril St Croix, *L'Esclave Blanche* (Paris, 1913).

19. Christabel Pankhurst, *The Great Scourge* (New York, 1969), p.41.

20. For a discussion of the legal battle waged see Peter Fryer, *The Birth Controllers* (London, 1965); Shirley Green, *The Curious History of Contraception* (London, 1971); Norman E. Himes, *Medical History of Contraception* (New York, 1936); Clive Wood and Beryl Suitters, *The Fight for Acceptance; A History of Contraception* (Aylesburg, 1970).

21. *La Femme Affrachie,* no.1 (Aug. 1904; April, 1905).

22. Barbara Leigh Smith Bodichon, *A Brief Summary in Plain Language of the Most Important Laws Concerning Women* (1854).

23. *Englishwoman's Domestic Magazine* (Sept. 1870), p.188.

24. For a discussion of the French woman's legal struggles see Frances I. Clark, *The Reaction of Women in Contemporary France* (Paris, 1937); René Viviani *et al., Cinquante Ans de Féminisme 1820-1920* (Paris, 1921); Léon Richer, *Le Code des femmes* (Paris, 1883); Charles Lefebre, *La Famille en France dans le Droit et dans les Moeurs* (Paris, 1920).

25. A.H. Halsey, *Trends in British Society Since 1900* (London, 1972); O.R. McGregor, *Divorce in England, A Centenary Study* (London, 1957);

R.H. Grareson, *A Century of Family Law.*
26. Zeldin, *France,* p.358. For a discussion of the necessity for reform in French divorce laws see Maurice Dupont, *Capacité de la Femme Mariée* (Paris, 1874); Dr Arsène Drouct and Emile Renier, *De la Nécessité Civile, Morale et Politique de Rétablissement du Divorce dans le Code Civil Français* (Paris, 1871); *André Mollier,* La Question du Divorce (unpublished thesis, Besançon, 1930); G. LeBras and M. Ancel, *Divorce I Separation de corps dans le monde contemporain* (Paris, 1952)
27. Edward H. Clarke, *Sex in Education* (1873).
28. Esmée Charrier, *L'Evolution intellectuelle féminine* (1931).
29. *La Femme Affranchie,* no.1 (August 1904).
30. *Le Journal des Femmes Organe du Mouvement Feministe,* no.8 (June 1892).
31. *Englishwoman's Domestic Magazine,* no.17 (March 1873).
32. *La Femme Affranchie* (January 1905).
33. Maris A. Vinovkis and Richard M. Bernard, 'The Female School Teacher in Ante-Bellum Massachusetts', *Journal of Social History,* Vol.10, no.3, (Spring, 1977)
34. Emily Faithful, *Woman's Work* (London, 1871)
35. *Le Journal des femmes* no.7 (Nov.1898).
36. *La Femme Affranchie,* no.2 (September 1902).
37. *Le Journal des femmes,* no.1 (December 1891).
38. Sophia Jex-Blake, *Medical Women* (London, 1886); Elizabeth Blackwell, *Pioneer Work in Opening the Medical Profession to Women* (London, 1972); Margaret Todd, *Life of Sophia Jex-Blake* (London, 1918).
39. *La Femme Affranchie,* no.2 (September, 1904).
40. A collection of leading French feminists' writing is located in the Bibliothèque Marguerite Durand in the Mairie of the 5th *arrondissement* of Paris.
41. 'During the last session of Parliament several measures have been discussed which prove the great advance that public opinion has made. . .First in order was the Women's Disabilities Bill, which will in all probability be passed next time it is brought before the House. . .' *Englishwoman's Domestic Magazine (Sept. 1870), p.188; no.12 (Feb. 1872), p.95.*
42. For a discussion of the peculiar nature of the Englishwomen's women's suffrage campaign see George Dangerfield *The Strange Death of Liberal England 1910-1914* (New York, 1935), pp.139-213; 364-88; William O'Neill, *The Woman Movement* (New York, 1969), pp. 81-8; Trevor Lloyd, *Suffragettes International* (New York, 1971), p.5; Andrew Rosen, *Rise Up, Women!* (London, 1975).

5 THE COMING OF AGE: WOMEN IN MODERN SOCIETY

Logically, a conclusion to a study of the development of women in modern society should integrate and relate the contemporary woman's experience to the historical framework. The contemporary woman's experience is as critical to the development of the modern woman's as was the nineteenth century woman's experience. However the task is, ironically, more difficult. Historical accounts of women often end with the chapter on the battle for suffrage, the assumption being that the gaining of the vote marked the coming of age of womankind. Anything thereafter was merely an appendix to the basic story. The contemporary woman's situation is far more complex and needs to be dealt with more seriously. While it is closely tied to developments in the nineteenth and early twentieth century, the woman today confronts a unique situation. For every account which proclaims that women have arrived there is another voice denying it. The rhetoric surrounding the women's issue today is as politicised, is not more so, than ever before in her history. Are we in the midst of a female revolution or close upon it? What is so distinctive about the contemporary woman's position from that of her great grandmother's, her grandmother's, even her mother's?

Before we venture forth we need to note a shift in emphasis in geographical locus in the story. The American woman today holds the place that the English woman held throughout the nineteenth and first half of the twentieth centuries. That is to say that the American woman is setting the pace and style of change. Having said this it is equally true that within the comparative framework similarities are far more striking than differences. As we will see the crucial issues confronting the contemporary woman in England and France will be quite familiar.

The resurgence of feminism on the continent, and especially in America, can again be seen as an expression of women in a critical stage of flux. Important problems have been solved, as we noted, but new problems have arisen and need to be sorted out and decisions made. Exactly what these decisions will entail is not known. Before we can begin to look into the future we need to examine the present as it was influenced by the past.

Women today have fully reaped the rewards of the changes in behaviour and social environment painfully achieved by their nineteenth century forbears. A pregnant mother no longer fears the perils of childbirth for she is confident that her pains will be treated safely and easily and she need not worry for her own or her baby's life. Maternal and infant mortality rates have dropped to insignificant levels in Western Europe and America. In countries like France, where there was a lag, patterns since the 1950s have shown a dramatic increase in the use of hospitals and doctors, and a reduction of mortality levels to norms common to other industrialised countries. Earlier battles for new educational opportunities have at least borne partial fruit. A host of traditional problems have thus found some response. However the twentieth-century woman's sense of restriction *vis-à-vis* her nineteenth century sister seems just as intense. As already suggested part of the explanation is that in coming to terms with traditional worries, women inevitably created new concerns that were more subtle and therefore more difficult to manage. To illustrate the phenomenon: the life cycle of women continues to change as family planning becomes more and more scientific. The progress in this field colours women's attitudes in youth and early adulthood and creates problems of self-image for them in their later years. Women are only beginning to understand the full dimensions of the path set out before them.

At the risk of labouring an analogy between human development and woman's history: women today are in what may be seen as the stage of adolescence. The adolescent struggles with the desire to direct and the needs to be directed. While women today are demanding their full rights of adulthood, to be free and independent agents, they are at the same time still reluctant to let go of the more familiar role — be it dutiful daughter or dutiful wife. External barriers to women's self-fulfilment have been under siege for over a century. In the nineteenth century it was proclaimed that when women attained their full political, legal, economic and educational rights they would have arrived. We have made important advancements towards most of the goals thought necessary in the nineteenth century. Yet the voice of female discontent is louder than ever. Is this because the battle goes on too long and women today grow more and more impatient with piecemeal reforms? Or is there something deeper within themselves that they find is cause for more anxiety and frustration?

In order to understand the subtleties involved in the woman's question as it stands today we should look first at those changes in recent decades that have shaped her life.

In confronting the contemporary woman's situation we must acknowledge changes in two areas not discussed earlier: fashion and leisure. One hears much today about the new look for women and the emergence of the leisured lady. Images of women in neat and brief tennis outfits, bikinis, even monokinis appear as sure signs of the new freedoms for women. While fashion and the rise of leisure were of growing interest from the 1870s, these phenomena now play a more substantial role in the life of the average woman than ever before in her history. In many respects it is quite correct to speak of a revolution in women's fashion and leisure life. Technological advances since World War II are basic to the startling advances in fashion and leisure activities. Innovations in chemicals and textiles, for example, have revolutionised the clothing industry. Fabrics are now cheaper, lighter, more revealing, and easier to care for than ever before. The latter feature of significance for it presumably has allowed more time for women to follow their new pursuits.

Now more and more women are caught up in the so-called fashion mainstream than was possible even in the nineteenth century. The development is most interesting. At one end it involves Parisian designers' dresses being quickly copied and mass produced in the sweatshops of Manhattan and Hong Kong. At the other end the mass market has a real influence on fashion design — witness the popularity of the mini-skirt and trousers. Looking at the evolution in women's clothing since the early nineteenth century, fads aside, one sees a definite trend toward the very aims that dictated change in women's family and work roles: greater self-expression involving personal comfort and mobility. Multi-layered petticoats, crinolines, whale-bone corsets, and chemises have given way to the more practical, the healthier, the comfortable — be it mini-skirts or maxi-skirts, shorts or trousers. Changes in fashion, like feminism, were an attempt on the part of the female to reshape her life-style, and these changes have been met with severe criticism. Since the nineteenth century there has been a running debate over the innovations in women's attire.

The controversy continues into the present and has taken on a new dimension. Have women become too fashion conscious, too absorbed with the superficialities of personal appearance? Strong criticism, from feminists circles particularly, follows from thinking that this is indeed the case today. Women have been duped once again by blatant sexism to worry more over the condition of their hair than the condition of their jobs or marriages. Many times women, for the sole sake of appearance, endanger their physical well-being through drastic diets, harmful drugs, even undergoing injections of foreign substances to fill out the curves fashion charts. The obsession with 'fashion' has kept women dancing to the same old tune of a sexist society and prevented them from tackling the 'real' issues. While one can sympathise with those who demand an end to the overt sexism displayed in the fashion market and support those who work to redirect women's concerns it is important also to keep in mind the needs of the woman herself. Every time a woman buys a new outfit, or a new lipstick or changes her hair style, she is in essence putting herself first. Women, as we have seen, have traditionally put others, be it their husbands, children, parents, or their brothers before them. These efforts however small are steps towards maximising their own self-interest.

Beyond this one must remember that the major impetus for fashion change arose from women's desire to expand their range of activities thus requiring adaptable clothes. Today a significant proportion of women spend increasing time in leisure activities primarily outside the domestic circle. The new interest in sports is perhaps the most obvious example. The female athlete, virtually unknown in the nineteenth century, gains increasing recognition. Even more important are the millions of women who pursue amateur recreational sports on a regular basis ranging from golf, tennis, swimming, bicycling to jogging. The development of the physically active woman is also a clear sign that women are redefining their roles. These activities are pursued for their own pleasure. They also indicate a more healthy individual. While the importance of exercise for good health was preached vigorously in the nineteenth century only a minority of women could indulge in it. The majority found their lives too restricted by repeated pregnancies and household chores. The smaller families of today have allowed more time for women to pursue leisure activities in their younger years than was possible a hundred years ago.

However all is not frills and fun for the contemporary woman. While one can point to the wide range of advantages to be reaped from the increase in free time it is also true that many women have not adapted well to this new development. One of the classic explanations of late nineteenth century feminism was the idleness of the middle-class woman. As a monocausal explanation this approach is severely limited, as indicated earlier. Nevertheless, the problem of the woman who feels increasingly useless arose in the late nineteenth century, and today it is a common experience. Some see in the new leisure forms pale substitutes for a real function in life.

There is some controversy even today as to how widespread this particular problem of the bored housewife is. Studies of women's work in the home indicate that women today spend most of their waking day performing traditional domestic chores.[1] [Despite the proliferation of labour-saving devices from automatic garbage disposers to electric can openers, the old housewife's lament — there are never enough hours in a day — continues to be heard.] Women today have considerably quickened the pace first set by nineteenth century housewives. What is considered a well-managed household is being upgraded constantly; for example, the levels of cleanliness have become absurd. In the nineteenth century, cleanliness ensured good health and a comfortable living. Today it is an obsession. Washing machines and driers have reduced the burden of laundering to such a point that women now do several washes daily. Houses no longer have to look clean — they have to smell clean. The amount of time and energy a woman puts into household chores continues to outstrip any savings from technology. Why? Perhaps in reaction to a growing sense of dysfunction, women today try to maintain their traditional means of identification by continuing to add new work for themselves. The harder they work the more important they feel. The function of the woman as household manager remains primary, and women carefully maintain the importance of the function as part of self-definition.

The more serious problem lies with the silent sisterhood who do not get involved in any activities. The lonely suburban housewife who is left to think about her home all day as husband and children go off in the morning not to return till late afternoon is waiting for help. A recent study shows a significant increase in depression among women.[2] A study of the role of alcohol and drugs in the lives of these women seems imperative. How to put meaning back into a life that has been reduced to a domestic function is as important as ensuring equal opportunities in women's work.

Wife and Mother: A New Balance

The decline of the family as a social institution is often seen as one of the main trends in present-day society but, although we can note changes in women's family roles and expectations, we see little sign of women wishing to take themselves out of a familial role.

The basic statistic is the rate of marriage. In England in 1901 the percentage of women married by the age of thirty-four was 71.8; in 1966 it was 89.2 per cent.[3] In 1960 over 90 per cent of all German women aged fifty were or had been married. The twentieth century maintains the trend of ever-rising marriage rates which, in the nineteenth century, so clearly marked a modernising pattern. Institutions that preserved adult women in the unmarried state, such as religious convents, have faced a steadily declining recruitment base, again a trend that began in the nineteenth century.

Several changes in marriage patterns account for the increased rate. Most obviously middle-class women have increasingly imitated working-class patterns, by reducing their age at marriage. The class gap in this respect has diminished though working-class girls have continued to push their marriage age lower. Teenage marriages, virtually unknown in nineteenth century Europe, have risen substantially since World War II. In England only 17.1 per cent of all girls were married by the age of nineteen in 1931; by 1968 the rate had soared to 67 per cent. Here was a trend that clearly transcended class, for when a majority of the population participated virtually every large social group was involved. The goal was not new, but its realisation came increasingly sooner and with increasing frequency.

In contemporary society most young women marry shortly after leaving school. Reduced marriage age is here combined with laws which increase the school-leaving age. In England in 1950 the percentage of girls remaining in school until the age of sixteen was only 11.7 per cent; fifteen years later, the rate had more than doubled, to 28.3 per cent.[4] Whereas in the nineteenth century a girl would spend from ten to fifteen years working or at home under mother's eye, contemporary young women go almost directly from schoolroom to their own new household. If they work at all before marriage, their jobs last but a few years.

The trend could not continue without creating new problems. Even more than in the case of the nineteenth century working-class girl, who first set the early marriage pattern, one must ask if the teenaged wife is prepared to cope with the responsibilities and burdens of domestic bliss, bearing in mind that she has no experience in the outside world, save for schooling. There may certainly be a correlation between the rush into marriage and the growing sense of malaise among wives in their twenties, some of whom feel isolated and unfulfilled.

The problems are complicated further for the new pattern does not end with early marriage; it includes early motherhood, another sign that traditional roles are taken very seriously. In England the fertility rate among women aged fifteen to nineteen increased by 88 per cent between 1954 and 1964, while among women of twenty to twenty-four it rose 33 per cent. In France a similar trend was clear, as fertility rates for girls under twenty increased by 56 per cent from 1911 to 1962, and for the age bracket twenty to twenty-four the increase was 61 per cent.[5] Fertility rates rose also for women in their later twenties, in what was a population boom period after World War II, but, particularly in France, by no means as dramatically as in the younger age groups. And for women over thirty there was an absolute decline in births — by 214 per cent in France.

A desire for motherhood has thus become firmly intertwined with family planning, two nineteenth century developments that in combination produced novel behaviour. The contemporary woman obviously plans a smaller family than her nineteenth century counterpart. The norm seems to be between one and two children. Exact family size proves to be variable in contemporary society. In the interwar period, with intense economic pressures and widespread social disruption, the birth rate plummeted, and many families were content with a single child. After War War II (even during the war in England), the birth rate rose again. Greater prosperity, extension of social welfare including direct payment to help support each child born, better hospital care and more convenient baby care products, ranging from prepared baby food to disposable nappies (diapers) — all can be associated with the 'baby boom' that lasted well beyond a normal post-war recovery. Compared, however, to population growth rates of the later eighteenth and the nineteenth centuries, this was a relatively quiet bang rather than a boom. The average family remains small, the number of births far below any traditional norm; family planning continues be practised. By the later 1960s birth rates dropped once again, confirming the conclusion that contemporary families may oscillate in size but within a context in which two factors remain constant: the desire not to be overburdened with excessive numbers of children and the willingness to use artificial contraceptive means to determine the desired birth rate.

Class gaps have narrowed in this regard also. The post-war 'baby boom' revealed new interest among segments of the middle class, particularly professional people, for slightly larger families — two children instead of one — although the white-collar group, always cautious, continues to record the lowest birth rate (1.2 children per family in England in 1961). Workers (both in town and country) have reduced their birth rate, though polls suggest that they still list number of children as a more important criterion of family success than is true of the middle class.

What is particularly new about contemporary motherhood,

is the life cycle commonly involved. Combining early marriage with birth control allows most women to have their children at a young age, and increasingly this is deliberately planned. By 1960 in Britain 58 per cent of all births were occurring within the first two years of marriage. This of course is not historically unprecedented, except insofar as marriage itself now occurs at an earlier age; most married women gave birth within the first year or so of wedlock. But now, if a second or even third child is desired, it is commonly produced in quick succession after the first. The most physical aspect of motherhood, the process of giving birth, is confined to a few years of the average woman's life, in dramatic contrast to all historical precedent.

For the student of contemporary women, the result of these patterns raises important questions. The first is familiar enough: why has the small family become the norm? The means involved no longer raise dispute: improvements in contraceptives make family planning a relatively sure thing. Post-war introduction of birth control pills and the intrauterine device (IUD) provided women with virtually full control over the number and spacing of births. Medical warnings against the pill have not reduced its use, for the dangers cited – primarily those related to cardiovascular disorders – have so far proved too remote to divert women from a major goal – control of their bodies – their lives – in regulating the pregnancies they are willing to experience. Should preliminary birth control methods fail, women can seek abortions. It would be statistically awkward to say that the abortion rate has increased, from late nineteenth century levels. The increase in the rate of legitimate abortions among both the middle and working classes indicates that abortion today is regarded as preferable to an unwanted child. Two overriding and not necessarily incompatible explanations emerge. Women eagerly have children early in their marriage as part of their expected role but then tire of the process and so stop; the responsibilities are awesome and the rewards less than anticipated at first. Or women now see motherhood, as they once viewed work in the nineteenth century, as a stage of life, not a life-time commitment. They rationally decide that they will be active, involved mothers from, say, the ages of nineteen to thirty-nine, and then new vistas will be open.

While the life-cycle of motherhood has changed, the concept of mothering preserves its continuity with nineteenth century patterns, thereby creating a host of new problems. Certain goals have become easier to achieve but standards are constantly being raised. A good mother obviously attends to her child's physical health and material needs. She has increasing assistance as pediatric medicine, the new specialisation in the early twentieth century, gains growing sophistication. The new, specially-prepared foods and clothing make aspirations for a healthy, attractive child easier to fulfil. Guidance from the extended family remains important and may indeed have increased even into the middle class. Working-class women continue to depend heavily on regular visits to their mothers, who among other things provide advice about what to do for children's problems.[6] Middle-class women, more mobile geographically, can use telephone and automobile to gain access to similar advice. Between science and other forms of guidance a number of haunting worries have been laid to rest. Mothers need not be seriously concerned that their babies will die at birth. Medical advance has brought a host of diseases that once caused damage to older children under control.

Concern remains but it has changed from worry over the physical to the psychic aspects of the child's development. As with housework there has been a tendency to maintain a constant anxiety level, simply substituting a new worry for a traditional one. The mother, particularly the middle-class mother, continues to assume the full burden for the well-being of her children. Today's mama has quickened the pace set in the nineteenth century. Indulgence increases, as middle-class mothers adhere to the philosophy new to the nineteenth century but basic to all child-rearing manuals today that each child has its own personality which needs individual care. Disciplinary necessities of the early twentieth century, such as firm, early toilet training (within the first 18 months) are relaxed in favour of a more gradual approach (20 to 24 months). The belief is that this is the more 'natural' process and therefore less likely to damage an infant's personality development. Here, however, class lines remain important. Working-class families, in crowded apartments with less likely access to laundry facilities, toilet train more rigorously. They are also more likely to employ corporal punishment. But even the working class attempts greater emotional rapport with its children.

A good illustration of how a woman's levels of anxiety have increased rather than decreased concerns the heightened interest of mothering and adolescents. In the nineteenth century the primary focus of worry for the mother centred on the infant and the young child. Most of the material directed at mothers dealt almost exclusively with the first six years of life (when childhood ended in the traditional view). Little was said on how to deal with the problems of children who lived beyond the early years; what types of problems one could expect were not even discussed. Nevertheless childhood was extending well beyond the age of six or seven into the teenage years. In the last quarter of the nineteenth century adolescent problems were beginning to be perceived as unique and requiring careful attention.[7]

Only recently have historians begun to grasp the impact of the 'youth cult' which emerged in the early years of the twentieth century and has been growing in the second half of the century.[8] The number of periodicals and manuals directed specifically to these most difficult years together with the new development in adolescent medicine is comparable to the developments of early infant care that we saw in the nineteenth century.

How has this new shift in emphasis or added concern affected women? How much has the extension of childrearing from between six and eleven years to eighteen to twenty-one years negated or at least seriously inhibited women's efforts to define themselves as individuals? Mothers, especially working-class mothers, are now subject to coping with the trauma of adolescence at much closer quarters and for a longer period (given the continual decline in the age of puberty and the extension of the legal definition of minor). With the continuing rise of education the departure of children from the mother is delayed. Adolescent problems are by no means novel or unique to post-World War II society. What is new is the heightened concern and its repercussions for the woman and the child.

It is not uncommon to hear a mother bemoaning the fact that her baby has grown into a teenager. For some mothers, caring for younger children, even though it requires greater physical exertion, is an easier task than trying to deal with the 'monster' years, the years of daily confrontation on the psychological battlefield. The problems that ensued were inevitable given the trends in childrearing developed in the nineteenth century and perhaps given the refusal of some women to break with tradition. The mystique developed in the nineteenth century was the love bond between mother and child, which could have led to difficulties over 'cutting the apron strings'. Yet while a mother is encouraged to prolong the nurturing of her child, the child is being encouraged to exert his or her individuality, to strive for independence from mama – both sensible courses of action in themselves but potential sources of conflict.

Tensions between first and second generations are not new. Historians have described the plight of the son who waits upon the good will of his father for his birthright.[9] The present situation is different in that what is needed from the parents is not so much material support as the relinquishing of their emotional bond; in this case the tie is usually with the mother. It is more difficult to deal with anger and frustration in an emotional relationship than in a financial one. How much guilt do mothers and children suffer today as a result of tensions which were historically very common and psychologically quite natural?

The mother who insists on doing everything for her child (in some cases beyond adolescent years) because she believes it is her duty is interfering with an age-old process. This is more critical for the female child than it is for the young male. The increased attention to the adolescent child may be directly related to the fact that most women do not have a young child to attend to because of the changes in the family planning patterns. Without a suitable function to replace that of mother, many women may simply have extended the role of mother beyond childhood into adolescent years in order to maintain their position of power.

The trend in the decreasing age of motherhood has caused concern recently. There are some who believe that the decline in the age of mothers has gone too far. The argument is that today's young mama does not possess the maturity, the knowledge, the sense of self-sacrifice necessary to fulfil the heavy responsibilities of motherhood. It is held that the young woman straight out of school, be it secondary or college, is not equipped with the emotional stamina to meet the demands of twentieth century mothering. Older mothers, women in their late twenties are more experienced with life and therefore better able to guide young lives. The argument is calling for a return to more traditional family patterns. Is this merely another example of the older generation's traditional carping at the ways of the younger generation? Or is there substance to the argument?

Until we have more data it is difficult to come to any real conclusions, but it would seem that the burdens of motherhood are proving too much for the younger woman. Increase in divorce rates among the very young is a good indication of this. Some young mothers themselves have expressed concern. There seems to be a small but significant number of younger women who are deeply concerned about what they feel is their lack of maternal feeling. How widespread this sentiment is, is not at all clear. At present it appears to be primarily an American middle-class dilemma. Other developments such as the continuing decrease in the number of children and the revolutionary increase in the number of young mothers working outside the home suggests also that perhaps this is a problem worthy of serious investigation.

For the historian of women two possibilities need to be examined in assessing the situation of the young mother today. First, the younger age of motherhood has no doubt contributed to a lack of self-confidence on the part of the woman. The continuing interest in advice on childrearing, while an expression of a desire to do best by the child, is also an indication that many are finding it a difficult task. The modern pattern of family planning does not allow a young girl the same kind of first-hand experience as the nineteenth-century girl. Since the one to two children are born today within a few years of each other it does not allow older children to see their mothers mothering, nor are they exposed as much to the chores which nineteenth century daughters had to do.

Second, the influence of other alternatives to motherhood (be it increased leisure activities or work) as the primary means of self-definition for women today must also be weighed. Is it possible that the underlying factor influencing smaller and smaller families is a growing sense of disillusionment on the part of women themselves with the role of mother? The concept of motherhood has become so deeply engrained in our culture that it is assumed that it has always been there – that it is indeed instinctive. But we have seen, it was a concept that took hold only in the nineteenth century. Even then women had to work hard to learn to cope with it. No doubt some women in the nineteenth century also found it difficult and unrewarding. But the sentiment was not articulated. Only very recently have we heard that women are finding mothering a less fulfilling role than it was for their mothers and grandmothers. For some, an extreme, it is viewed as the bondage of womanhood.

There is yet another factor even more difficult to assess. How much has the need to express and fulfil individual needs conflicted with the image of the self-sacrificing mother? It would be a grave injustice to minimise the crisis which these conflicts can produce. Efforts are being made by women themselves to resolve the inherent conflicts in the new situation. As we will discuss more fully, women are turning to work roles in combination with their family roles. There has also been a slight increase in importance of the father's role which alleviates some of the woman's responsibilities. Whether these are the best solutions, and whether the problems are superficial or fundamental also remains to be seen.

Added to the complexities of the modern woman's experience is the state of flux in the concept of wife. The emotional satisfaction sought from relationships with husbands has never been greater. As a result the sense of frustration is also on the increase. As one feminist sociologist notes, 'Never has marriage been taken more seriously, never have young couples looked forward so much to their union'.[10] The high rates of marriage and the earlier age at marriage which are stabilising indicate this clearly. The nineteenth-century commitment to a concomitant relationship between two equal and loving individuals has been deepened. The commitment to sharing shows in the new roles taken by husbands in domestic matters. It shows also in the growing emphasis on mutual sexual fulfilment primarily from the female's point of view. It shows in prosaic but vital matters such as shared decision-making about household economics. It shows in the expansion of leisure activities pursued by the family unit. A survey of British workers a few years ago captured the new sense of commitment denouncing the 'old-fashioned idea of being a master' in favour of 'we share responsibility' or 'full partners: we must agree in everything', or still more graphically, 'One leg of trousers for each of us'. Working-class husbands spend more time with their wives than ever before in history. 'When we are married all the company we need is at home'. 'We are quite happy at home, just the two of us'. 'We are complete in ourselves.'[11] It is even possible that with respect to time spent at home working-class husbands have outdistanced many middle-class men in dealing directly with domestic matters.

However the twentieth-century marriage does not promise a rose garden and too few realise this today. While British workers express satisfaction about their relationships with their wives and general contentment with their domestic life it is not at all clear that their wives feel the same sense of contentment. The modern marriage is significantly different from even the nineteenth-century one. Demographic realities have made it a much more complicated deal. Expectations nourished and encouraged by youthful romances can easily be deceived. New expectations, early marriage age plus the declining rates of overall mortality add up to the fact that today the potential life-cycle of a marriage is much longer. A married couple today can reasonably expect to spend virtually 50 years together as against the 35 years of the nineteenth century and the 25 in pre-industrial society. The consequences of this phenomenon have not been fully anticipated.

Marriage in traditional society was viewed as a life-long undertaking. But, as we noted, outside forces, primarily death, made this commitment relatively short. A life-time commitment for marriage was necessary in pre-modern society given the late age at marriage, the high levels of infant and maternal mortality and the low level of fecundity.

It took a life time to establish a family. Today a life-time commitment means much more and many are finding it difficult to adapt the traditional commitment to a modern life-style which is based and nurtured on change.

The most significant new feature in marriage today is divorce. Divorce is part and parcel of the very force that brought about an increase in the numbers of marriages and the decline in the age of marriages – the surge of sentiment. Since the late 1960s divorce has become a fact of life for more and more women. In the early 1960s ten per cent of all marriages in England and France ended in divorce. Within a few years by 1965 the rate was up to 16 per cent in England. The rate in both countries continues to rise. The most dramatic divorce statistics concern America where current reports show that more than 50 per cent of all marriages end in divorce. The rise in the divorce rate plus the decline in marriage rates in the mid-1970s has stirred a sense of alarm. Two questions loom large: Why the increase in divorce rates and how can we put an end to it?

Without hard data from substantial studies on the exact nature of divorce and family patterns it is difficult to answer either question. For the woman historian this phenomenon is most critical given the fact that most women are still confronting a culture which defines their existence primarily through marriage.

The little information available to us at this time points to the possibility that as modern couples strive to reach their ideas of marital harmony, they are also more ready to abandon it when reality is not what they expected. Everywhere, the most striking divorce increase occurs in the young married groups. In France between 1911 and 1962 divorce rates among married couples between the ages of 20 and 24 increased over five-fold. In England the percentage of divorces occuring among couples married less than five years was nine per cent in 1931, but 16 per cent in 1968.[12] Whatever the age bracket it is important to note that it is the woman who most commonly files for and is most commonly granted divorce. Whether this is an indication of increasing discontentment among women or merely a function of legal strictures needs to be investigated.

There can be no question of the difficulty in interpreting the rise in divorce rates. It is not clear whether current divorce rates are challenging the traditional institution of marriage since the rate of remarriage is still very high. However, women do not re-marry as soon or at the same rate as men. Obviously, this is in part due to the fact that the divorced woman is looked upon as an economic liability. It is possible also that there is a conscious decision made by more and more women that marriage, or at least the traditional concept of marriage, is no longer functional to their growing-up process.

The changes in the function of marriage are grossly under-estimated. Marriages seemed to work better in pre-modern society when the basis was economic – and the function procreative. Today these functions are secondary. As we saw, the cultural definition of marriage has changed from one stressing the economic and reproductive functions to emphasising the emotional union between two individuals. This new goal has proved extremely difficult to achieve for a significant minority of women. For some it is possible that the institution of marriage is not the best means of expressing one's love for another. While the institution of marriage remains an important step in most women's growing-up process its meaning has dramatically altered from that of their nineteenth century sisters.

The most novel development since World War II in the husband and wife relationship has been the sharing of economic roles. The spread of employment among married women has been truly revolutionary in terms of numbers especially for the middle-class family. Interpreting this phenomenon is as difficult as analysing the divorce rates. With a direct contributory role to family income the woman's balance in the decision-making process is obviously increased. How significant this increase is, given the added burdens the modern wife and mother has assumed with her new work role, is yet another unanswered question.

In women's history this new economic development comes closest to a break with the past. For this reason and because the working mother has become the common experience we need to examine the ramifications of the new decision on the part of women to combine two separate roles: the family role and work role.

The Working Woman: The Common Experience

The new work role for married women is related to their new life-cycle. Whatever the intent in limiting child-birth and concentrating it in the early years of marriage, women, by the age of thirty find themselves with continuing responsibilities of motherhood but are free during much of the day, while their children are at school, to develop other interests. By the age of forty their children are gone, and their active, day-to-day mothering functions terminated. New rewards in the relationship with the husband may compensate for this change. And a new focus outside the home may develop through formal employment.

Let us look first at the few facts available. The number of women in the active work force has soared since 1940. In England they constituted 42.2 per cent of the total labour force in 1966, as against 27 per cent in 1931.[13] In Germany women constitute 37 per cent of the labour force; over one woman out of two of working age has a job, well above the early-twentieth century in which women barely approached 30 per cent of the total labour force. Even in France where women workers had always retained a greater stake in the total working population, 39 per cent of the labour force was female in 1973 and by 1975 the percentage has risen to over 43 per cent. Expansion thus continues, no matter what the work patterns of women during the first stages of industrialisation. There has been a change not only in numbers but also in the nature of the woman worker. In striking contrast to the pattern of the nineteenth century the average woman worker today is older, married and a mother.

Most people are unaware of the dynamics involved in this new development. The impression persists that the typical woman worker is a young woman; polls suggest a belief that her average age would be no more than twenty-five.[14] But the impression is culture bound; the average now is far closer to forty-two.[15] There are few women under twenty now in the labour force, given changes in school-leaving requirements, marriage age and early childbirth. In France the percentage of women working in non-agricultural labour, between the ages of 15 and 19, decreased from 49 per cent in 1929 to 37 per cent in 1962. Work is now a two- to four-year experience for the young girl between school and marriage, not one of eight to ten years. By the mid-1960s girls approached the halfway mark in percentage of attendance in secondary schools (49 per cent in England, 52 per cent in France, 44 per cent in Germany).[16] Though a far smaller group from both sexes is involved, the percentage of women in higher education, compared to men, has risen also: to 38 per cent in England, 42 per cent in France, 39 per cent in the United States and 24 per cent in Germany.

The typical teenage worker, so dominant not only in the industrial age but also in pre-industrial society, becomes a rarity. The inflation in the number and percentage of women working occcurs in the older age groups. The number of French women, aged 45 to 49, formally employed increased by 28 per cent between 1936 and 1962; the increase in the fifty to fifty-four group was even greater, at 37 per cent.[17] In England between 1931 and 1966 there was a decline of 6.6 per cent in the number of women working under twenty-four years of age, but a rise of 116 per cent of those aged thirty-five to forty-four and an increase of 161 per cent in the forty-five to fifty-four age bracket.[18] In Denmark, quite typically, the largest decennial group of women working by 1966 was in the group aged forty-five to fifty-four. More older women are formally employed and more married women work outside the home than ever before. Whereas in 1900 in countries like England and Germany the number of married women working outside agriculture amounted roughly to 10 per cent of the total female work force, the figure had risen to 50 per cent by the second half of the 1960s. Married women have come to constitute the majority of the female labour force. Some of them, of course, have completed their active mothering cycle; hence the impressive concentration from the later forties to the fifties age group. But a substantial percentage — 50 per cent in the United States — of women with children over the age of six are employed; in Germany the number of employed mothers with children under the age of fourteen increased by 319 per cent between 1950 and 1974.[19]

Again changes in life-cycle and school requirements (and educational aspirations beyond formal school-leaving age) explain this dramatic evolution in part. The increased availability of grandmothers to serve as babysitters with increased longevity and the earlier age at which the average woman becomes a grandmother could also be viewed as significant. But before we speculate further, it is best to look at what changes, if any, occurred in the types of jobs available for women since World War II. Key traditional bastions of women's work declined: in France, female agricultural workers dropped by 20 per cent between 1954 and 1968. The textile industry is no longer the important source of employment it was for the young female worker in the nineteenth and early-twentieth centuries. Some women have taken up jobs in metalwork, engineering, and electronics. In Germany the number of women employed in metallurgy increased 162 per cent between 1950 and 1961; in France the gain was less spectacular but still amounted to 50 per cent. Women employed in German electronics showed a rise of 313 per cent, France 73 per cent, the United States 82 per cent between the early 1950s and the early 1960s.[20]

In addition women have advanced in professional occupations. By the mid-1960s 25 per cent of all English doctors were women; 22 per cent in France; 20 per cent in Germany (as against only 6 per cent in the United States). Gains in the male-dominated legal bastion were predictably less impressive; 19 per cent of all French lawyers were women by the later 1960s, 7 per cent of all German lawyers, 4 per cent of all English lawyers. Higher education has granted more jobs. In France 20 per cent of the professional staff of higher educational institutions was female in 1964; in England, 15 per cent, in Germany 6 per cent and in the United States 22 per cent. These figures, even in their diversity, show marked gains for women. They also, as feminists quickly and correctly point out, fall far short of equality; the problems of becoming a professional woman remain formidable. The disparity between the advance of women as a percentage of university students and the advance in most formal professions indicates this;[21] because of prior cultural conditioning, continuing bias, and possibly a desire for early marriage women do not enter professions at a level commensurate with that of men. This is not necessarily a sign of high tragedy, for work expectations between men and women continue to differ; but it is a danger signal to any women seeking rough equality between the sexes in employment. Women do not obtain their numerical share of professional or management jobs.

Having noted the key areas of breakthrough in new work channels for women, we must acknowledge that the majority of women in today's work force are following trends set in the nineteenth century. Women today concentrate in the service sector as they began to do a hundred years ago from semi-professionals such as teachers to secretaries. This constitutes an obvious continuity in the female work experience, in that women have always disproportionately 'served', from their employment as servants in peasant households to their present concentration as nurses or secretaries. It also constitutes an obvious attunement to modern work patterns. If women suffered from exclusion from formal, outside-the-home, productive employment in the nineteenth century, they have more than compensated by their ability to dominate the service sector, which has turned out to be the major employment category in a modern industrial society. Women constitute 63 per cent of all lower grade civil servants in France, 77 per cent of those in Germany; 82 per cent of all telephone employees in Germany and 95 per cent of those in France and the United States.[22] In a modern industrial society between 70 per cent and 80 per cent of all employed women are in the employer-white-collar worker category. Female dominance in education has extended; in 1961 62.5 per cent of all teachers at secondary as well as primary levels in Germany were women.

Women thus are found preferable as workers in the service category though usually below formal professional levels; they themselves often find these jobs more desirable. The revolution in numbers and the dramatic shifts in ages of women workers has not substantially altered the kind of work women perform. Discrimination and cultural conditioning continue to affect job choice. One must also recognise the persistence of the female work ethic first developed with modern economic developments, now over a century and a half ago. The reason women say they work echoes responses that would have been given, had pollsters been present, in the earlier stages of industrialisation. The family remains the focal point of employment. A study of married women working in England in the early 1960s revealed that most saw their work not as a goal in itself but as an extension of family duties. Their earnings were destined to supplement family income, to buy more home furnishings, more toys and educational equipment for the children and — reflecting the newer family role — better vacations.[23] Because work remains supplementary to the family role, women workers continue to accept jobs that are lower-paid, that offer fewer chances for mobility, than those available to their husbands. And this is in spite of equal pay for equal work legislation, common in many industrial countries.

Women on the job continue to stress sociability and companionship as chief goals. Like the servant who entered the factory seventy years ago, the married woman who has a job that gets her out of a purely domestic environment will accept a host of routine assignments if the job allows contact with others; this of course remains one of the reasons that white-collar work is preferred. Work, though an actively sought diversification in life and an increasingly vital component of the family income, remains a secondary identification. Hence part-time jobs, lower status positions, frequent job changing and early retirement ages (55, on the average, compared to the male tendency toward 62-65) reflect the persistence of the special female work ethic.

It is in this area of women's self-perception and society's expectations that the internal conflicts of a cultural lag loom largest as a barrier to fuller female participation and fulfilment in today's society. The culture today that defines a woman's place, despite constant and vigorous criticism even beyond feminists circles, is one that remains bound to nineteenth-century conceptions. While sentiments about 'equal rights' and 'equal opportunities' for women are expressed widely the primacy of the domestic function maintains itself.

The inherent conflict between image and reality is most pressing for women today than at any point in their development in modern society. What women are *supposed* to be doing and what they *think* they are doing and what they *actually* are doing are quite different. Despite the fact that today women are educated on equal terms with their male counterparts (one need only glance at women's enrolment figures in higher education to witness this new development); despite the fact that women are crucial to the labour force, the image of wife and mother developed in the nineteenth century (as opposed to the image of the pre-modern era) has become deeply rooted. As we observed in the discussion of the evolution of women's role in the family the role of mother and wife became all-consuming for the woman.

Today any suggestion that this may not in fact be the exclusive domain for a woman incites reactionary sentiment. One need only look at the current debate over the Equal Rights Amendment in the United States to see the level of hysteria that can be aroused when there is any serious discussion of redefining a woman's place beyond home and hearth. The conflict at the public level is serious but not as serious as the conflict within women themselves. Reality is so out of tune with the image. As we have seen, it becomes increasingly difficult for a woman to maintain a functional self-image of wife and mother given the relatively short-lived experience as part of the modern female life-cycle. Whether it is proper for a mother to work or not is really becoming a semantic debate given the statistics of married women's employment patterns. The fact is that women *are* working. Understanding the opposing forces one sees that something has to give: either the cultural image or the woman herself. Women are now assuming the full burdens of motherhood, housewife and labourer with little support from either their immediate surroundings or the outside world. Maintaining the burdens of a dual career is taxing the mental and physical resources of the woman, as a recent study of the incidence of depression among married women workers has shown.[24] While women are working they still believe that they should be at home. A poll taken in the 1960s in Germany showed that there was an overwhelming confirmation that *no* woman should work before her youngest child reaches age ten. Yet reality showed that most married women were in fact beginning employment prior to that point. How much guilt is being repressed by women who enjoy work more than domestic chores is not known. How healthy a situation this is for women's growing-up process needs to be seriously investigated. While there is much that could and should be done in the public sector in the way of day-care facilities, providing tax benefits for household maintenance etc., a more subtle, and therefore more difficult, problem lies within women themselves. How are women today dealing with their internal conflicts arising from their challenge to the image that their great-grandmothers set?

One of the practical solutions that some women have implemented in dealing on a day-to-day basis with the dual roles is to rely upon their own mothers to take over domestic chores for them. This no doubt helps to relieve some of the anxiety and sense of guilt for the working mother. Also, it helps remove the feeling of uselessness for the grandmother, that we noted earlier, in that now she is able to re-establish her primary means of identity to her grandchild. For those who are able to make such arrangements the problem seems to be resolvable to everyone's benefit. Yet for this historian an important question comes to mind when viewing the situation. Here we need to return to the problems of the mother-daughter relationship as it has developed since the nineteenth century. Sociologists and psychologists attested to the growing importance, especially for the twentieth century, of what is termed the *Demeter tie:* the tie between mother and daughter. Studies have shown that even when a woman marries and has her own home and family, she continues to maintain close contact with her mother. In the working-class community the contacts are almost daily since often the daughter lives in close proximity to her mother. In middle-class communities the ties are not so visible but the telephone and the car go a long way in giving life to the *Demeter tie.* In an earlier chapter we discussed that this type of support particularly for the working-class woman helped her adjust to a strange and at times hostile environment. No doubt with the continued decline in age at marriage more and more women felt the need to rely upon their mothers for a sense of stability. While positive gains were made from the continuation of the mother-daughter bond perhaps there are underlying negative aspects that have to date been ignored but must be considered in evaluating the usefulness of the *Demeter tie.*

Sociological studies have shown that the one serious problem from the new mother-daughter bond is the husband who finds himself a stranger in his own home. A study of East End London conducted in the 1950s found that husbands complained at times of the omnipresence of their mothers-in-law or the absence of their wives.[25] Obvious tensions of this sort limited the concomitant relationship. A more serious problem for the historian of women is the impact of this strong tie on the woman herself. While it is true that for many women the Demeter tie has enabled them to venture forth beyond the home and assume new roles in society at the same time it has added to her state of *dependency*. Her mother is very much a part of her life even as an adult. The question is, can a woman really assume full status as an adult and a proper self-image if she remains the 'dutiful daughter' even if this is only part-time? The point was raised in the earlier discussion about retarding influence of working-class mothers on their daughters' behaviour with regards to adoption of birth control, even childrearing practices, in the nineteenth century. The influence of the older generation inhibited innovation considerably. The problem for the contemporary woman is more complex. The dividing line between a mother's help and a mother's constant interference is very fine. How many women today find that their sense of frustration is most real as they relate to their own mothers whose constant criticism is severely undermining their sense of self as opposed to broad issues of social discrimination?

Herein lies an important difference between the growing-up process for a woman compared to a man. It is far more difficult for a woman to mark clearly her entrance into adulthood, her independence, her ability to stand on her own two feet. The struggle for independence for a woman is most difficult for it is fought on two fronts: the familiar front — the dependent nature of the husband-wife relationship — and the less recognised problem, the dependent mother-daughter relationship. Efforts have been made and are continuing to be made to correct the imbalances of the first state of dependency as we saw in the discussion of the growing commitment to a concomitant relationship between husband and wife. The second problem needs to be seriously investigated. With increasing longevity the problem becomes most complex. At least in the nineteenth and early-twentieth centuries a woman could expect that her mother would overlap her life as an adult for about ten years to fifteen years at most. Today many a mother and daughter grow old together (given the small differences in age between them also). This discussion is not to raise the macabre. It is merely to suggest potential problems that have heretofore been underestimated in the development of the *Demeter tie.* An important aspect of women's growing up process depends upon their ability to cut the silver threads. As we have noted a mother's need to continue to mother her children, especially her daughter, even when she is herself a mother may not be totally beneficial. It would also be interesting to test whether the number of divorces today would be as high as they are if the young woman was not able to return home to mama as readily as she can.

Herein lies a host of open questions, some of which are perhaps not strictly within the realm of historical analysis and are best pursued in tandem with psychoanalysis. However, with history we can see the complexities of the new developments confronting the contemporary woman. How important the work role will be in the lives of the modern woman has not yet been established. For this historian it would appear that it is here to stay. If one views the nineteenth century and early-twentieth century as a period of transition as women adjusted to the traumas of change in moving from an agricultural to an industrial complex, it is plausible to see the cessation of work in the nineteenth and early twentieth centuries as merely temporary and the new work role as re-integration of the lost economic role of the pre-modern world (although it is now on a significantly improved level in terms of equality *vis-à-vis* men). The new work performance, affecting not only women's lives but the whole economy, cannot be downplayed or viewed as a short-term phenomenon which will dissipate with an improvement in the economic cycle. It is fundamental to the woman's growing-up process. For middle-class women the development is even more startling. For the first time in their modern history, the average middle-class woman can expect to work; this is one vital source of the new female work force. Marriage, for working, as well as middle-class women is no long a barrier to formal economic independence. The ultimate effects of the new work role on the family itself is far from clear. Without fuller investigation into the family patterns and family life-cycles we can venture no further than to say that it is inevitable that there will be dramatic changes primarily in the relationship between husband and wife. How to implement these changes in order to avoid serious stresses and strains for both man and woman needs to be examined immediately.

The Feminist Revival

It is not at all surprising that the last decade has seen a great resurgence of feminist agitation. As we have seen, feminism continues to be an integral aspect of women's confrontation with changing life-styles. As was true in the nineteenth century, feminism today is articulating the many problems with which women are coping on a personal basis be it the right to abortion, or equal work, or a release from the burdens of motherhood. It is also true that there are different sets of priorities among the various feminist factions throughout Europe and America. The strongest and most publicised of the feminist movements are those centred in the United States. But the women's question looms large throughout Western Europe. Regardless of geographical location, the major thrust behind feminism today is the challenge to the exclusiveness of the family focus for women instilled by education and entertainment media from the earliest years. Feminism is the articulation of the very problems we have discussed in this section. Feminists' strivings today are centred on finding more meaningful outlets beyond the domestic sphere for women who find their lives becoming increasingly dysfunctional.

Specific demands from feminists are familiar enough: improved facilities for higher education; better jobs; rewards commensurate with performance. Key issues of principle and practice remain unresolved. Yet this is not to say that the female's lot has not improved. As we noted in the very first pages of this study, the facts show that women have significantly altered their position of society *vis-à-vis* themselves.

There is a new element in the feminists' criticism of the workings of society today. There is a strong emphasis on the psychological dimensions of the problems between the sexes. Sex stereotyping is seen as a major problem limiting women from fulfilling their full potential. Advances whether they be legal, political or economic provide little if the image of the woman's primary place in the home remains unchanged. Thus efforts are made today to alter the cultural conditioning process in order to provide women with a fuller range for participation in today's society.

As with earlier feminism, most feminist leaders are well-educated, middle-class women. Their approach, however, has been more broadly based and they are more aware of the problems of all women. This is seen in the efforts to get legislators to provide day-care centres, and in efforts to organise effectively women workers, particularly white-collar service personnel such as teachers and nurses. An even more dramatic break with earlier patterns has been the active participation of feminists in sexual matters. Eliminating sexual exploitation of women is among the top priorities of many feminists. One prime example of this new concern has been the full support feminists have given to the liberalisation of abortion laws.

The impact of feminists on legal changes such as the abortion issue must not be minimised. But at the same time it has to be realised that even today the feminist movement remains a minority movement and is harshly received in conservative quarters. As with earlier feminism of the nineteenth century, the call for consciousness raising has roused antagonism among some women. The frontal assault on the domestic role offends many women who, for better or worse, devote their lives to this role. Specific campaigns for abortion bring strong counterattacks from women who, out of religious conviction or out of subconscious fear of losing their role, find this method of birth control highly immoral.

Yet the new wave of feminism strikes a strong chord of concern among all women. Most women have made significant changes in their domestic roles, particularly as mothers. In seeking work outside the home they have found a new if partial means of identification. Women today are more vocal and actively involved in protest than ever before in their history be it campaigns to liberalise abortion or amend legal codes to provide equal rights for women or to protest food prices. Even strikes among women against the age-old discrimination in wages are becoming important concerns for employers. (In 1968 women workers struck for three months in a Belgian arms factory.) Women's union membership has risen from 13 per cent of the total in 1936 in England to 27 per cent in 1966. This is not to say that these are signs of a massive commitment to formal feminism. They are not. Feminism is only one expression of a new sense of self on the part of women; of a new sense of militancy in defending and demanding their place in society. 'Up with woman power' is a sentiment expressed in many languages. To a greater extent than ever before, by building upon foundations set in the nineteenth century, the life of the contemporary woman is multi-faceted. The feminist movement reflects this most clearly. Women have come from behind closed doors to claim their place. Now that they have ventured forth to the outside however, they find that their task has only just begun. Diversity of roles involves more stamina and mental and physical strain than required of her in her domestic role.

Since one of the underlying purposes of this book was to show women that they have not been the dupes many historians have said they were, that they indeed have a history to be proud of, one of progress in many directions, it is only appropriate to end on an optimistic note despite the fact that since the undertaking of this task this historian has become an angry young woman. The modern woman is best described as an integrated woman, crucial to the well-being of the whole society at its most intimate level, the family; and at its most public, be it political or economic. There are many problems unresolved and no doubt new problems will arise tomorrow. But basically the modern woman has made the decision to attempt to deal with her problems for her own self-satisfaction. Her success will be crucial to us all, male and female. For *her* story is as fundamental to the working of modern society as *his*tory.

Notes

1. See the work of William O'Neill, *Everyone Was Brave: The Rise And Fall of Feminism in America* (1971).
2. For an example of today's French advice literature on how to stop the process of ageing see Janine Alaux, *101 Trucs Pour Vaincre Le Coup de Vieux* (1973).
3. A.H. Halsey, ed., *Trends in British Society Since 1900* (1972), p.43.
4. Halsey, p.175.
5. Evelyn Sullerot, *Woman, Society and Change* (1974), pp.69-70.
6. For a discussion of working-class wives see the work of John Goldthorpe, *et al*, *The Affluent Worker in the Class Structure* (1969); F. Zweig, *The Worker in An Affluent Society* (1961); Colin Rosser and Christopher Harris, *The Family and Social Change* (1965); Standish Meacham, *A Life Apart* (1977).
7. G. Stanley Hall, *Adolescence* (New York, 1904).
8. J. Coleman, *The Adolescent Society*.
9. See Philip J. Greven, *Four Generations: Population, Land and Family in Colonial Andover, Mass.* (New York, 1970); Lutz, Berkner, 'The Stem Family and the Developmental Cycle of the Peasant Household: An 18th Century Austrian Example,' in *American Historical Review*, 77 (1972), pp.398-418.
10. Sullerot, *Woman*, p.58.
11. Zweig, *Worker*, pp.31, 29.
12. Halsey, *Trends*, p.50.
13. Halsey, *Trends*, p.118.
14. Sullerot, *Woman*, p.99.
15. For a discussion of the period in America see William Chafe, *The American Woman* (1972).
16. Judith Ryder and Harold Silver, *Modern English Society: History and Structure 1850-1970*, p.328.
17. Sullerot, *Woman*, p.101.
18. Halsey, *Trends*, p.118.
19. Dr Ingrid Sonnerhorn, *Women's Careers: Experience from East and West Germany* (1970), p.21.
20. Sullerot, *Woman*.
21. For a good discussion of women in modern society see the collection of essays in R. Patai, *Women in the Modern World* (1967). The essay by Helge Prosse on the situation for German women is most important. See also the excellent essay by Tim Mason, 'Women in Germany, 1925-1940: Family, Welfare and Work. Part II', *History Workshop*, Vol.2 (Autumn 1976).
22. Sonnerhorn, *Women's Careers;* Sullerot, *Woman*, p.142.
23. Silver, *Modern English*, p.258.
24. According to Dr. Helen DeRossi author of the *Book of Hope: How Women Can Overcome Depression,* any time there is a change there is conflict and anxiety and these are the roots of depression. There are numbers of depressed women who have devoted themselves to their families and are now 'becoming more aware of their feelings, and coming out of the closet with their unhappiness, admitting their unhappiness and regretting the role of mother which leads to feelings of guilt'.
25. See Michael Young and Peter Willmott, *Family and Kinship in East London* (London, 1952).

Inevitably this overview will raise much criticism; hopefully it will help formulate new questions. To anticipate some critics, I would like to raise several philosophical points concerning the implications of the pattern forged by women in the last 200 years. We grant comparative differences in the overall process, but the process has been fundamental and grows increasingly similar among modern women across sectional and to an extent class boundaries. Hence the fundamental question: was the female response a sensible response? Who is to judge? By what criteria does one measure success for *women*? Yet even without clear norms judgements are inevitably made. Most historical accounts of women have either explicitly or implicitly concluded that the female response has ranged from less than adequate to absolutely detrimental. The by-word of women's history has been 'she stoops but never conquers'. Is women's history the history of the duped? Is being female merely the expression of male whims? Obviously the focus of the preceding pages vigorously argued against such sexist interpretations. The purpose of this overview has been to explain the 'why' of women's history of the past 200 or more years. Explanations, however, do not mean that the female response has been totally successful. To illustrate change is not to say that the process or response is complete either, even if it seems headed in a fruitful direction.

A case in point is the 'functionless' middle-aged woman, or even more the widow, who has adopted new recreational patterns, sometimes new jobs, but retains ties with traditional norms of behaviour. While one can grant that the trite American jingle, 'You've come a long way, baby', is historically perceptive, one cannot forget that stress and strain, anxiety and frustration are the toll paid by women as they have grown up in modern society.

Which brings us to a second but related question: how women have coped with the traumas of change brought about by the urban-industrial network? One of the important aspects of women's adaptation has been that while modern women have overcome traditional hazards such as maternal mortality and economic dependency, they are faced inevitably with newer problems. Can we really speak of progress/success given the fact that women continue to battle against blatant inequities? The concept of modernisation makes no claims to be the universal solution to problems be they male or female. A belief in progress is not a search for utopia. In fact, the very time modernisation takes place is when society is besieged by problems and must be willing to change. To reject the concept of modernisation for women because it has not created a problem-free society is like throwing the baby out with the bath water.

Given the fact that the female pattern was distinctive (from that of the male), one is ultimately forced by students and other historians to ask how it compares with modern male history, and, second, whether the two models will remain distinctive. The questions are not unrelated. The answer to the latter depends very much on the growing-up process of males in modern society.

As heretical as it may sound, men's adaptation to modern society has lagged behind women's in crucial areas. How can one make such a statement when all around men hold the reins of power? We are not disputing the fact that males dominate the political and economic scene (although we have observed that challenges to the male sanctum have been made). The more important question is whether this is the whole of men's history. We have realised that the accomplishments of great women were not the all of women's past. Just because men can make up a longer list of 'greats' is it more true for them? Men's history has suffered as much as, perhaps even more than women's from this elitist approach. Political and economic dominance are important aspects of modern society but for the majority they are only of peripheral interest. Let's face it: most men will never be political leaders or financial magnates. Does that mean that they have failed as well? How do most men measure personal success? Unlike the female experience since 1750, the male's role in society has changed very little. Life for men has been dominated primarily, if not exclusively, by a job, as their only means of self-expression.

In spite of the biological-social restraints put upon women, their multi-role experience allowed them a broader spectrum for self-expression. Women also have learned to cut some of their losses when a role became too demanding, as witnessed in the birth control movement. On the other hand, for modern man work became an end in itself, but it has been a far from glamorous role. Have the rewards justified the sacrifices? What opportunities were passed by as work consumed the male identity? This was a point raised in the discussion of the family. We went to great lengths to discuss the changing role of women in the family. Through her role as household manager and mother she explored new avenues for self-expression. The male interaction however was perforce minimal, largely due to the demands of a work role which segregated him from his home, his primary potential source of emotional sustenance. Alienation is a topic discussed by labour historians, but alienation goes well beyond the job. It is part of a man's family history in modern society. Where is he to find full self-expression, not to say anything of the growing need in modern society for emotional support?

Even if we consider work as the primary means of self-expression the male lags behind the female. Women have not been as successful materially in that monetary returns from work are still overbalanced in the males' favour. But can a man's pay cheque satisfy his need for satisfaction (especially given the fact that more often than not he turns it over to the woman)? How many men would have liked to change their jobs as often as women did and do, to retire as early as women do? To push the analogy into the future, the modern economic system presents far more problems for men than it does for women. Work *per se* (especially male-type work) has been declining with the process of industrialisation. Distinctive chances to display masculine physical strength have waned with mechanisation. The number of hours one works in a day, the number of years one works in a life-time declines steadily. Women accepted this and have adapted with some success; shorter hours of work and earlier retirement were adopted by women years ahead of men. Men have been more ambiguous in their response. The male faces two serious problems. The first is obvious. How is he to sustain himself and his family? (The working of the welfare state has ameliorated some of the crucial economic concerns such as health, education and old age insurance but it has not provided full economic security.). Since World War II women have, furthermore, been willing to share this responsibility. The second problem is just as real but has not been recognised. As the male's economic role in society diminishes (*vis-à-vis* his actual work role and the advancement of women into the labour force) so does his only means for self-expression. Men without work suffer identity problems. (This was seen in several studies of the unemployed.) This is becoming a very common problem with the rise of mandatory retirement. Males have far more difficulty adapting to retirement than women in part because women have developed a more integrated life-style.

One can add to the examples wherein the male is at a distinct disadvantage compared to the female. The disparities between female and male health are well known. Males, quick to the defence, retort that this is due to the demands of their economic role, and there is no denying this. Women have been able to modernise their personal well-being in part because they have not had to bear the full physical strains of productive employment. In the extreme, men were given far less option to be sick. More broadly, the need for self-expression, a crucial aspect of the growing-up process, has found male opportunity ironically limited. Perhaps this accounts for the fact that more men than women find themselves addicted to drugs or alcohol or find suicide the only answer. Whose pattern of adaptation was best depends more on a measurement of the quality of life rather than the number of power positions in government and industry. This type of evaluation process has not yet been accomplished. Again this is not meant to imply that the barriers to women in these areas should remain. The struggle against female inequities is real and deserving of a successful attack, but woman should be careful not to lose herself in the process.

We have noted throughout this study the many areas that need to be investigated for a fuller understanding of the modern woman's experience. In conclusion we should note the real need for a social history of men. Women's history is probably the first successful attempt, even if incomplete, to deal with the quality of life as it affected the common people's experience. Through this overview we have seen that one's experience is not just work, or family life, or the political arena but an integration of these various facets. A woman's life was and remains complex and only in its complexities can it be fully perceived historically. The need to do the same for men seems to cry out in almost every sector. Why do men work? What is a father? Or even what is a lover? Why is it that so many folk songs sing of the trials of men as lovers? It is as unfair to men as it is to women to generalise their history as one of exploitation. Ideally one should be able to deal with the human experience since 1750 for this is really the making of modern society. The fact is that women's adaptation is closely related to men's and existing inequities reflect a lag in men's modernisation. As long as 'vive la différence' prevails, modernisation, interpreted in its most basic sense as individual satisfaction, will be impeded. Without invoking overt cheers for feminists — it remains a point to be pondered — men have much to learn from the female experience.

BIBLIOGRAPHY

General Histories of Women

Beauvoir, Simone de *Le deuxième sexe*, 1949
Chombart de Lauwc, Paul Henry *La femme dans la société*, 1963
Clark, Francis *The Position of Women in Contemporary France*, 1937
Crow, Duncan *The Victorian Woman*, 1971
Cunnington, C. Willet *Feminine Attitudes in the 19th Century*, 1935
Dallin, Alexander; Dorothy Atkinson; Gail Lapidus (eds.) *Women in Russia*, forthcoming
Dumas, Francine *Femmes du XXe Siecle*, 1965
Dunbar, Janet *The Early Victorian Woman; Some Aspects of Her Life 1837-57*, 1957
Fussel, G.E. and K.R. *The English Country Woman: the Internal Aspect of Rural Life 1500-1900*, 1953
Hartman, Mary, and Lois W. Baunner (eds.) *Clio's Consciousness Raised* 1974
Klein, Viola *The Femine Character: History of an Ideology*, 1949
Lyttkins, Alice C. *Krinnan boer jar rakna*, 1973
—— *Krinnan finner en Foeljeslagare Den Svenska Krinnans Historia från Forntid till 1700-tal*, 1972
Meyer, Gerhard *German Women and Modern Problems*, 1915
Patai, R. (ed.) *Women in the Modern World*, 1967
Ravera, Camilla *La donna Italiana dal primo al secondo Risorgimerto*, 1951
Rowbotham, Sheila *Hidden From History: Rediscovering Woman in History from the 17th Century to the Present*, 1975
Shield, Betty *Women in Norway: Their Position in Family Life, Employment and Society*, 1970
Stenton, Doris Mary *The English Woman in History*, 1957
Sullerot, Evelyn *Woman, Society and Change*, 1971
Thompson, Patricia *The Victorian Heroine, A Changing Ideal*, 1956
Vicinus, Martha *Suffer and Be Still*, 1972

Women and Work

Anderson, Adelaide *Women in the Factory: An Administrative*

Adventure 1893-1921, 1922

—— *Les Attitudes des travailleurs et des employeurs à l'égard de l'emploi*, 1973

Bath, Slicken von *Work in the Agricultural Revolution*

Bell, E. Moberly *Storming the Citadel: Women's Entry into Medicine*, 1953

Bennett, A.M. *English Medical Women*, 1915

Boserup, Ester *Women and Economic Modernization*, 1970

Brittain, Vera *Women's Work in Modern Britain*, 1928

Butler, C.V. *Domestic Service; An Enquiry by the Women's Industrial Council*, 1916

Drake, Barbara *The Tea Shop Girl*, 1913

—— Women in Engineering Trades, 1918

—— *Women in Trade Unions*, 1920

Garrison, Dee 'The Tender Technicians: The Feminization of Public Librarianship, 1876-1905', *Journal of Social History*, 1972-3

Gendall, Murray, *Swedish Working Wives*, 1963

Gilman, Charlotte Perkins *Women and Economics*, 1912

Goodnow, Minnie *Nursing History*, 1953

Guibal, Paul *La femme mariée commerçante*, 1920

Guilbert, M. *Fonctions des Femmes dans l'Industrie*, 1966

Hallsworth, Joseph, and Rhys Davis *The Working Life of Shop Assistants*, 1910

Hamp, Pierre *La France, pays ouvrier*, 1916

Harvey, E.C. *Labour Laws for Women and Children in the U.K.*, 1909

Hecht, J. Jean *The Domestic Servant Class in 18th Century England*, 1956

Hewitt, Margaret *Wives and Mothers in Victorian Industry*, 1958

Holcombe, *Victorian Ladies at Work*, 1973

Horn, Pamela *The Rise and Fall of the Victorian Servant*, 1975

Hunt, Audrey *A Survey of Women's Employment*, 1968

Hutchins, B.L. *Women in Modern Industry*, 1915

Klein, Viola *Britain's Married Women Workers*, 1965

—— *Women Workers* 1965

LeRoy, Robert *Essai sur la population active*, 1968

Lobsenz, Johanna *The Older Woman in Industry*, 1921

McBride, Theresa *The Domestic Revolution*, 1976

Morley, Edith J. (ed.) *Women Workers in Seven Professions: A Survey of their Economic Conditions and Prospects*, 1914

Neff, Wanda *Victorian Working Women 1832-50*, 1929

Odencrantz, L.C. *Italian Women in Industry*, 1919

Parey, Agnes *The Story of the Growth of Nursing as an Art, a Vocation, and a Profession,* 1953

Perrot, Michelle *Les ouvriers en grève en France 1871-1890,* 1974

Peterson, M. Jeanne 'The Victorian Governess: Status Incongruence in Family and Society.' in M. Vicinus (ed.) *Suffer and Be Still,* 1972

Pflaume, Eberhard *Frauen im Industriebetrieb,* 1943

Philips, M., and Tomkinson, W.S. *English Women in Life and Letters,* 1926

Pinchbeck, Ivy *Women Working in the Industrial Revolution,* 1931

O'Neill, William *Women and Work,*

Pross, Helge *Gleichberechtigung in Beruf,* 1973

Rich, R.W. *The Training of Teachers,* 1933

Salaff, Janet 'Working Daughters in the Hong Kong Chinese Family' in *Journal of Social History,* 1976

Schoonbroodt, Joseph *Les femmes et le travail,* 1973

Scott, Joan, and Louise Tilly 'Woman's Work and the Family in Nineteenth Century Europe' in Charles E. Roseberg (ed.) *The Family in History,* 1975

Serrais, J.J., and J.P. Lauret *Histoire et dossier de la prostitution,* 1967

Stearns, Peter W. *Lives of Labor; Work in Maturing Industrial Societies,* 1975

Tropp, Asher *The School Teachers,* 1957

Tuckwell, Gertrude, *et al. Women in Industry from Seven Points of View,* 1908

Ulshoeten, Helgard *Mutter Beruf: Die Situation der werbstätigen Mütter in neun Industrieländern,* 1969

Walkewitz, Judith R., and Daniel J. Walkewitz '"We are not beasts of the field": Prostitution and the Poor in Plymouth and Southampton under the Contagious Diseases Act' in Hartman and Baumer (eds.) *Clio's Consciousness Raised,* 1974

Yudkin, Simon, and Anthea Holme *Working Mothers and their Children,* 1963

Family

Anderson, Michael *Family Structure In Nineteenth Century Lancashire,* 1971

Aries, Phillippe *Centuries of Childhood,* 1962

Banks, J.A. *Prosperity and Parenthood,* 1954

Betham, Edwards *Home Life in France,* 1905

Bordesure, H. *Le Mariage,* 1921

Branca, Patricia *Silent Sisterhood,* 1975

Calhoun, Arthur W. *A Social History of the American Family from Colonial Times to the Present*, 1917-19

Cheron, André *La Femme mariée anglaise en Angleterre et en France*, 1906

Cobbold, Helen M. *Statistical Analysis of Infant Mortality and its Causes in the United Kingdom*, 1910

Cominos, Peter T. 'Innoral Femina Sensualise in Unconscious Conflict', in M. Vicinus (ed.) *Suffer and Be Still*, 1972

Cyril, Pearl *The Girl with the Swan Down Seat*, 1955

Degler, Carl N. 'What Ought to be and What Was Women's Sexuality in the 19th Century', *American Historical Review*, 1971

Delzons, Louis *La Famille française et son evolution*, 1913

Demos, John *A Little Commonwealth: Family Life in Plymouth Colony*,

Findlay, Joseph J. *Children of England: A Contribution to Special History and to Education*, 1923

French Institute of Public Opinion *Patterns of Love and Sex: A Study of the French Woman and Her Morals*, 1961

Fryer, Peter *The Birth Controllers*, 1962

Gathorne-Hardy, Jonathan *The Rise and Fall of the British Nanny*, 1972

Gillis, John *Youth and History: Tradition and Change in European Age Relations, 1770-Present*, 1974

Gordon, Michael (ed.) *The American Family in Social-Historical Perspective*, 1973

Graham, Harry *Eternal Eve: The Mysteries of Birth and the Customs that Surround It*, 1960

Grareson, R.H., and F.R. Crane *A Century of Family Law, 1857-1957*, 1957

Greven, Philip Jr. *Four Generations: Population, Land and Family in Colonial Andover, Mass*, 1970

Hunt, David *Parents and Children in History*, 1970

Kirkpatrick, Clifford *Nazi Germany: Its Women and Family Life, 1938*

Laslett, Peter (ed.) *Household and Family in the Past Time*, 1972

—— *The World We Have Lost*, 1960

Lefebre, Charles *La Famille en France dans le droit et dans les moeurs*, 1920

Lelière, Jacques *La Pratique des contrats de mariage chez les notaires en Chatelet de Paris de 1769 à Hoy*, 1959

Martin, André *La Protection de la Maternité en France*, 1912

Mause, Lloyd de (ed.) *The History of Childhood*, 1924

McGregor, O.R. *Divorce in England: A Centenary Study*, 1957

Morgan, Edmund S. *The Puritan Family*, 1966

Oakley, Ann *Woman's Work: The Housewife Past and Present*, 1974

Oren, Laura 'The Welfare of Women in Laboring Families: England 1860-1914', in Hartman and Baunner (eds.) *Clio's Consciousness Raised*, 1974

Pearsall, R. *The Worm in the Bud: The World of Victorian Sexuality* 1969

Pinchbeck, Ivy, and Margaret Hewitt *Children in English Society*, Vols.I and II, 1969

Rabb, Theodore K., and Robert I. Rotberg (eds.) *The Family in History*, 1973

Radcliffe, Walter *Milestones in Midwifery*, 1967

Roe, Fredrich Gordon, *The Victorian Child*, 1959

Rosenberg, Charles (ed.) *The Family in History*, 1925

Segalen, Martine *Nuptialité et alliance; le choix du conjoint dans une commune de l'Evre*, 1972

Sennett, Richard *Families Against the City: Middle-Class Homes of Industrial Chicago 1872-1890*, 1970

Shorter, Edward *The Making of the Modern Family*, 1975

Stearns, Peter W. 'Working-Class Women in Britain 1890-1914', in M. Vicinus (ed.) *Suffer and Be Still*, 1972

Sussman, George D. 'The Wet Nursing Business in 19th Century France', *French Historical Studies*, 1975

Taylor, G.R. *Sex in History*, 1964

—— *The Angel Makers, A Study in Psychological Origins of Social Change 1750-1950*, 1958

Thabaut, Jules *L'Evolution de la législation sur la famille*, 1913

Wells, Robert V. 'Family History and Demographic Transition', *Journal of Social History*, Vol.9, No.1, 1975

Wood, Ann 'The Fashionable Diseases: Women's Complaints and Their Treatment in 19th Century America', in Hartman and Baunner (eds.) *Clio's Consciousness Raised*, 1972

Wood, Clive, and Beryl Suitters *The Fight for Acceptance: A History of Contraception*, 1970

Young, Michael, and Peter Willmott *Family and Kinship in East London*, 1952

—— *The Symmetrical Family: A Study of Work and Leisure in the London Region*, 1973

Yudkin, Simon, and Anthea Holme *Working Mothers and their Children*, 1963

Women in the Wider Society

Abensour, Léon *Le Féminisme sous le régime de Louis Philippe et en 1848*, 1913

Anthony, Katherine Susan *Feminism in Germany and Scandanavia*, 1915

Barthélemy, Joseph *Le Vote des femmes*, 1920

Bertin, Célia *Le Temps des femmes*, 1958

Biasc, Paola Gaiott de *Le origini del movimento cattolico femminili*, 1963

Bortolotti, Franca Pieroni *Alle origini del mori monto femminile in Italia 1848-1892*, 1963

Brittain, Vera *The Wives of Oxford*, 1960

Callet, C. *Place des femmes*, 1973

Chabaud, Jacqueline *The Educational Advancement of Women*, 1970

Clarke, A.K. *A History of Cheltenham Ladies College 1853-1953*, 1953

Crofts, Marel *Women Under English Law*, 1925

Daric, Jean *L'Activité professionelle des femmes en France*, 1947

Duhet, Paul-Marie, *Les Femmes et la Révolution*, 1971

Flexner, Eleanor *Century of Struggle*, 1973

Fulford, Roger *Votes for Women. Story of a Struggle*, 1958

Goland, Fernand *Les Féministes françaises*, 1925

Goodsell, Willystyne *Education of Women, Its Social Background and Problems*, 1923

Guclaud-Leridon, Francoise *Recherches sur la condition féminine dans la société d'aujourd'hui*, 1967

Guilbert, Madeleine *Les Femmes et l'organisation syndicate avant 1914*, 1966

Hutchins, Elizabeth Leigh *Laws for Women in France*, 1907

Jenness, Linda (ed.) *Feminism and Socialism*, 1972

Kann, Josephine *Hope Deferred: Girl's Education in English History*, 1965

—— *How Different From Us: Miss Buss and Miss Beale*, 1958 1958

Köhler-Wagnerova, Alenz *Die Frau im Sozialismus*, 1924

Kunstmann, Antje *Frauenemanzipation und Erziehung*, 1972

Laclos, Pierre Ambroisie *De l'Education des Femmes*, 1903

Merfield, Mechthild *Die Emanzipation der Frau in der sozialistischen Theorie und Praxis*, 1922

Michel, Andrée, and Geneviève Texier, *La Condition de la française d'aujourd'hui*, 1964.

Mitchell, David *The Fighting Pankhursts,* 1967
Mitchell, Hannah *The Hard Way Up,* 1920
Morgan, David *Suffragists and Liberals,* 1975
O'Neill, William *The Women's Movement,* 1969
Ramelson, Marian *The Petticoat Rebellion: A Century of Struggle for Women's Rights,* 1967
Rosen, Andrew *Rise Up Women!,* 1975
Rousselot, Paul *Histoirie de l'éducation des femmes,* 1903
Rover, Constance *Love, Morals and the Feminists,* 1970
Sauna, L. *Figures Féminines 1909-1931,* 1949
Sullerot, Evelyn *Histoire de la presse féminine en France des origines à 1848,* 1966

INDEX